GABRIEL CHANEL

GABRIELLE CHANEL

FASHION MANIFESTO

Thames & Hudson

CONTENTS

Modern photographs
of Chanel pieces by
Julien T. Hamon

Gabrielle Chanel in the 1930s. Photograph by André Kertész.

'Chanel works with her ten fingers,
with her nails, with the side
of her hand, with her palms, with pins
and scissors, right on the garment,
which is a white cloud with long pleats,
speckled with crystal drops.'
Colette on Chanel, *Bravo*, April 1930, p. 36

Gabrielle Chanel was a legend in her own lifetime, a legend that she wove herself and continued to expand throughout her career. From the 1930s onwards, the press in France and abroad repeated the contradictory biographical snippets that accentuated her deliberate vagueness around the subject of her life and the fascination that her personality had already begun to stir up. Since her death in 1971, many books have tried to shed light on the facets of her history and personality. These works have attempted to delve into the mystery of her origins, the keys to her success, her relationships with artists and lovers and, more recently, her conduct during historical events, especially during the Second World War. They have allowed us a better understanding of the complex character of Gabrielle 'Coco' Chanel, while generating more debate and controversy.

The Palais Galliera in Paris, in its capacity as a museum of fashion, has chosen to concentrate on the couturière's work, which made her one of the most influential designers of the 20th century. The exhibition that this book accompanies is the first retrospective of Chanel's work ever held in Paris, and aims to analyse her career trajectory, the birth and evolution of the famous Chanel style, the characteristics of her work and her legacy within the world of fashion.

From the start of her career, in the early years of the 20th century, and right up to the end of her life, Gabrielle Chanel spoke out against the fashion of her time, with its swiftly changing trends and stereotyped view of women and femininity. In her youth, she decided to appropriate men's clothes, which allowed her both to move freely and to look distinguished, while also arousing amazement and fascination. Chanel became a female dandy, switching from borrowing clothes to designing them, and reinterpreting the comfort, functionality, restraint and elegance of the male wardrobe to suit women. In a similar manner, she advocated the idea of a modern uniform for a new kind of woman who was emerging as the century progressed, a woman who aspired to a new way of living and a freedom that had only been dreamed of before. Through extensive experimentation with techniques, reinterpreting the traditional craft of tailoring by using soft and flexible fabrics, such as jersey and tweed, she began to introduce her own version of the suit and the little black dress in the 1920s. In the 1950s, these became the symbols of a new kind of femininity, on both sides of the Atlantic.

Chanel developed her own recognizable and timeless style, which endured in the face of the ever changing collections, trends and fleeting fancies of fashion. The Chanel style was based on the principles of comfort and respect for the female anatomy, but also lay in the details, a subtle but exact combination of technical, decorative and symbolic touches that made up the world of the great designer. Rejecting superfluous decoration, Chanel always made bold and appropriate use of colours, prints, fabrics and techniques, emphasizing the balance and harmony of the whole. The sophisticated restraint of her clothes contrasted with the opulence of her jewelry – inspired by ancient or faraway civilizations – and her plentiful way of wearing it. Her first perfume, Chanel N° 5, became a landmark in perfume history, thanks to its abstract fragrance and the sharp lines of its bottle. Since its creation in 1921, this iconic perfume has been an invisible but vital accessory for the modern woman.

In the 1950s, Gabrielle Chanel was forced to defend her position in the world of fashion. Faced with the rise of Christian Dior and women's willing return to a wasp-waisted silhouette, she refused to submit to the dictates of a style she abhorred, rediscovered the fighting spirit of her early years and once again set out to oppose the dominant trend. Taking her own principles to the extreme, the designer presented a purified and pithy version of her style, which was completely in keeping with the vision that had guided her since the beginning. The suit of the 1920s became a modern uniform in 1954, and served as a fashion manifesto in itself. The jewelry and accessories designed after Chanel's comeback, including two-tone shoes and the '2.55' bag, became key elements of the house style.

Gabrielle Chanel's success was based not only on the functionality, comfort and chic elegance of her designs, but also on her ability to grasp and interpret the needs and desires of the women of her time. Chanel embodied her own style better than anyone; she was her own best model and the perfect representation of the intangible qualities than women wanted to see reflected in themselves: independence, youthfulness, freedom and ambition. She made use of her own image and built up her own legend in order to draw women from all over the world into a new way of being, a new way of moving, a lifestyle that could become theirs if they dressed like her. Understanding the power of her own image, the designer embraced a strategy of self-duplication, surrounding herself with women who looked like her and conveyed the qualities that made her a legend: Coco Chanel, an endless seeker of seduction.

The countless portraits of Chanel bear witness to the importance she placed on her public image. Many of them were taken by famous photographers, including Adolph de Meyer, Man Ray and Richard Avedon, for whom Chanel posed in one of her signature outfits, looking relaxed but alert, serene but defiant, with a penetrating gaze that never allows us to forget that she runs an empire. In the 1930s, André Kertész took a series of photographs showing the hands of the great designers of Parisian haute couture, Gabrielle Chanel among them. In this portrait, we see a Gabrielle Chanel that we're not used to seeing: serious, pensive, engaged, her mind at work. Unaware that her face was also in Kertész's frame, she dropped her guard: the character vanished, the legend disappeared, leaving only Gabrielle, the couturière.

Gabrielle Chanel devoted her long life to creating, perfecting and promoting a new kind of elegance based on freedom of movement, a natural and casual pose, a subtle elegance that shuns all extravagances, a timeless style for a new kind of woman. That was her fashion manifesto, a legacy that has never gone out of style.

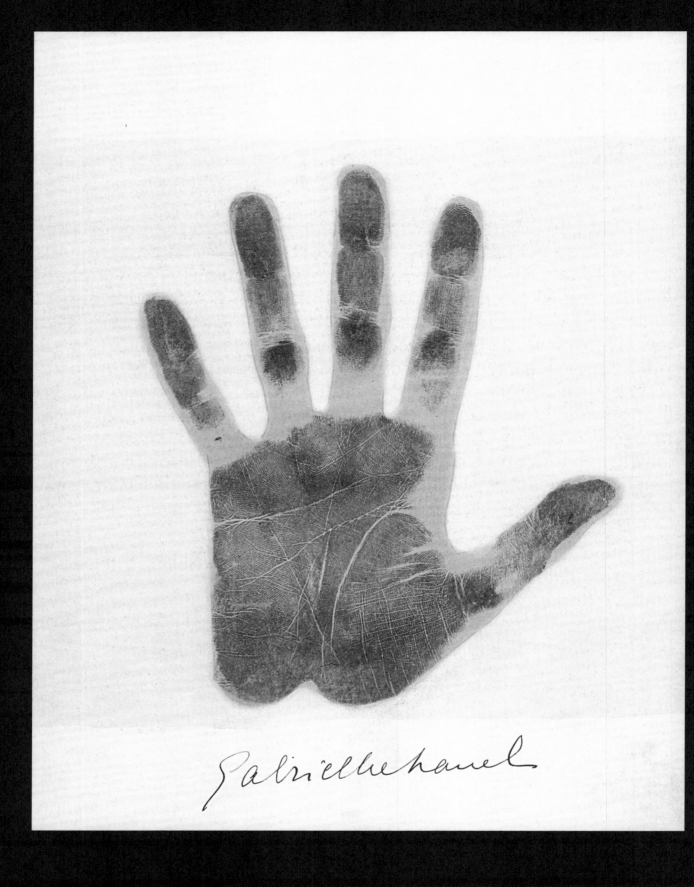

Handprint and signature of Gabrielle Chanel, 1939.
Patrimoine de CHANEL collection.

Olivier Saillard

THE MANY CHANELS

Mademoiselle Chanel lived at the rue Cambon but retired each night to sleep at the Ritz. In a modestly sized apartment, located one floor above the haute couture salons, she reigned over a silent realm of decorative objects that served as motifs for her entire life. The walls were lined with a dense tapestry of leather-bound books. Strange mirrors reflected back not the solitude of the great couturière's everyday world but her constant efforts to mask it. Not an inch of space or wall was left bare. While the clothes Chanel designed were a form of architecture for the body, the upholstering of her personal space created an extra layer of protection that kept the real walls at bay. If one of them reached out towards her, she deftly smothered it beneath golden coverings, heavy with menace. The alcoves encouraged confessions, while screens muffled, rebuffed or disguised them. Mademoiselle Chanel knew something of this, being someone who traded in truth and lies with equal disdain, since ultimately everything was part of the business of the self, the business of *her*self, which was her only true raison d'être. Lost amid the depths of an outsized sofa, she seemed to shrink and age inside the armature of her clothes. In the days before a show, she would lose more weight. Like an everyday person, she would take in the waistband of her skirt with a safety pin. Like an old lady, she would tuck a handkerchief inside her jacket sleeve. Seated on the plump cushions of her boat-like couch, she was a puppet without strings, a ventriloquist's dummy of herself, incapable of containing her own rages. Her success was there for all to see – in the iron scrollwork of a chandelier in the shape of her initials, in the

scentless camellias bursting from the painted screens, in the bouquets of wheat-ears moulded in metal. Incapable of holding her tongue about anything she disliked, Chanel railed endlessly against an entire decade – the 1960s. In a television interview in 1969, she could not refrain from telling a journalist: 'You know, I don't belong in the present day,'[1] which was her way of saying that things were better before. But who else was left to rail against? Were the 1960s – the final years of her life, which she would observe from the top of those famous stairs – not the peak of her success as well as her solitude? All those whose style inconvenienced her had either died or stepped aside. The greatest names among them, Jacques Fath and Christian Dior, died in 1954 and 1957 respectively. Her great rival, Elsa Schiaparelli, was no longer a major player; her firm closed its doors in 1954. The couturiers who had created Parisian chic – Lucien Lelong, Mainbocher, Molyneux and Robert Piguet – had also downed the tools of their trade. Paul Poiret, from whom Chanel had snatched her success, died in the bleak surroundings of a servant's room. Chanel, on the other hand, owing to her down-to-earth shrewdness and practicality, had secured herself a comfortable future. As for the avant-garde couturiers who had recently arrived on the scene, they were merely a source of amusement rather than irritation; they brought a smile to Mademoiselle Chanel's lips, because she knew that, ultimately, they would never be competing on the same playing field. Meanwhile, between the heirs to a lost world of fashion and good taste and the newcomers who were attempting to reinvent haute couture, there was barely room for those designers who had jumped on the fashion bandwagon with varying degrees of success. There was little left to ruffle the feathers of a couturière who had twice changed the face of fashion and who had women everywhere completely under her spell.

From the *monstres sacrés* of the fashion world to the 'revolutionaries', as Pierre Bourdieu called them, nobody could 'escape the law that relegates the latest thing to the realm of the out-of-fashion, and forces the designer to do everything all over again: it is the privilege of the greatest – Chanel for example – to halt fashion time for a moment, a supreme form of distinction.'[2] Despite the cast-iron certainty of the Chanel suit, whose fixed nature befitted a style rather than a fashion, Mademoiselle Chanel was on her guard. Ferocious, shrewd, waspish and intelligent, and as attuned to her instincts as an animal at bay, she recognized the need to confront a new and formidable enemy. This enemy had nothing to do with Italian couture or frilly extravagances; its address was neither the avenue Montaigne nor some wealthy private residence. And the couturière, who was still dominating her profession at the age of eighty-six, can be forgiven for getting emotional, anxious and mistrustful over this enemy, who ruled the 1960s: its name was youth.

'Something new appeared, in our society, which the new couturiers tried to interpret and codify: a new class was born that the sociologists had failed to predict: the young. Since all they possess is their bodies, the young need not concern themselves with looking common or classy: they simply *are*.'[3] The Chanel style, based on a kind of 'forgetting of the body [which was] entirely protected and absorbed by the social distinction of clothes',[4] was now obliged to do battle with the near-nudity of the baby boom generation. 'Take the Chanel woman: we can locate her social milieu, her jobs, her leisure activities, her travels. Then take the Courrèges woman: we do not ask what she does, who her parents are, what her income is – she is young, necessarily and sufficiently so.'[5] Fashion occupies a strange realm. It keeps its eye focused on the high peaks of art but somehow always ends up in the boxing ring. In the 1960s, the battle between Chanel and Courrèges set the respectable doyenne of haute couture against a young buck who had recently gone solo after years at Balenciaga. By the end of the decade, the battle between Chanel tradition and Courrèges innovation had cost the Spanish couturier his company. In 1968, no longer able to see himself in the world of fashion, Cristóbal Balenciaga announced in the press that he was retiring. Prêt-à-porter had won the day.

In her room at the Ritz – a room described as monastic in its simplicity – Mademoiselle Chanel retired each night to sleep, alone among the vestiges of a bygone age, as lone in her splendour as the column in the Place Vendôme.

Every day of every week that made up the months and years of the 1960s, the couturière, who once said 'I can think of nothing more ageing than trying to make oneself look younger,'[6] fought, campaigned, spoke out, and above all maintained the dignity of a profession that others were already beginning to lose sight of, thanks to the power of the mass media. In her own little corner of Paris, Chanel continued to design clothes by stripping away clutter. In the 1920s, the era of the little black dress, [ill. 4 p. 290] and in the 1950s, which marked her return to fashion and the advent of the famous Chanel suit, she tossed the frills and furbelows of an entire age out of the window. In response to the extravagances of Paul Poiret and the Ballets Russes, she emptied the feminine wardrobe of all its unwieldy artifice. As she said to Paul Morand, 'At about that time, I remember contemplating the auditorium at the Opéra from the back of a box. All those gaudy, resuscitated colours shocked me; those reds, those greens, those electric blues, the entire Rimsky-Korsakov and Gustave Moreau palette, brought back into fashion by Paul Poiret, made me feel ill. The Ballets Russes were stage décor, not couture. I remember only too well saying to someone sitting beside me: "These colours are impossible. These women, I'm bloody well going to dress them in black."'[7] The 'exterminating angel of nineteenth-century style' invented 'poverty for billionaires (all the while dining off gold plates), extravagantly expensive simplicity, seeking out what did not attract attention... Never was snobbery better directed against oneself.'[8] The little black dress was a definitive statement, the abstract ideal of a dress that women could wrap around themselves like a silent shadow. But Chanel went further. As well as dimming the colours of the previous decade, she steeped her garments in everyday jersey, decapitated dresses, sliced off collars, removed and stripped

away excess, erasing the ornamental armoury of the kind of fashion she wished to reject.

People thought she had faded into the background, that she was slumbering quietly, bundled up in the mink coat left to her as a cruel testament by the 1940s. But this was not the case. When Chanel, perched like a hawk on a clifftop of her own making, witnessed the revival of Belle Époque fashions and the success of the New Look, her reaction was fierce. Confronted with the likes of Dior and Balmain, couturiers with a talent for drawing and a penchant for girdles and corsets (the very garments she had discarded) and the kind of elegance that trapped women in petticoats and frills, Chanel headed straight back to the atelier and began sharpening her scissors. She could not bear this stylistic archaeology that sought to bring back the splendours of Versailles. Seven years after the New Look had dropped like a bombshell, followed by the 'Jolie Madame' silhouette and flounced dresses, Mademoiselle Chanel set off shockwaves no less dramatic than those caused by the little black dress in the 1920s. In restrained tweeds, the couturière sought retribution for women trapped by the prison of fashion. She invented the Chanel suit, trimmed with braid and weighted with chain at the hem, which allowed women to move freely once again from morning till night. With this suit in its many variant forms, Chanel knocked the designs of the male couturiers off-course. Once when Chanel – dressed all in black – bumped into Paul Poiret, in the 1920s, and he asked for whom she – this style icon of a new era – was in mourning, Chanel saucily replied: 'For you, Monsieur.' And indeed, she lived to see him laid to rest.

In the 1950s, she did the same thing with the ruling fashion trends, the elaborate gowns, the vestiges of the past that she would never approve of. She routed the bombastic style of the decade and became a spiritual guru for the young Courrèges and Saint Laurent. Her architectural garments – more like uniforms than swiftly changing fashions – became a blueprint for the couturiers of the sixties, who began to strip back fashion in the same way. As Chanel cast a black veil over the success of Dior and Fath, they themselves were forced to concede, and neither outlived the 1950s, the decade they had shaped. She saw them to their graves, just as she had Poiret. After the war, Schiaparelli – whom Chanel had allegedly steered into a lighted candelabra at a costume ball – was no longer even a rival. The Italian couturière's costume went up in smoke that evening; by the 1950s, Schiaparelli's surreal creations were barely even a memory, let alone fashion currency. Once again, Chanel looked on as another rival was laid to rest. A high priest as well as an abbess, she launched fashions and consigned those of others to the realm of the dead. Even her friend Balenciaga, whom Chanel clearly admired, got into a skirmish with her – Balenciaga kindly sent her a caricature of herself by A.M Cassandre, but Chanel immediately returned it to sender. She was not content with merely decluttering jackets and evening dresses; close friends and society acquaintances could be cast aside too. Only in matters of the heart was Chanel not in control of her enforced exile and increasing solitude. It was the men she loved and bedded who decided the fate of the relationship, not Chanel herself. Thus, as Hubert de Givenchy recorded, every evening after supper, the great Mademoiselle Chanel found herself torn – scornful of the company she had gathered around her table, yet fearing the loneliness of the spartan room that awaited her at the Ritz. Beneath the awning of the grand hotel, her guests had to wait patiently while she talked and talked, delaying the moment when she would have to climb the staircase alone. A Chanel wardrobe was like a fashion X-ray: just the bare bones with everything else stripped away. In Chanel's life too, the same process occurred. Throughout her life, Chanel had always preferred the romance of a dreamed-up childhood to her real memories – to the point of chasing away locals so that they didn't appear in photographs. Biographers came into uneasy collision with her fictions. Louise de Vilmorin was unable to write anything especially meaningful after interviews that focused more heavily on spiritualism than introspection. The resulting 'memoirs' were far blander than the life story Chanel had embroidered for herself. We have to look elsewhere to locate a true portrait of Mademoiselle Chanel. 'Convinced that the abandonments were the source of the abandonments, she refused to abandon herself so as not to be abandoned,'[9] Louise de Vilmorin later wrote in the foreword to an edition of *La Princesse de Clèves*. The line cannot help but remind us of Mademoiselle Chanel. Paul Morand's biography *The Allure of Chanel* was a polished and unparalleled exercise in style, taking his interviews with Chanel and stitching them together with literary flourishes. A skilled writer and a kind man, Morand took care not to trespass on the couturière's past or the intimacies of her private life. Morand's book contains no catches or hidden traps tucked between the covers or the folds between pages, or between the deftly chosen words and the rustle of memories, and remains the most fair of all the portraits of Chanel. Edmonde Charles-Roux, meanwhile, worked like a criminologist piecing together a case, building an entire edifice of facts to support the poor little girl from Moulins. Here too, some elements have yet to be improved upon. Accounts by female friends and collaborators, such as Claude Delay and Lilou Marquand, kindly and circumspectly held back details that Chanel, more out of shame than arrogance, preferred to keep concealed behind her painted screens. She could not bear to see herself in paintings either, refusing to pay the bill issued by Marie Laurencin, whose pallid portrait of Chanel seemed so far off the mark. Perhaps surprisingly, it was with photography – the art that supposedly never lies – that Chanel felt most at home. In 1937, she became the first woman of her rank to pose for an advertisement for her own perfume, Chanel N° 5. Leaning against her own mantelpiece, Chanel had the advantage of being very slim and cut a magnificent figure.[ill. 1 p. 98] Decade after decade, she was happy to be photographed. Whether in flattering close-ups by Horst P. Horst and George Hoyningen-Huene, or laid bare by the realism of Willy Rizzo, who produced the finest portraits of the couturière at work, Chanel seemed to forget herself. Neither painting nor text was capable of maintaining the illusion of her presence in the way that a photograph could.

Between her past, which she kept close to her chest like a hand of cards, and the future, which she could only conceive by building it herself, Chanel was very much of her time. In truth and in lies, in cruelty and in passion, in fashion and in life, she was never anything other than bare.

1

'Mademoiselle Chanel', *Panorama* broadcast, including an interview (in colour) conducted by Micheline Sandrel, Office National de Radiodiffusion Télévision Française, 31 July 1969.

2

Pierre Bourdieu with Yvette Delsaut, 'Le couturier et sa griffe: contribution à une théorie de la magie', *Actes de recherches en sciences sociales*, vol. I, no. 1, January 1975, p. 17.

3

Pierre Bourdieu with Yvette Delsaut, 'Le couturier et sa griffe', p. 27.

4

Pierre Bourdieu with Yvette Delsaut, 'Le couturier et sa griffe', p. 27.

5

Roland Barthes, 'Le match Chanel-Courrèges', *Marie Claire*, no. 181, September 1967, pp. 42–43; reprinted in Roland Barthes, *The Language of Fashion*, trans. Andy Stafford, London: Bloomsbury, 2013, pp. 99–103.

6

'Mademoiselle Chanel', 31 July 1969.

7

Paul Morand, *The Allure of Chanel*, trans. Euan Cameron, London: Pushkin Press, 2008.

8

Paul Morand, *The Allure of Chanel*, 2008.

9

Madame de Lafayette, *La Princesse de Clèves*, foreword by Louise de Vilmorin, Paris: Le Livre de Poche, 1958.

ill.1 **Gabrielle Chanel wearing one of her own hat designs,** *Comœdia Illustré*, **1 October 1910.**

Sophie Grossiord

Famous stage performers appeared in articles that showed them relaxing at home or taking a holiday. In advertisements, they vaunted the merits of stockings, corsets, cosmetics and perfumes, Lucky Strike cigarettes, automobiles and more. Advertisements for Cadum soap even used the faces of Régina Badet, Gaby Deslys and Geneviève Vix as evidence of its high quality.[5]

THE EARLY DAYS OF THE 'ARTIST OF THE RUE CAMBON'[1]

'GABRIELLE CHANEL'S STYLISH DESIGNS'

While Gabrielle Chanel's success in the early 1910s had its origins during her time with Étienne Balsan, it also owed a great deal to the world of the theatre. On 15 September 1910, the cover of *Comœdia Illustré* showed Lucienne Roger starring in *Le Mariage de Mademoiselle Beulemans*,[6] wearing a hat described as the 'creation of Gabrielle Chanel, 21, rue Cambon', a detail that also appeared in the theatre programme.[7] Chanel's name was then only known to a handful of people. 'I have just written a name that requires an introduction for those of my readers to whom it may be unfamiliar still,' wrote the columnist. 'In this column, we present to you two delicious designs by the refined artist Gabrielle Chanel. …We intend to publish the entire range here this winter, with the many creations of this highly distinguished artist, who designs hats for our prettiest society ladies … as well as our most elegant artistes.'[8]

In the early years of the 20th century, the bustling world of the Paris stage was one of fashion's favourite parade grounds. The sheer number of performances was a guarantee of success, and a glance at the theatrical magazine *Comœdia Illustré* shows the role that actresses, dancers and singers played in popularizing new styles.

The milliner Gabrielle Chanel, who opened her first shop in 1910 at 21, rue Cambon – in competition with the likes of Ida-Marguerite, Madame Lenthéric, Lewis, Lucienne, Lucie Hamar, Maria Guy, Marie Crozet and Marie-Louise – was no exception to this rule. *Comœdia Illustré* was soon singing her praises and her designs featured on several full-colour covers.[2] The images in this elegant magazine, as well as *Les Modes* (1912–14) and *Le Théâtre*, are valuable sources of evidence, given that very few of the young Chanel's hats have survived the passage of time.[cat. 2]

The close collaboration between couture and theatre goes back a long way.[3] Leading actresses were photographed by Félix, Talbot and Henri Manuel in costumes designed by Béchoff-David, Callot Sœurs, Chéruit, Dœuillet, Jenny, Margaine-Lacroix, Martial et Armand, Paquin, and others. These women were hugely famous, and the reviews lyrical. Parisian haute couture could rely on a source of guaranteed publicity – constant, effective and free – in press articles and theatre programmes that specified that a particular actress had been dressed for the stage or for town by a particular couturier. Meanwhile, the public could gaze upon the fashions of the day in all their splendid diversity. It was a process of exchange in which everyone benefited.[4]

The tone was set and success was beckoning. Chanel, with her hair pinned up, also posed for the camera herself – something of a special event. 'Gabrielle Chanel's exquisite profile shows to advantage two designs from a truly impeccable collection.… These hats have the hallmark of distinction, like the artist of the rue Cambon herself,'[9] we read in *Comœdia Illustré* on 1 October 1910.[ill.1] In the pre-war years, Zina Brozia, Simone Damaury and Mlle Frémont all modelled hats by Chanel for the magazine.[10] The portrait of celebrated singer and dancer Régina Badet wearing a plumed turban teamed with a fur coat, published in December 1910,[11] was reused in a Cadum soap advertisement without any mention of Chanel's name. Resplendent in a voluminous black velvet toque decorated with matching bird-of-paradise feathers, soprano Geneviève Vix posed for *Comœdia Illustré* and *Les Modes* in November 1912,[ill.3] and once again in June 1913,[12] wearing a feathered black straw hat. Juliette Rudy was also photographed for *Les Modes* in a Chanel hat.[13]

Gaby Deslys was another celebrated actress who served the Maison Chanel well. 'Gabrielle Chanel's stylish designs are increasingly sought after by pretty women both in the theatre and in town,'[14] observed *Comœdia*. Indeed, the milliner's name was linked to several popular styles of hat, and the theatre was clearly a key part of her growing success. The cover of the 1 March 1911 issue, illustrated by Paul Iribe, featured Iribe's wife, actress Jeanne Dirys, making her stage debut in *Le Cadet de Coutras*.[15] Several hats in the play originated in the rue Cambon, although neither

ill. 2 **Paul Delaroche, sketch of Gabrielle Dorziat in** *Les Éclaireuses*, **Comédie Marigny, Paris, 1911. Bibliothèque Nationale de France, Paris.**

ill. 3 **Geneviève Vix wearing a hat by Gabrielle Chanel,** *Les Modes*, **November 1912, p. 6.**

the programme nor the critics mentioned Chanel's name. Indeed, although the reviews dwell at length on the play itself, the actors' performances and the sets, the costumes are barely discussed, but mention is made of Jeanne Dirys's dress and coat in royal blue and black satin worn in Act III, teamed with a black tagal hat adorned with blue feathers, as well as the suit she wore in Act V, in aubergine satin, teamed with a tagal hat in lime green.[16]

MADEMOISELLE DORZIAT: 'ARBITER OF FEMININE ELEGANCE AT THE THEATRE'[17]

Chanel met Gabrielle Dorziat in her early days at Royallieu and the actress occupied a central place in Chanel's circle of friends. The press remarked upon their staunch friendship, which was evident from the number of Chanel hats that Dorziat wore and promoted. One of these was the design photographed for Les Modes in May 1913, a reproduction of which also exists with a Spanish caption.[18]

Regularly photographed and eulogized for her talent and her elegance, Gabrielle Dorziat was very much in the public eye and happy to play the publicity game. Although she loved Chanel, she also posed for other milliners, including Marie-Louise, Esther Meyer, Alice Nora and Lucie Hamar,[19] and while she wore outfits by Chéruit, Jenny and Revillon,[20] her favourite couturier was Jacques Doucet.[21]

Two photographs in a programme for a Ballets Russes production at the Théâtre du Châtelet, in June 1911, show the modernity of Chanel's designs. Dorziat wears a huge wide-brimmed hat decorated with white feathers,[ill. 4] teamed with an abaya, sold under the Babani label but designed by Mariano Fortuny, whose love of liberating the body suited the needs of his emancipated and artistic clients.[22]

Dorziat's loyalty to Chanel and Doucet was also expressed on stage. Late in 1911, the actress was appearing in a production of Peau neuve,[23] and could be seen on the cover of Comœdia Illustré wearing an outfit by Doucet and a hat by Chanel. The following year, the play Bel Ami[24] included costumes by Paquin and Buzenet, as well as Gabrielle Dorziat dressed in outfits by Doucet. Chanel's hats were featured alongside designs by Lewis and Camille Roger. 'The hats worn by Mademoiselle Dorziat in town and at the theatre are all designed by Gabrielle Chanel,'[25] the programme states. There were at least three of these, possibly four.[ill. 5] 'Mademoiselle Dorziat wears an exquisite hat by Madame Gabrielle Chanel, whose excellent taste has been given an opportunity to produce masterpieces and win approval from the most demanding of audiences,' Le Théâtre enthused. 'The female audience of Bel Ami are familiar, moreover, with the elegant creations of this delightful milliner, who is among those most renowned today.'[26] The month of March saw Dorziat once again wearing hats by Chanel, in her role as the singer Minuccio in Carmosine, a play by Alfred de Musset.[27]

Le Diable ermite,[28] in late 1912, consolidated this success, with Gabrielle Chanel designing at least six, possibly seven, hats for Gabrielle Dorziat, Alice Nory and Andrée Barelly. Chanel's name featured prominently in the programme, ensuring excellent publicity. Gabrielle Dorziat wore outfits by Doucet, Andrée Barelly by Buzenet and Alice Nory by Drécoll.

The play Les Éclaireuses (1913)[29] was a significant milestone and a personal triumph for Gabrielle Dorziat. She only wore one Chanel design in the final act, a 'hat in Nattier blue taffeta garnished with a rosette and two ribbons in the same taffeta',[30–ill. 2] but it was highly symbolic. This feminist play criticized marriage and tackled issues such as work and women's suffrage, divorce and common-law relationships. 'Yes, I'm free because I work... I'm interested in the work I've chosen. I'm fascinated by it!' exclaims the character of Germaine Luceau in the very first scene. 'Let me repeat that nobody has the right to control what I do; I'm not answerable to anyone else,' proclaims the independent Jeanne, the role played by Gabrielle Dorziat (Act II, Scene 5). There are unmistakable echoes here of the way that Chanel herself thought, and the way she lived her life. 'The hats worn by these young feminist heads have a genuine importance in Les Éclaireuses,' declared Comœdia Illustré. 'As for Mlle Dorziat, her hat, which strove like her dresses for absolute simplicity, blended with the gentle atmosphere of the final act.... Gabrielle Chanel ... as always struck just the right note.'[31] The stage directions state: 'Jeanne enters. She is dressed for a journey, having thrown a travelling coat over a house dress, and put on any old hat. Everything is unmatched and unplanned.'[32] The simplicity of Chanel's style responded beautifully to these requirements.

Unsurprisingly, contemporary actresses embraced modernity and the liberation of the body. Dancer and actress Régina Badet posed on roller skates on the cover of Femina on 1 January 1910, while Gaby Deslys was filmed in Deauville wearing a swimsuit.[33] Gabrielle Dorziat played golf, Lucienne Roger loved tennis, Geneviève Vix went rowing and, like Gabrielle Chanel at Royallieu, was photographed on horseback.[34] In 1916, Jane Renouardt, filmed by Gaumont Pathé, strolled down the Champs-Élysées wearing a comfortable dress designed by Chanel, and a year later Hilda May wore a jersey suit to ride a motorized scooter, as if it was the most natural thing in the world.[35] One particular shot of Jeanne Dirys, with short hair, lying in a meadow, is reminiscent of some photographs of Gabrielle Chanel[36] – whether by coincidence or deliberate imitation, who can say? A new milestone came in 1917–18. For the first time, Gabrielle Chanel designed costumes for actresses – Cécile Sorel in L'Abbé Constantin,[37] and Charlotte Lysès in La Dame de chambre. The programme for the latter listed Chanel's name alongside those of Martial et Armand, Buzenet and the couture house Aux Montagnes Russes, as well as the milliners Odette and Amélie, but the critics made no mention of the costumes. Significantly, Lysès wore her hair cropped short beneath a large hat with a draped crown by Chanel. Her outfits included a dress 'in dark brown satin embroidered with gold ... and trimmed with moleskin', with a matching cloak, and another in ivory jersey, with a broad band of beaver fur.[38] The play ran for 250 performances and there can be little doubt that the costumes attracted attention.

Véra Sergine wore a Chanel dress in Henry Bernstein's *Samson*, and then again in *Le Secret* (1919) by the same author. Recognizing the role of theatre in popularizing certain styles, a caption in *Femina* referred to 'Outfits seen on stage and which lend themselves readily to evening wear'.[39]

'I have never had actresses as customers. As far as fashion is concerned, actresses no longer existed after 1914. Before that, they dictated the fashion,'[40] Chanel told Paul Morand in 1946. But whether this was an accurate reflection of the situation is unclear. Might Chanel in fact be saying that she regarded those women as friends rather than actresses? Numerous celebrities, from France and elsewhere, would continue to reflect Chanel's close relationship with the stage. They included Cécile Sorel, who posed in front of a Coromandel screen in 1923, and Chanel's singer friend Marthe Davelli, who declared in 1925 that for daytime she wore nothing but Chanel,[41] as well as Mary Marquet, Gloria Swanson and Ina Claire. [ill. 5 p. 224] Film later took over where the theatre left off, with Michèle Morgan [ill. 4 p. 253] and later Brigitte Bardot, Jeanne Moreau, [ill. 1 p. 250] Anouk Aimée, Delphine Seyrig, Romy Schneider, [ill. 5 p. 253] Marlene Dietrich and Elizabeth Taylor all flying the Chanel flag, both on screen and in town.

Mˡˡᵉ GABRIELLE DORZIAT
Chapeau créé pour *BEL-AMI*, au Théâtre du Vaudeville
par GABRIELLE CHANEL
21, rue Cambon

ill. 5 Gabrielle Dorziat wearing
a hat designed by Gabrielle Chanel
for the play *Bel-Ami*,
Théâtre du Vaudeville, Paris,
Le Théâtre, 1 March 1912.

Le "Chapeau" en 1911   549

Mlle Gabrielle Dorziat
de la Porte-Saint-Martin
Photo Félix

Chapeau Création Gabrielle Chanel, 21, Rue Cambon.

ill. 4 Gabrielle Dorziat wearing
a hat by Gabrielle Chanel,
Comœdia Illustré, 1 June 1911.

1

My thanks, for their invaluable help, to Laurence Decobert, Laurence Rey, Anne-Lise Chatard, Manon Dardenne (Bibliothèque Nationale de France, Département des Arts du Spectacle) and Flora Triebel (BnF, Département des Estampes et de la Photographie), Martine Boussoussou (Bibliothèque Forney) and Sylvaine Lambert (Bibliothèque Historique de la Ville de Paris).

2

15 September 1910, 1 March 1911, 15 January 1912, 15 March 1912.

3

See *Modes à la ville à la scène*, Moulins: Centre National du Costume de Scène; Paris: Somogy, 2017.

4

Paul Poiret referred to the existence of contracts between actresses and couture houses; see *King of Fashion: The Autobiography of Paul Poiret*, London: V&A Publishing, 2009, p. 58.

5

BnF, Arts du Spectacle, 40ICO PER 1279 (1 and 2), 7394 (1), 26837.

6

Le Mariage de Mademoiselle Beulemans was a comedy in three acts by Frantz Fonson and Fernand Wicheler. First performed in Brussels, at the Théâtre de l'Olympia, on 18 March 1910, it opened in Paris at the Théâtre de la Renaissance on 7 June, with Lucienne Roger and Jules Berry. The 200th performance was in November 1910. The photograph used on the cover of *Comœdia Illustré* was reprinted in the programme for *L'Amour en cage*, which played at the Théâtre de l'Athénée in November 1911, but with no mention of Chanel's name (BnF, Arts du Spectacle, WNA-12).

7

BnF, Arts du Spectacle, ICO THE-3715.

8

Lucienne Roger wore two more hats by Gabrielle Chanel in the same issue. *Comœdia Illustré*, 15 September 1910, pp. 727 and 730.

9

Comœdia Illustré, 1 October 1910, pp. 28–29.

10

Comœdia Illustré, 1 November 1910, pp. 86 and 89; 15 November 1910, pp. 119–120; 15 December 1910, pp. 189–191; 1 April 1911, pp. 400 and 410.

11

Comœdia Illustré, 1 December 1910, p. 150; BnF, Arts du Spectacle, 40 ICO PER 1279/2.

12

Comœdia Illustré, 5 November 1912, p. 126; *Les Modes*, November 1912, p. 6; *Les Modes*, June 1913, p. 9.

13

Les Modes, February 1914, p. 28.

14

Comœdia Illustré, 1 May 1911, pp. 475 and 477.

15

Le Cadet de Coutras was a comedy in five acts by Abel Hermant and Yves Mirande, starring Jeanne Dirys, Ellen Andrée, Mademoiselle Dherblay, Roger Puylagarde, Jean Dax and Jean Joffre, first performed at the Théâtre du Vaudeville on 9 February 1911.

16

BnF, Arts du Spectacle, RF62274, pp. 40 and 41.

17

Comœdia Illustré, 20 November 1912, p. 162.

18

Les Modes, May 1913, pp. 19 and 32. 'Chapeau en tagal noir, orné de crosses claires'; 'Sombrero paja negra, adornos paradis', BnF, Arts du Spectacle, 40 ICO PER 7899 (2). See the photographs of Gabrielle Dorziat in *Comœdia Illustré*, 15 December 1911, *Les Modes*, May 1912 (pp. 8 and 28), July 1912 (pp. 10 and 28), August 1912 (pp. 10 and 24) and January 1913 (pp. 8 and 31). This last design was worn by Gabrielle Dorziat in *Le Diable ermite*.

19

See *Comœdia Illustré*, 15 December 1910, 15 August 1911 (p. 717). BnF, Arts du Spectacle, 40 ICO PER 7899 (2).

20

BnF, Arts du Spectacle, 40 ICO PER 7899 (2 and 3).

21

The programme for *La Dame de chambre* (Théâtre de l'Athénée, May 1924) states that 'Mademoiselle Gabrielle DORZIAT in Town and on Stage always wears designs by DOUCET, 21, rue de la Paix.' BnF, Arts du Spectacle, RF 59746.

22

Paris, Palais Galliera, B744. See *Mariano Fortuny. Un Espagnol à Venise*, exhibition catalogue, Paris: Palais Galliera/Paris Musées, 2017, cat. 230, p. 201. See also *Comœdia Illustré*, 1 June 1911, p. 549.

23

Peau neuve was a comedy in three acts by Étienne Rey, with Gabrielle Dorziat, Madeleine Lély, Alice Nory, Lucien Rozenberg and J. Laurent, performed at the Théâtre Michel. *Comœdia Illustré*, 15 January 1912. See also *Le Théâtre*, 1 February 1912, pp. 17–18.

24

Play in eight tableaux by Fernand Nozière, adapted from the novel by Guy de Maupassant, with Jean Dax, Gabrielle Dorziat, Véra Sergine and Madeleine Dolley, first performed at the Théâtre du Vaudeville, 24 February 1912.

25

On the cast page, the programme mentions milliners Camille Roger and Lewis, but not Gabrielle Chanel; see BnF, Arts du Spectacle, RT-3474.

26

Comœdia Illustré, 1 March 1912; *Le Théâtre*, 1 March 1912.

27

Comœdia Illustré, 15 March 1912, cover, p. 437.

28

Le Diable ermite, a comedy in four acts by Lucien Besnard, with Jean Dax, Harry Baur, Charles-Alexandre Guyon, Gabrielle Dorziat, Alice Nory and Andrée Barelly, was first performed at the Théâtre de l'Athénée on 15 November 1912. Programme: see BnF, Arts du Spectacle, WNA-12; *Comœdia Illustré*, 20 November 1912 (pp. 162–166) and 5 December 1912 (pp. 188–189). The same design was reproduced in *Les Modes*, January 1913, p. 8.

29

Les Éclaireuses, a four-act play by Maurice Donnay, with Gabrielle Dorziat, Marcelle Lender, Alice Nory, Claude Garry, Blanche Toutain and Henry Roussell, was first performed at the Comédie-Marigny on 26 January 1913.

30

Les Modes, March 1913, pp. 22 and 40.

31

Comœdia Illustré, 5 February 1913, pp. 433, 435 and 437.

32

BnF, Arts du Spectacle, RF57097.

33

BnF, Arts du Spectacle, 40 ICO PER 1279/2, 7394 (1).

34

BnF, Arts du Spectacle, 40ICO PER 7899 (2), 22655, 26837.

35

La Mode à Paris. Mademoiselle Jane Renouardt, artiste de théâtre au Palais-Royal, Gaumont Pathé Archives, ref. 1623GJ 00012; see *Femina*, June 1917, p. 12.

36

BnF, Arts du Spectacle, 40 ICO PER 7702. See Edmonde Charles-Roux, *The World of Coco Chanel: Friends, Fashion, Fame*, New York: The Vendome Press; London: Thames & Hudson, 2005, pp. 139–141 and 144.

37

L'Abbé Constantin, a comedy in three acts by Hector Crémieux and Pierre Decourcelle, based on the novel by Ludovic Halévy. See *Vogue US*, 1 May 1918.

38

La Dame de chambre, a comedy in three acts by Félix Gandera, with Charlotte Lysès, Jane Danjou, Lucy Ritto, Geneviève Béry, Lucien Rozenberg and Georges Mauloy, was first performed at the Théâtre de l'Athénée on 8 January 1918. It reopened at the Théâtre de l'Athénée in May 1924, with Gabrielle Dorziat in costumes by Doucet and hats by Valentine About; BnF, Arts du Spectacle, RF 59746. See *Femina*, March 1918, pp. 23 and 32.

39

Femina, March 1919 (p. 24) and April 1919 (p. 45).

40

Paul Morand, *The Allure of Chanel*, trans. Euan Cameron, London: Pushkin Press, 2013, p. 181.

41

Femina, October 1923, p. 17. A very similar dress is conserved in New York, at the Costume Institute, Metropolitan Museum of Art, 1995.468.1a-c; see *Vogue*, 1 May 1925, p. 56.

Hat by Gabrielle Chanel,
between 1913 and 1915,
black woven straw,
black silk satin ribbon.
cat. 2

ill.1 **Gabrielle Chanel playing golf in Saint-Jean-de-Luz, 1910s**

Miren Arzalluz

FREEDOM AND ELEGANCE ON THE BASQUE COAST

'Biarritz was the perfect setting for shopping.... Boy [Capel] advanced the funds and Gabrielle opened a *maison de couture*, offering a selection of dresses priced at three thousand francs each. ...It gave the Biarritz enterprise a solid base. Gabrielle began in July and had everything in place by September. And she did not have to wait long to discover the value of her initiative.'[1]

In her vivid account of Gabrielle Chanel's life and career, Edmonde Charles-Roux discusses the couturière's decision to open an establishment in Biarritz in 1915, and grasps better than any of Chanel's other biographers the significance of this episode in her professional trajectory. The Biarritz venture was the third major strategic decision in Chanel's career. In 1910, she opened a milliner's shop, Chanel Modes, at 21, rue Cambon in Paris. The extreme simplicity of her hat designs and the loyalty of a handful of the most celebrated actresses of the age swiftly combined to launch Chanel in the world of Paris fashion. Then in 1912 – recognizing the potential of such a fashionable resort with its emphasis on sophistication and its flourishing commercial life – she decided to open a shop in Deauville,[ill.1] and Parisians holidaying by the sea fell in love with her accessories and her sports clothes. Spurred on by her Deauville success, Chanel turned her thoughts to another key beach resort that attracted visitors from both France and abroad: Biarritz.

The Empress Eugénie played a pivotal role in transforming Biarritz into a holiday destination of international repute.[2] Eugénie de Montijo knew the place well. Following her marriage to Napoleon III, the imperial couple were invited to visit by the Biarritz authorities. They were charmed by the place and decided to build a palace there, the Villa Eugénie, making it their summer home. From 1855 onwards, Biarritz became a magnet for the principal royal families of Europe, the aristocracy, the political elite and major industrialists from all over the world. The arrival of the railway on the Basque Coast, that same year, facilitated the influx of these illustrious visitors, who tended to travel with a large retinue and a well-equipped wardrobe.

Despite the presence of the imperial court and its European counterparts in Biarritz, life at the Villa Eugénie was simple and free from the rigid etiquette of palace routine. As recorded by Ernest Barthez, the court doctor, days were punctuated by walks on the beach, visits to the shops in Biarritz, excursions into the countryside and sea bathing – something that the imperial couple did in public, alongside other regular bathers.[3] Writing several years later, Victor Hugo describes the atmosphere of freedom and spontaneity he found so delightful: 'They bathe at Biarritz as at Dieppe, as at Havre, as at Tréport; but with a certain unconventionality inspired by the beautiful skies and tolerated by this delicious climate. Women, wearing the latest Parisian styles of bonnets, enveloped from head to foot in great shawls, with lace veils on their faces, with downcast eyes disappear into one or another of the canvas booths with which the beach is dotted, and a moment later they come out again bare-legged, dressed in a simple brown linen chemise, which in many cases reaches scarcely below the knee, and with merry laughter they run down and jump into the sea. This freedom ... has its grace.'[4]

During the last three decades of the 19th century, after the emperor and empress had gone into exile, Biarritz continued to develop as a seaside resort, putting in place an extensive leisure infrastructure capable of hosting and providing entertainment for the increasing number of visitors to the Basque region. In the early years of the 20th century, numerous bathing establishments, hotels, casinos, cafés and restaurants, sporting facilities and upscale shops selling luxury goods ensured the elegant and cosmopolitan colony of summer holiday-makers an experience on a par with their expectations. The Russian, English and Spanish communities, whose presence on the Basque Coast dated back to the early years of the 19th century, were particularly well represented. Fashion played a fundamental role in this lofty society and Biarritz became a showcase for elegance; haute couture was breezily paraded along the sea front, on the beach at the bathing hour, on the golf course and the tennis courts, on the café terraces and in the salons of the casino. The modern urban experience, the product of careful town planning, acquired a new dimension in a place where promenading up and down, observing and being observed, were essential ingredients of everyday life. [ills.3, 4]

THE GREAT WAR: POVERTY AND OPPORTUNITY

Even though the circumstances may have seemed inauspicious, Chanel recognized the potential that Biarritz offered. The First World War, one of the bloodiest conflicts of the 20th century, had the paradoxical effect of favouring the microclimate – the leisured atmosphere and lavish consumerism – that was associated with the watering holes that lay along the Basque Coast. After war was declared in 1914, Biarritz opened its arms to those who, fleeing the horrors of the war, sought refuge in their sea-front residences and devoted themselves to a life of escapism and idle recreation. And, thanks to its proximity, Spain – which had remained neutral – offered the security of a fallback in case of need and was a reliable source of provisions. Just over the border, moreover, San Sebastián, the summer residence of the Spanish royal family, the court, politicians and financiers since the end of the 19th century, was another watering place of key importance. Chanel thus recognized the potential for a wealthy and elegant clientele on both sides of the border.

On 2 September 1915, at the height of the summer season, a local newspaper announced: 'We are delighted to learn that Paris's Maison Gabrielle CHANEL has opened its Sales Rooms at Villa de Larralde, 6, Descente de la Plage, in Biarritz.'[5] Chanel had made the decision to rent the Villa de Larralde – a medieval-style building dating from 1867, owned by the Larralde-Diusteguy family – based on its prime position in the centre of town, opposite the casino and just a few yards from the beach.[6] In this grand residence, Gabrielle Chanel established her first couture house and showed a collection of dresses, a new step and a qualitative leap in her as yet still short career.[7] Within a few days of its opening, the Maison Chanel announced in the local press that it was looking for 'a good seamstress'.[8] Other advertisements appeared at regular intervals in the months that followed and throughout 1916.[9] The Biarritz venture was an immediate and unqualified success, and when Chanel returned to Paris it was as a famous couturière, assured of a new and promising clientele. In her absence, her sister Antoinette managed the business in Biarritz, while Marie-Louise Deray supervised the workshops, which employed around sixty seamstresses.[10]–ill.7

'In Paris,' Edmonde Charles-Roux tells us, 'one of her ateliers worked only for Spanish clients. Now, like a general deploying his reserves according to the needs of war, Gabrielle recruited in Paris whatever personnel she lacked in Biarritz and, in a riskier manoeuvre, nagged Basque mothers into letting their daughters go to Paris, and this despite the zeppelins. Defeated, the mothers surrendered.'[11] In July 1916, 'Maison Gabrielle Chanel, Robes, Modes, Jerseys' (the title was followed by the addresses in Paris and Biarritz) informed its Spanish clientele that the Villa de Larralde establishment would remain 'open all year'.[12] This strategic decision set the Maison Chanel apart from the Paris couture houses that only showed their collections on the Basque Coast in high season. In 1918, Chanel purchased the Villa de Larralde from Marie Antoinette de Larralde-Diusteguy, Vicomtesse de L'Hermite – irrefutable proof of the financial success of her bold enterprise.[13]

OVER THE BORDER

From 1917 onwards, the effects of the war were also felt in Biarritz, and Chanel's international, and especially Spanish, clientele became increasingly important, to the point where Chanel took a new step by showing her collections on the Spanish side of the border. She began in September 1917, at the Hotel María Cristina, the most fashionable establishment in San Sebastián,[14] upon which the royal family and the court, the Spanish aristocracy and the powerful Basque industrial bourgeoisie all converged. Cristóbal Balenciaga, then aged twenty-two, had just set up as a couturier in town. Years later, he recounted how he had summoned up the courage to introduce himself to Chanel, whom he admired enormously, on one occasion when she was playing baccarat at the casino.[15] The two of them went on to become genuine and lifelong friends. After San Sebastián, Chanel showed her collections in Madrid, in the salons of the Ritz and Palace hotels between 1918 and 1920,[16] and later at the Ritz in Barcelona, where she began showcasing her innovative designs in 1920.[17]

Queen Victoria Eugenie of Spain played an undeniable role in the success Chanel found with a Spanish clientele in the early years of her career. Granddaughter of England's Queen Victoria and wife of Alfonso XIII of Spain, Victoria Eugenie was a great lover of fashion and she introduced Parisian haute couture to the austere Spanish court of the dowager Queen Maria Christina. The Infanta Eulalia recorded in her memoirs: 'From the moment she arrived in Spain, Victoria set the tone of Madrid fashion... She and her ladies were illustrious models who, in San Sebastián, Santander and Madrid, laid down the rules and set the direction of travel.'[18]

Thanks to her English education and the customs of her native England, Victoria Eugenie was an energetic woman, keen on open-air activities and sports such as tennis, golf and sailing, all of which she practised regularly. Favouring comfort and freedom of movement, she particularly liked a restrained style of dressing, stripped of extravagance and superfluous ornamentation. There were some occasions when her royal duties and the strict etiquette of the Spanish court demanded a more conservative elegance, and she would then rely principally on the House of Worth,[19] historically the supplier to most of Europe's royal houses. From 1915, the queen was a regular client of Gabrielle Chanel, whose creations she loved for their perfect balance between freedom and sophistication. The queen's private accounts, along with the contemporary press, demonstrate her fidelity to the Maison Chanel during the 1920s.[20]

COSTUMES DE JERSEY
Modèles de Gabrielle Chanel (fig. 257, 258 et 259)

Planche XI. — Supplément des " Élégances Parisiennes " N° 4.

Le Gérant : H. Bernard.

ill. 2 **Jersey ensembles
by Gabrielle Chanel,**
Les Élégances parisiennes,
July 1916, pl. XI.

ill. 3 **An elegant woman walking
her dog, Biarritz,
between 1900 and 1910.**

ill. 4 **Beach promenade, Biarritz,
between 1900 and 1910.**

A RADICAL VISION OF FASHION

The garments Chanel designed for her first collections, with their simple lines and use of light, supple fabrics like jersey, appeared particularly well suited to the demands of a holiday lifestyle involving long, relaxed days socializing in the open air. [ill. 2] In her quest for practical solutions, Chanel found that the traditional masculine wardrobe and working attire offered unexpected materials and an apparently neglected aesthetic that complemented life on the Basque Coast. Like Victor Hugo's, in the previous century, numerous testimonies record the bustle, the dynamism and the insouciance that reigned in Biarritz in the early years of the 20th century. In 1910, in an article for the American daily *The Boston Globe*, Idalia de Villiers described the elegance of women in Biarritz, comparing their style to the style then prevalent in Trouville, another of France's key watering holes: 'There are few, if any, seaside resorts where one sees more attractive toilets than at Biarritz. In its own way it is quite as fashionable as Trouville and Deauville, but it does not at all resemble either of these exotic watering places. ...At Biarritz the fashionable women, for the greater part, like an open-air, natural life. [ill. 5] They swim, they play golf, [ill. 1] they play tennis, they ride and drive. And I am speaking of women of many different nationalities: English, American, French, Spanish and Russian. Everyone is active at Biarritz....' [21]

In August 1914, writing for *The Washington Post*, Claude Cherys declared that, while women in Deauville dressed in a sophisticated way, in Biarritz they were 'more genuine, more like true sportswomen'. [22] And, in Biarritz, he added, 'There is a touch of manlike utility about the pure white linen costumes worn on the Grande Plage in the early morning. The wide-brimmed sailor hats seem just a trifle more severe and correct.' [23]

Gabrielle Chanel's radical take on fashion, apparent from the earliest days of her career, was immediately admired and adopted in Biarritz, where freedom of movement, functionality, casualness and distinction were non-negotiable elements of the accepted dress code. On the Basque Coast, Chanel found both the ideal testing ground for her innovations and a clientele who were willing to grant her creative recognition and bolster her financial position. She had always intended to capitalize on her success in Biarritz by establishing a major couture house in Paris, fashion's holy of holies. In 1918, she achieved that ambitious objective when she opened a business in her own name at 31, rue Cambon. In August of the same year, *Harper's Bazaar* brought its readers up to date regarding her latest designs: 'Chanel, in her pretty new salons in the rue Cambon, is making many new models of tricot for Biarritz, where Chanel frocks at least half the "beach". This transparent Jersey and thick, soft Jersey, trimmed with a furry sort of tricot, are made into cloaks and one-piece frocks, which are such desirable garments at the seaside, being at once cool and warm... Not only is tricot worn at the seaside and in the country, but in Paris as well, where we are beginning to array ourselves in "tailored" frocks of tricot.' [24]

After conquering Biarritz, Chanel's style triumphed in Paris and, during the final months of the war, the capital of fashion regained its status as the primary arbiter of elegance and style. The society that emerged from the conflict was profoundly changed, and Parisian haute couture had to grapple with the needs and aspirations of women in this new world. Gabrielle Chanel, yet again, showed herself to be one of the most influential creative forces of her age.

ill. 5 **Stormy day in Biarritz, August 1918. Photograph by Jacques Henri Lartigue.**

1

Edmonde Charles-Roux, *The World of Coco Chanel: Friends, Fashion, Fame*, New York: The Vendome Press; London: Thames & Hudson, 2005, pp. 130–131.

2

See Pierre Laborde, *Histoire du tourisme sur la Côte basque (1830–1930)*, Biarritz: Éditions Atlantica, 2001; and *Biarritz, huit siècles d'histoire. 250 ans de bains de mer*, Biarritz: Éditions Atlantica, 2008.

3

Ernest Barthez, *La Famille impériale à Saint-Claude et à Biarritz*, Paris: Calmann-Lévy, 1913.

4

Victor Hugo, *Victor Hugo's Letters to his Wife and Others (The Alps and the Pyrenees)*, trans. Nathan Haskell Dole, Boston: Estes and Lauriat, 1895, p. 143.

5

La Gazette de Biarritz, Bayonne et du littoral, 2 September 1915, p. 2.

6

See Edmonde Charles-Roux, *L'Irrégulière*, Paris: Grasset et Fasquelle, 1974, p. 256.

7

Edmonde Charles-Roux, *L'Irrégulière*, p. 256.

8

La Gazette de Biarritz, *Bayonne et du littoral*, 12 September 1915.

9

La Gazette de Biarritz, *Bayonne et du littoral*, 20 April, 9 August, 30 September and 5 October 1916.

10

Amy de la Haye, *Chanel: Couture and Industry*, London: V&A Publishing, 2011, p. 26.

11

Edmonde Charles-Roux, *The World of Coco Chanel*, p. 131.

12

La Correspondencia de España, 23 July 1916, p. 7.

13

See the deed of purchase of the Villa de Larralde, dated 14 and 23 November 1918, from Gabrielle Chanel to the Vicomtesse de L'Hermite, in the presence of Maître Blaise, notary in Biarritz; recorded in the French Mortgage Registry on 23 December 1918.

14

La Voz de Guipúzcoa, San Sebastián, 24 September 1917, p. 2.

15

Prudence Glynn, 'Balenciaga and la vie de chien', *The Times*, 3 August 1971.

16

ABC, 24 October 1918, p. 24; *La Época*, 13 March 1919; *El Sol*, 12 March 1920, p. 2.

17

La Vanguardia, 24 October 1920, p. 2.

18

Memorias de Doña Eulalia de Borbón, Barcelona: Editorial Juventud, 1967, pp. 132–133.

19

See the General Palace Archives, dossier 333, box 597.

20

See the General Palace Archives, general administration, dossier 1153; *La Correspondencia de España*, 4 April 1920, p. 11.

21

Idalia de Villiers, 'Modes of the moment', *The Boston Globe*, 2 December 1910.

22

Claude Cherys, 'The Craze for Striped Coats at the Fashionable French Summer Resort', *The Washington Post*, 23 August 1914, p. 4.

23

Claude Cherys, *The Washington Post*, 23 August 1914.

24

'Paris whispers of autumn in her late summer frocks', *Harper's Bazaar*, August 1918, pp. 39–40.

ill. 6 **Gabrielle Chanel on the beach at Biarritz, c. 1920. Patrimoine de CHANEL collection.**

ill. 7 **Gabrielle Chanel and her staff in the courtyard of her Biarritz couture house during a St Catherine's Day celebration, c. 1915. Patrimoine de CHANEL collection.**

Loose blouse with sailor collar
by Gabrielle Chanel,
Summer 1916, ivory silk jersey.
cat. 1

**Dress and jacket ensemble,
between 1922 and 1928,
ivory silk jersey.**
cat. 7

**Evening dress, 1924,
gold lamé, gold lace embroidered
with gold cabochons.**
cat. 40

Cape, Spring–Summer 1925,
black silk crêpe,
black rooster feathers.
cat. 111

Cape, Spring–Summer 1925,
ivory silk crêpe,
white rooster feathers.
cat. 110

Evening dress, Autumn–Winter
1926–27, midnight blue
crêpe georgette, silk fringing dyed
in graduating shades of blue.
cat. 112

Evening dress, Spring–Summer
1927, ivory silk fringing and crêpe.
cat. 113

Previous pages

Short evening dress,
Autumn–Winter 1927–28,
blue silk crêpe embroidered
with blue glass beads.
cat. 115

Short evening dress, 1927,
black silk crêpe embroidered
with white glass beads.
cat. 114

44

Previous pages

**Evening dress, Autumn–Winter
1929–30, pink silk tulle
embroidered with pink sequins.**
cat. 105

**Evening dress, Autumn–Winter
1929–30, blue silk tulle
embroidered with fancy
blue sequins.**
cat. 104

Evening dress
cat. 104

**Evening dress, c. 1921,
navy crêpe de chine embroidered
with navy sequins,
midnight blue pongee, royal
blue crêpe georgette.**
cat. 116

**Evening ensemble
with dress and jacket,
Autumn–Winter 1934–35,
ivory Moroccan crêpe,
silk tulle embroidered
all over with copper sequins.**
cat. 44

**Beret, c. 1935,
black nylon and cellophane.**
cat. 108

ill.1 **Sem, sketches for a portrait of Gabrielle Chanel, 1923, black pencil and graphite on paper. Patrimoine de CHANEL collection**

Laurent Cotta

SEM AND CHANEL: BUILDING AN IDENTITY[1]

Gabrielle Chanel described herself in the following fashion: 'I see myself with my two menacing arched eyebrows, my nostrils that are as wide as those of a mare, my hair that is blacker than the devil, my mouth that is like a crevice out of which pours a heart that is irritable but unselfish; ...My dark, gypsy-like skin that makes my teeth and my pearls look twice as white; my body, as dry as a vine-stock without grapes; my worker's hands with cabochons that resemble an American knuckle-duster. The hardness of the mirror reflects my own hardness back to me; it's a struggle between it and me: it expresses what is peculiar to myself, a person who is efficient, optimistic, passionate, realistic, combative, mocking and incredulous, and who feels her Frenchness.'[2]

This encapsulation of Chanel's physical and mental characteristics is strikingly reminiscent of three caricatures drawn between 1913 and 1923 by Sem,[ill. 6] the nom de plume of Georges Goursat,[3] a renowned arbiter and critic of elegant society. These witty portraits were published as plates – with pochoir colouring – in three different albums and summed up the first decade of Chanel's career. The artist captured his subject's silhouette and characteristic expressions so well that she became as iconic and as immediately recognizable as Charlie Chaplin in his role as the Little Tramp. Known as portraits-charges ('loaded' portraits), these caricatures mirrored Chanel's own efforts to build her own public identity for advertising purposes. The angular silhouette and equally angular face, the glowering eyes and tight lips, the hair tucked up under a hat, and later cropped short, were the recurring elements that transformed the youthful Chanel into a figure who would remain distinctive to the end of her life.

In 1913, in Sem's Tangoville album, illustrating Deauville society, Gabrielle Chanel appears as a somewhat grim-faced trophy wife being swept off her feet by a polo-playing centaur in the form of Arthur 'Boy' Capel, who financed her millinery business.[ill. 2] There are clear allusions to Chanel's craft, such as the hat perched on top of the polo stick, which resembles one of her own designs. But, above all, Chanel herself is represented as an eccentric figure – no classical beauty, but one half of a couple very much in the public eye.

In Sem's album Le Nouveau Monde, published in 1923, a short-haired Chanel – now smiling and the very picture of success – lounges on a couch, observing the goings-on in her salon.[ill. 3] The scene is framed by the unmistakeable outlines of a Chanel Nº 5 bottle and symbolizes the rise of the new queen of perfume and couture, the two realms that Chanel revolutionized. Between these two illustrations falls a third, executed in 1919 and published in Le Grand Monde à l'envers, and rather more complex to interpret. It is the most crudely caricature-like of the three.[ill. 4] In it, Chanel – with little apparent conviction – is showing the actress Jacqueline Forzane a selection of somewhat battered-looking hats. Neither woman has been spared by the illustrator. Forzane's chin is particularly exaggerated, as is her characteristic stance – hips thrust forward, stomach pulled in, shoulders thrown back, to such a degree that her body appears to be pulling in different directions. Chanel's stance is similar, if a little less exaggerated, and reflects a typical posture adopted by fashionable women in the 1910s, one that Chanel herself emulated throughout her adult life and demanded from her models: 'Push your pelvis forward and pull your shoulders gently back...'[4] was the injunction. Both women are depicted wearing Chanel outfits, which the artist has made to look loose, even shapeless. Chanel herself has a drooping bosom (quite unlike her actual shape) and her stockings are wrinkled. She looks more like a concierge in a comic play than the very embodiment of Parisian chic.

The cartoonist's pen is particularly vicious, and arguably rather unfair. Sem's comments in Le Vrai et le Faux Chic (1914), nevertheless seem to suggest that the kind of fashion Chanel was selling was exactly what Sem believed was needed. 'It is odd', he wrote 'that women are seeking such excessively complicated outfits at the very moment when male apparel tends towards absolute simplicity, and automobile manufacturers ... are reducing bonnets and bodywork to a series of clean lines.'[5]

This could perhaps be viewed as the bad faith of an illustrator who was prepared to do anything for the sake of a successful caricature. That would be reductive, however. To be sketched by Sem was a cast-iron guarantee of one's position in Paris society, and Sem's illustrations can be read on more than one level. As a way of recording the major changes among the upper classes, who were unsettled by the First World War, the author of Le Grand Monde à l'envers took it upon himself to portray the leading lights of pre-war Deauville being forced to work in order to survive in a now-hostile world: Boni de Castellane was depicted in the guise of a junk dealer; Robert de Montesquiou as a hairdresser; the Aga Khan as a carpet seller. Within the satirical logic of this album, therefore, Gabrielle Chanel's wrinkled stockings are something of a triviality.

Nor does Chanel appear to have criticized these caricatures; in any event, there is no record of her ever having done so. According to Madeleine Bonnelle, the great-niece of Sem, his friendship with Chanel dated back to the time when she was living with Étienne Balsan, at Royallieu.[6] In 1910, her shop 'Chanel Modes' at 21, rue Cambon, where Arthur Capel set her up in business, was only a few doors away from Sem's apartment.[7] Their friendship grew over the years, and is evidenced by documents now in the archives of the Association Sem: photographs of Chanel and Sem with the Duke of Westminster on a yacht, and letters Sem sent Chanel from Biarritz, describing society life in the seaside resort with a caustic wit that must have delighted the recipient.[8] Their relationship was based around a similar sharp sense of humour, but also a similar aesthetic. In the family memoirs, Madeleine Bonnelle describes her great-uncle's apartment at 15, boulevard Lannes, where Chanel apparently helped with the interior decor. Recorded in photographs, the curtains and lampshades, which were made for him at Chanel's atelier, are strangely reminiscent of the white faille furnishings that the couturière later installed at her own holiday home, La Pausa, in around 1930. The description of Sem's sitting room, with its white walls and little white couch in unbleached linen, garnished with cushions in every shade from beige to dark brown,[9] demonstrates the similarity of their tastes in interior design. In an article written in 1929, Sylvia Lyon describes the famous staircase lined with mirrors at Chanel's rue Cambon boutique, where celebrities of the age often gathered; among them was the vitriolic caricaturist,[10] who was a regular visitor.

Sem's three images of Gabrielle Chanel may well be uncompromising. However, the caricature from 1913 can be interpreted as an artistic homage, and one that helped to launch the young milliner's career. In one fell swoop, she became an equal of the most celebrated figures of the immediate pre-war period.

Chanel and Sem certainly both loved luxury and elegance as long as it was discreet, restrained and comfortable. A handwritten note by Sem from the early 1930s comments on Chanel's style with a perceptiveness that suggests they shared a point of view: 'Subtle elegance – nothing superfluous, nothing artificial, nothing useless, lacking in point or purpose… No false buttons or laces, no tabs, no elastic, no fasteners or clips, no useless complications: clean – very simple – belts, a logical fastening system, no useless eccentricity – it's coherent, a masterpiece of logic and ingenuity, like the wing of a bird or its tail, which is also ornamental, or like the wings of an insect… or the reproductive organs of a flower: nothing silly, fussy, absurd or over-fanciful, whimsical….'[11] From 1911 onwards, Sem wrote a column on men's fashion in *Le Journal*, entitled 'Le Vrai et le Faux Chic' ('Real and Fake Chic'). In it, the illustrator went further than using his customary wit to critique the excesses and

ill. 2 **Sem, plate from the album** *Tangoville*, **1913. Palais Galliera, Paris.**

absurdities of fashion. In articles entitled 'Do Not Modify Nature' and 'Do Not Dress Richly', he dispensed valuable advice to his readers on true elegance – which meant dressing simply, with an economy of means and without superfluous decorative details. Sem's concept of masculine elegance tallied in many respects with that of Adolf Loos in Vienna, who was also applying the same rationalist principles to architecture during the same period. It was Chanel who began incorporating these principles into women's fashion. In 1914, however, she was not sufficiently well known for her name to be mentioned in Sem's album *Le Vrai et le Faux Chic* alongside those of Worth, Chéruit, Paquin or the milliner Marcelle Demay; but, as Edmonde Charles-Roux noted, the hat worn by Jacqueline Forzane on page 41 of the album has all the characteristics of a Chanel creation,[ill.5] although no designer's name is given.[12]

Sem explained his working method in an issue of *Le Journal* on 2 December 1913: 'A likeness, a true likeness, which not only retains the appearance of a face but also reveals the model's soul, does not come about through the juxtaposition, the more or less exact assemblage, of traits servilely reproduced. … It's not a question of copying a face, but of *recreating* it. …From that moment on, I pursue my model mercilessly, my eye drinks them in so greedily, I identify with them so completely, that, by a curious phenomenon of telepathy, through a heightened sensibility, I reflect like a mirror the tiniest nuances of their physiognomy, all the phases of their expressions, their demeanour, their looks. …If the subject is female, I tear off her veil in a sort of sadistic frenzy; my pencil ferrets around in her nostrils; beneath her makeup, which I scrape off, I scour her wrinkles plastered with white grease, I reveal the mauve of her jam-coloured lips, I rumple her fake curls. It's a fight to the death: I pluck her alive.'[13]

These lines provide a context for the fifty or so preparatory sketches[ill.1] that Sem made for the 1923 print depicting Chanel inside a bottle of Nº 5 perfume.[ill.3] The same ambivalence can be perceived, a balancing act between cruelty, admiration and sympathy. Chanel looks rather swan-like due to the elegantly haughty way she holds her head, while her mobile face is by turns charming, laughing, grimacing, astonished. She was forty at the time but seemed ageless. The visionary Sem had captured the very essence of his subject, prefiguring the iconic figure she would ultimately become.

ill.3 **Sem, plate from the album**
Le Nouveau Monde, **1923.**
Palais Galliera, Paris.

ill. 4 **Sem, plate from the album**
Le Grand Monde à l'Envers, **1919.**
Palais Galliera, Paris.

discrètement dissimulées au milieu de ce défilé de mi-carême, non pas quelques-unes, mais des milliers de Parisiennes exquises, habillées avec un goût sûr par une élite de couturiers et de modistes qui savent encore soutenir le bon renom et la suprématie de Paris.

Voyez cette petite robe d'un bleu cendré, comme pastellisé par la lumière modérée de Paris. C'est un rien : une tunique retenue par une ceinture sur une jupe droite. Mais quel petit chef-d'œuvre de simplicité harmonieuse et discrète ! Le buste fragile de cette jeune femme se meut aisément dans ce souple velours adouci d'un col et d'une bande de fourrure, tandis que la jupe claque allégrement entre les pieds alertes, à la cadence de la démarche réglée sur l'amble du lévrier. Il faudrait avoir des yeux bien peu exercés, de bien mauvais " callots ", dirait une arpette indignée, pour ne pas deviner à première vue que cette charmante promeneuse s'est échappée des mains divines des deux sœurs fées que l'univers nous envie.

ill. 5 **Sem,** *Le Vrai et le Faux Chic*, **1914,**
p. 41. Musée Carnavalet –
Histoire de Paris.

ill. 6 **The caricaturist Sem, c. 1914.**

1

I would particularly like to thank Sem's great-great-niece Élisabeth Bonnelle-Rombach, and Xavier Chiron and Dominique Gouyou-Beauchamps, respectively honorary president and secretary of the Association Sem. The information they provided has been extremely helpful and I am grateful for their willingness and generosity in allowing me access to their collections and archives.

2

Paul Morand, *The Allure of Chanel*, trans. Euan Cameron, London: Pushkin Press, 2008, p. 143.

3

Georges Goursat (1863–1934), better known as Sem, caricaturist, columnist and poster artist.

4

Lilou Marquand, *Chanel m'a dit*, Paris: Éditions Jean-Claude Lattès, 1990, p. 72.

5

Sem, *Le Vrai et le Faux Chic*, Paris, 25 March 1914, p. 40.

6

Madeleine Bonnelle and Marie-Josée Méneret, *Sem*, Périgueux: Pierre Fanlac, 1979, p. 143.

7

Xavier Chiron, *Collection Sem*, vol. II, Tokyo: Kawashima, 2008, p. 123.

8

Élisabeth Rombach and Xavier Chiron, *Feuillets Sem*, no. 70: *Sem, Chanel et le Pays basque*, September 2014, pp. 3–6.

9

Madeleine Bonnelle and Marie-Josée Méneret, *Sem*, p. 154.

10

Sylvia Lyon, 'Chanel', *The Bystander*, 10 April 1929, p. 70.

11

From a handwritten note by Sem, cited in Élisabeth Rombach, 'Le talent de Chanel vu par Sem', *Les Feuillets Sem*, no. 70, Association Sem, September 2014, p. 10

12

Edmonde Charles-Roux, *Le Temps Chanel*, Paris: Chêne / Grasset, 1979, pp. 115–116.

13

'L'art d'obtenir une ressemblance', *Le Journal*, 2 December 1913, p. 6.

THE DRAGONFLY AND THE BULL

They were worlds apart – the little orphan girl from a family of market traders from the Cévennes region, and the bourgeois Parisian born into wealth and culture. The former instinctively sought out powerful men as her protectors, while the latter – upon whom fate had smiled from the moment of his birth – needed only to publish his first handful of poems to conquer Paris. The gulf between them might never have been bridged, had it not been for the extraordinary determination of Gabrielle Chanel, now a couturière, to make her mark as a patron like her friend Misia Sert, right at the moment when the Ballets Russes were staging *Parade*, with a libretto by Jean Cocteau.

Lively, witty and highly strung, Cocteau saw fashion as much more than a manual trade, which was rare in those days. In 1917, Chanel was happy merely to listen, and she found herself at ease with Cocteau the writer and his penchant for aphorisms. His monologues were littered with gems waiting to be picked up, applied and recycled. 'Fashion dies young. That's what makes its levity so serious' (*Le Grand Écart*, 1923). 'Fashion becomes unfashionable' – to which Chanel added 'Style never,' with her innate ability to cut to the chase. There was also this barb from Cocteau's *Thomas l'imposteur* (1923) – 'On some women, the finest pearls look like fakes, while on others, fake pearls look like the real thing.'

The friendship between the two sprang from the meeting of two visions, fuelled by a shared determination to make an impact. Cocteau was bursting with an intelligence that was almost exhausting; Chanel dreamed of encapsulating her own experience as pithily as he could – an aspiration so successful that we still do not know which of them actually said 'Fashion creates beauty, which will grow ugly in time; art creates ugliness, which will become beautiful.' Cocteau was unquestionably the more erratic of the two; but Chanel was also constantly shedding her skin – the supreme goal of the world of couture.

In the wake of the Great War, they were both pioneers. Chanel set the fashion for slender bodies and cropped haircuts, while Cocteau promoted the craze for suntanned skin, once fit only for 'peasants'. Both favoured the use of clean lines to create an essentially graphic silhouette; both were curious about the sailor/fisherman/working man lifestyle: coarse-weave garments coupled with sun-bronzed skin fed into the Chanel style – producing the sporty feminine look (in which women were acknowledged to have muscles) – and the Cocteau aesthetic with its focus on biceps and sailor shirts. Through her contact with the younger Cocteau – who regarded reality merely as an unfinished work of fiction – Chanel learned not only to tell her own story, but to reinvent herself.

Étienne Balsan and Boy Capel introduced Chanel to Paris society, a world to which couturiers had previously been denied access. Seeing her bring to fashion the rules and the rigour that had previously only been applied by painters and musicians, Cocteau pushed Chanel towards the world of art, to work alongside his friends Pablo Picasso and Igor Stravinsky. Chanel already had something of a connection with poetry thanks to her relationships with Max Jacob and Pierre Reverdy, both of whom eventually became recluses. Cocteau embodied a kind of writing that was more compatible with society life, although Chanel recognized in him the same refusal to be satisfied, the same determination to extract a poetic 'essence' from his very being, and the same drive to work constantly without stopping, even at the risk of his mental and physical wellbeing.

The bond between them was forged in 1923, when Cocteau returned from a working holiday in Cap Ferret with Raymond Radiguet, who was suffering from typhoid. Chanel saw to it that the twenty-year-old Radiguet was admitted to hospital and went on to organize a white funeral for him at the church of Saint Honoré d'Eylau, with the assistance of Misia. Overwhelmed with grief at the young man's death, Cocteau began to believe that Radiguet was trying to communicate with him from beyond the grave – an obsession that Chanel understood, given her own tremendous sense of loss following the death of Boy Capel, her mentor in esoteric matters.

Both Chanel and Cocteau were superstitious, believing in astrology, symbolism, predictions and the significance of certain numbers (5, 19). Chanel read his cards; Cocteau read her palm. Both believed in the existence of a secret world, hidden behind the deceptive world of appearances and where the dead and the living supposedly dwell together. Whether in the rue Cambon or the rue d'Anjou, their respective (and nearby) residences, they both longed to pass through the mirror to see their lost loved ones on the other side. When a Hindu stranger came to her with news of someone she had known and loved, Chanel knew he must be talking about Capel.

All the elements that made them legends were there from the start. They shared a loose relationship with facts and a similar need to bare their souls to one another: two 'lies that speak the truth', in Cocteau's words. But running a busy workshop full of seamstresses was a far cry from penning a poem. While the poet dwelled in daydreams, the couturière had to be unflinchingly realistic: they were a matched pair, completing each other but also generating friction. Chanel had not worked for the stage before Cocteau enlisted her services in 1922 for his play *Antigone*. But it is *Le Train Bleu* (1924), a ballet full of sun, sea and sport, [ill. 3 p. 289] that gives us the best picture of their collaboration, thanks to the instructions recorded in Cocteau's notebook. [cat. 3] After giving his directions to the choreographer, Bronislava Nijinska (sister of Vaslav Nijinsky), Cocteau issued this challenge to Chanel: 'The costumes must be elegance itself, with no hint of theatricality. This ballet must be fashionable; it must hit exactly the right spot. It's impossible to deceive fashionistas about fashion.' This meant the beach robes that would be draped around the bathers' bodies, as well as the swimsuits and sunglasses. The tennis player wore white wool, while the golfer sported a Prince of Wales blazer and a mottled sweater. The coquettes and gigolos would be flamboyantly, absurdly, attired – 'the silliness of operetta, marble, fashion, sport, all meld together', noted the librettist before adding: '*Le Train Bleu* is a faux operetta, in which the couplets and chorus are mimed and the fashion is sculpted. It's not a frivolous work but a monument to frivolity.' With his gift for pithiness, Cocteau concluded these directions to Chanel – of whom he calls himself a friend and admirer – by declaring: 'The ballet should go out of fashion within a year and remain an image of 1924.'

Chanel designed costumes for several of Cocteau's plays, but their happiest collaborations were those based around figures from classical mythology, such as Antigone, Orpheus and Oedipus. For *Antigone*, Chanel chose a heavy woollen fabric to express the heroine's toughness and defiance: according to one critic, the actress looked like a Greek samurai, [ill. 2] with her white face and sweeping painted eyebrows. On his journey to the Underworld in Cocteau's 1926 play, *Orpheus* – a symbol of the reversibility of all things – meets the figure of Death, dressed in a splendid ball gown of pink chiffon and a chinchilla coat, assisted by surgeons with masked faces and rubber gloves – this was Chanel's answer to the question of how to bring ancient Greece up to date, and one that reflected her legendary love of simplicity.

Their views diverged during the making of *La Machine Infernale* (1934), when Cocteau found himself more in tune with his set designer Christian Bérard. For *Oedipus Rex*, in 1937, he came up with the idea of having Jean Marais appear naked on stage, with his dazzling physique diverting attention from his dubious thespian talents. Chanel went a step further by wrapping the actor's gorgeous body in bandages, emphasizing the eroticism and demonstrating her own sense of stagecraft: she drew a comparison between outer layers of clothing and the first act of a play.

Their collaboration was commercial as well as artistic. Chanel had little talent for writing or drawing, so it was Cocteau who transcribed the 'novel' she wrote for herself – the novel that was her life. Many were those who had served as her scribes, only to be rejected. Cocteau rewrote her press interviews, sketched jewelry and costumes, and assisted with window dressing at the rue Cambon, in exchange for a generous monthly retainer. In her role as patron, Chanel wore the trousers. Knowing what precarious lives artists sometimes lead, she would send her doctors and masseurs to Cocteau when he was ill – which was frequently – and paid his hospital bills along with his travel expenses and hotel bills.

When Cocteau became keen to pull back from his mother, upon whom he relied both emotionally and financially, Chanel invited him to live with her in the rue du Faubourg-Saint-Honoré. There, he was free to smoke opium as a means of forgetting Radiguet's terrible death. And when he sought to free himself of the addiction that eroded what little connection he retained with reality, Chanel paid for his many detox treatments, throughout the 1920s and 1930s.

'People who hang on to things have nothing,' Misia Sert used to say. 'You're only rich if you throw your money around.' A disciple-turned-rival, rather like Eve in Joseph L. Mankiewicz's *All About Eve*, Chanel extended her generosity to her protégé's own protégés. When Cocteau introduced her to a hotel lift attendant who had fallen in love with him, Chanel gave this man, Maurice Sachs, the job of assembling a choice collection of books for her – enabling the untrustworthy Sachs to lead a lavish lifestyle until Reverdy discovered that Chanel was paying a king's ransom for 'signed' editions that Sachs had forged.

In 1927, when asked to help with a staging of Stravinsky's oratorio *Oedipus Rex*, with a libretto by Cocteau, Chanel was strangely reluctant. Misia tried to persuade her – 'We're waiting for you, my darling! You're the one with the money!' – but to little effect. Chanel was usually more compliant, however. It was at her townhouse in the rue du Faubourg-Saint-Honoré that Cocteau sought refuge in 1928, before receiving invitations to Villefranche-sur-Mer and later to the Villa La Pausa. Their collaboration was so fruitful that there were press rumours about a potential marriage – an unlikely event that only occurred in his mother's dreams.

In 1937, Cocteau met Al Brown, a drug-addicted former boxer from Panama who was earning a living as a Paris cabaret performer. Reminded of his own difficulties, Cocteau became determined to relaunch Brown's boxing career, even though Cocteau knew nothing whatsoever about the sport and the boxing world had given Panama Al Brown up for dead. Cocteau convinced Chanel to pay for a rehab programme and a stint at a farm in the country where the boxer could regain his fitness by skipping for weeks on end and using sacks of grain as punching bags. Insulted by the sporting press, who called Brown a has-been, his fans rallied in support. The boxer nicknamed the 'Black Spider' managed to regain the world title that he had lost three years earlier in a rigged bout.

In the 1930s, while Chanel was establishing her fashion empire, Cocteau was struggling to deal with the same 'difficulty of being' that inspired one of his finest books. The gulf between them was growing, and their destinies seemed to be inverted: everything Chanel touched turned to gold, while everything that

Cocteau did cost him dearly and proved fruitless. 'You are good fortune,' he wrote in 1927 to the orphan girl who now ruled the world; the poet's life, by contrast, seemed to be governed by a darker star.

As Cocteau kept slipping back into opium addiction, Chanel was often tempted to stop the rehab treatments, which only seemed to encourage him to smoke more. She was tired of Cocteau's attempts to blackmail her by designing jewelry and accessories for her rival Elsa Schiaparelli, and she even hung up on a desperate midnight call from Jean Marais, begging her to cover the costs of hiring a theatre to stage Cocteau's *Les Parents terribles*: having failed to find a backer, Cocteau was threatening suicide. But Chanel liked tough-minded people, so when Marais locked her out of his dressing room on the play's opening night, she was rather impressed. In 1939, when Marais was drafted into the army, she became a fairy godmother to his company, then stationed in the Somme: each soldier received gloves, sweaters and plaids from the couturière's ateliers in the rue Cambon. 'Everyone is amazed by the blankets she's making for you. They're unlike the ones that are usually sent,' wrote Cocteau from Paris. 'She wants you to have blankets and balaclavas that she'd use herself, double-thick, not scratchy, retaining their warmth even when wet.'

It was in a sports car driven by Violette Morris – a racing driver and former athlete who had had an elective mastectomy so she could compete more effectively against men – that Cocteau delivered these winter supplies to the Front, along with Thermos flasks and cigarettes; trucks laden with bottles of wine and more cold-weather provisions followed. Chanel also got the details of the soldiers' families and sent them toys, clothes and jewelry as Christmas gifts, anonymously, as if they had come from the absent fathers and husbands. Marais's popularity rose hugely as a result and Cocteau's faith in magic was renewed.

The rue Cambon 'charity office' – as publisher Bernard Grasset called it – closed its doors between 1939 and 1954, and it would never again show such largesse, even after it reopened. Cocteau found himself a full-time patron in Francine Weisweiller and Chanel continued to find fault with him. She still invited him for the occasional lunch at the rue Cambon, and she also donated a 2.84 carat emerald for Cocteau's ceremonial sword when he joined the Académie Française. But she was no longer very interested in him. Alone with Cocteau, she would grow vindictive, overwhelming him with monologues in which he would hear some of his own maxims repeated. The frailty of the ageing dragonfly made the little bull turn fierce and cruel.

Cocteau fell so low in Chanel's esteem that she considered burning the books he had dedicated to her. Her admiration spent, she turned from guardian angel to exterminating angel. Cocteau was distressed to learn that the woman he had introduced to the world of theatre and so often praised in the press was now reviling him at society dinners and telling the papers that she was tired of his 'classical jumble-sale' (Chanel had designed the costumes for all his Greek plays). And he was almost reduced to tears on reading interviews in which the woman who had borrowed so many of his maxims called him a snobbish little pederast who had spent his whole life stealing from other people. Their longstanding relationship had widened the gulf between their personalities. Chanel was a predator by nature; Cocteau was prey. Only in death were they reconciled. Cocteau was the first to depart this world, in 1963, and when Chanel appeared at his funeral, she once again resembled the Chanel that Cocteau had described, with 'her angry outbursts, her spitefulness, her fabulous jewelry, her creations, her whims, her extravagances, her kindnesses and her humour and her generosities, making a unique person who is engaging, attractive, repellent, extreme....'

ill. 2 **Génica Athanasiou in *Antigone*, directed by Jean Cocteau, costumes by Gabrielle Chanel, Théâtre de l'Atelier, Paris, 1922. Photograph by Man Ray.**

Amy de la Haye

FASHIONING FLOWERS

A rare photograph,[ill. 2] taken by André Taponier in around 1908, shows a young Gabrielle Chanel wearing a white dress that draws stylistic references from the Grecian chiton and peplos. The edges of the skirt fabric, which encircle the body, are decorated with self-fabric flowers and the waist is similarly girdled. It is a technique that, drawing upon the modernist mantra of 'truth to materials', does not rely upon extraneous decoration – such as artificial flowers – and was to characterize much of Chanel's articulation of fashion flowers from the late 1920s.

This essay identifies which flowers Chanel favoured, and explores how and when she incorporated them into her designs and her own appearance. With the exception of the signature camellia, it is an aspect of her work that has not previously been examined. Here, flowers are explored in relation to Chanel's biography, classical (Greek and Roman) dress and romantic modernist expression, within broader fashion and sociocultural contexts. In the 1930s, flowers were the height of chic and this was when the couturière worked with and wore them most profusely.

PERMANENT BOTANICALS

'You must love flowers and love your trade to succeed: apprenticeship lasts all your life.' – Artificial flower maker, Paris, 1910[1]

When she was about 15 years old (c. 1898), Chanel was given a leghorn hat with an artificial rose above the brim. She hated it: 'It looked awful on me. I knew even then what suited me.'[2] Once independent, she defied the vogue for elaborate millinery bedecked with flowers and instead wore simple straw boaters. As a fashion designer, Chanel generally eschewed extraneous ornamentation on apparel, preferring jewelry as decoration. However, contrary to many of her design preoccupations and reported statements, she adorned the fashionable body and hair with artificial flowers, in clusters as well as singly and in pairs. 'Permanent botanicals' was the name commonly used to describe artificial flowers, which originated in ancient Egypt, Greece and Rome, cultures in which flowers were worshipped and worn. The artificial flower trade emerged in Paris in the 14th century and had become established by the early 18th. It was in this city that the craft attained its most refined and creative expression. Indeed, the very finest flowers were so true to nature, that their makers supplied artists as well as dressmakers. One of the oldest firms, established in the rue Blondel in 1727 (now the rue de Petits-Champs), the Maison Legeron became a family business. The Maison Lemarié, founded in 1880, has supplied flowers to the most exclusive fashion houses and brands, including Chanel, for three generations. Artificial flower making flourished from the mid-19th century onwards, when it became an ancillary to the haute couture houses and elite milliners, until the mid-20th century when hat wearing went into decline. Chanel also ordered flowers from the atelier of Noémie Fromentin.

Artificial flowers were originally made when the earth no longer yielded flowers. However, although available all year, they were mostly worn during the summer months, when those they imitated were still in bloom. Chanel applied them both winter and summer, on tailored daywear, including overcoats, as well as dresses and gowns. These strategies served to partly mitigate the advanced modernity of her linear designs. By 1927, a softly tailored black silk *garçonne* suit, teamed with an ivory-coloured blouse, is striking for its clean lines and elegant understatement. The sole ornament, placed on one shoulder, is a flower executed in raw-edged silk chiffon, dyed to match the tonal contrasts of the ensemble. Chanel also utilized pairs of flowers, one that matched the dark material of the suit and the other the lighter tone of the blouse or sweater.

In 1927, Chanel opened a London house, for whose clientele she designed fashionable ceremonial dress for elite social life, which revolved around the monarchy and social season. Court presentation dresses for debutantes were conventionally full-length; Chanel's modern variants incorporated the irregular hemline fashionable that year and extended it to form the requisite train.[ill. 3] A lavish artificial flower was stitched to one shoulder. Perhaps the couturière's most bountiful use of artificial flowers was a cluster of red and pink silk roses applied as a corsage to a pink silk satin evening gown for Spring–Summer 1928, featured in the February issue of French *Marie Claire* magazine. Chanel's atelier also used the sculptural qualities of heavily sequinned fabric to form self-fabric dress and hair ornaments.

Artificial flowers are scattered throughout Chanel's collections from the 1920s, 1930s and 1950s. For her Spring–Summer 1954 'comeback' collection, she presented a strapless evening dress, with clusters of three overblown roses placed on the left waist and on each of the three pagoda-like tiers. After the late 1960s, flowers began to disappear from the work of international designers, with the exception of Chanel's signature camellia.

CUT-OUTS AND GARLANDS

'...It is the material that makes the dress and not the ornaments that one can add.' – Gabrielle Chanel[3]

Chanel made only occasional use of green fabrics and it appears that she gave thought to the spaces in which nature's most verdant colour would be worn, informing a future biographer: 'A green dress on a lawn is perfectly acceptable.'[4] An afternoon ensemble from 1929 comprises an abstract flower-printed silk chiffon dress and green wool coat, lined with the same fabric as the dress. [cat.15] The edges of the flower motifs have been cut out and meticulously finished to create the alluring effect of fluttering petals. Chanel's delicate silk chiffon gowns from the 1930s incorporate the same kind of detailing. This labour-intensive technique served to elevate and transform a pretty printed silk fabric into a supremely beautiful haute couture garment.

A 1929 lace evening dress, printed with a rounded floral design, features cut-outs around the hemline of the peplum (a derivation of the peplos) and skirt. [ill.4] A matching circlet at the neck might be likened to Roman flower garlands that were bestowed for acts of virtue and heroism, at a time when flowers were not gendered as feminine. Chanel's enamel flower jewelry crafted by Maison Gripoix, [cats. 215, 216] such as the camellia earrings and brooch in pink and white, with rhinestone centres and imitation dew-drops, might be similarly compared (c. 1937–38).

Dresses and capelets made using solid colour fabrics were also trimmed with self-fabric cut-out petals. For Christmas 1929, Vogue declared: 'Chanel's lovely geranium red velveteen frock trimmed with petals is a good choice for the debutante, the material is young and the long and picturesque skirt is still good for dancing.'[5] A pale green dress in silk tulle from her 1930 Spring–Summer collection is constructed with elongated, vertical, slightly curvilinear panels on the skirt, a technique that creates the impression of a corolla, the collective name for the petal components of a flower. [cat. 86]

Flower motifs can also be seen in the many lace fabrics she used, particularly in the 1930s and 1950s, mostly in black, but also in white, pale yellow, beige, ivory and flesh tones. [cat. 78] Lace flowers were also cut out and when lace was worn sheer next to the skin, in the form of long sleeves or gloves, for instance, the effect created was one of flowers overlaid onto the female body.

WILD AND ABSTRACTED FLOWERS

'I asked wholesalers for natural colours, I wanted women to be guided by nature.' – Gabrielle Chanel[6]

Chanel spent much of her early life in rural spaces and later evoked within her collections the wild meadow flowers (and also the wheat) of her youth. The definition of a wild flower is one that grows freely and is resilient, qualities that we might associate with Chanel herself. It is an analogy that conflicts with the popular, moralistic and sentimental Victorian language of flowers and much flower symbolism that has classified women in terms of transient beauty, fragility and fertility – interpretations that we may find offensive today. Later in her life, Chanel recalled the London home of her 1920s lover, the Duke of Westminster, 'with its hundreds of gardeners who cultivated roses, carnations and orchids all year round. But,' she said, 'he preferred to pick the first daisies from the fields for me.'[7]

Printed fabrics were used extensively in the 1930s: it was the cheapest form of ornamenting fabric in a time of depression that impacted many couture clients; they were also ideal for the complex cut and styling of 1930s fashions. Chanel used prints with small scattered motifs and large flower patterns. [cat. 13] Some depicted realistic flowers, while others are abstracted but can be likened to daisies, poppies or cornflowers. For Spring–Summer 1937, American Vogue lauded 'Chanel's "Kate Greenaway" innocence done in poppy-printed crêpe.'[8] An artificial flower adorned the right shoulder and there were flower cut-outs along the hem. [cat. 14]

In 1935, Cecil Beaton photographed the actress and model Mary Taylor for Vogue magazine; she wore a long, full-skirted, black silk dress with sheer, 1830s-style balloon sleeves with a bunch of artificial violets on the bodice. Chanel was well read and she was also superstitious: it is likely she would have been well-versed in the various cultural and symbolic meanings attributed to flowers, including this flower with five petals – her lucky number. In ancient Rome, violets were associated with death, but by the 19th century they had become emblematic of modesty, love and faithfulness; the mauve of their petals was associated with spirituality and calm.

EXOTIC AND CULTIVATED FLOWERS

'...romantic as rose petals diamonded with dew is Chanel's idea of a really feminine dress to contrast with tailored clothes.' – Vogue, December 1935[9]

Chanel actively fed into the 1930s fashion for neo-romantic Victorian revival styles. Having rejected the structure and frou-frou that characterized women's fashions in her youth, she – perhaps rather unexpectedly – delighted in the 19th-century revival that was expressed most eloquently for evening. As in the Victorian era, flowers were used in abundance. Chanel created gowns with long, full skirts that were

ill. 2 **Gabrielle Chanel, c. 1908.**
Photograph by Studio Taponier.

CHANEL

*Les mousselines à fleurs à fond teinté sont les plus en vogue.
Chanel a choisi pour cette robe un dessin multicolore sur fond
crème. Deux panneaux superposés descendent sur l'un des côtés
au-dessous du bas de jupe, dans le prolongement de l'écharpe*

ill. 3 **Chanel dress in printed**
chiffon, *Vogue* **France,**
1 June 1927, p. 16.

likened to crinolines, dresses with bustle silhouettes and corselette waists. Full-length lace gloves and upswept hairstyles, adorned with flowers, provided finishing touches. [ill.1] Chanel was photographed wearing these styles both as fashion and as historical fancy dress; her friend, the neo-romantic artist Christian Bérard (1902–49) illustrated them poetically and Cecil Beaton and Horst captured them in images. The flower most associated with Chanel is the camellia, which is revered for the symmetry of its petals, a quality that has fed into modernist interpretations of the designer's fashion aesthetic. The flower is native to East and Southeast Asia: in Japan, it symbolizes the divine and the coming of spring. In the West, since the 19th century, camellias have been associated with longevity, desire and perfection and universally, like the rose, they symbolize love.

Chanel selected the pure white camellia and reproduced it in silk. She wore both these and the natural flower on her clothes and in her hair, appreciating the latter's absence of fragrance that negated any clash with her own perfume. Chanel adored the smell of flowers: her now legendary cubist bottle for N° 5 houses precious extracts of rose and jasmine, from flowers grown in Grasse. Here, parallels might be drawn with the integration of flowers and modernity into her fashion designs.

Chanel's use of all-white in the 1930s and the manner in which her fashions were depicted within fashion print media contributed to the neoclassical revival. For its March 1938 issue, *Vogue* commissioned Horst to photograph a model wearing a Chanel gown comprising 'Drifts of white organdie. Hundreds of yards of white baby ribbon frosting to the skirt, elaborating the bodice. A circlet of white camellias for a necklace. White carnations in the hair.'[10] In the same season, the magazine reported that, 'Chanel binds the head with wide ribbon in which she thrusts hand-spun blossoms, chrysanthemums, camellias....'[11] The leaves of a white fan were made from feathers that would have fluttered, flower-like, in motion.

A striking evening coat (c. 1927) of black and white ombré silk crêpe, also offered in black and brilliant green, is emblazoned with brocaded gold metal thread chrysanthemums. Chanel also exploited gold floral brocaded fabrics for capri-trouser and skirt suits in the late 1960s, while her final collection of Spring–Summer 1971 included a tunic-style dress with a woven design of gold roses. [cat.336]

Examining surviving garments, fashion images and portraits of Chanel through the lens of flowers – for which she is not especially well-known – is a fascinating process, prompting fresh insights into her use of autobiographical references, design expression and personal choices. Wild and exotic flowers were present in her work in the form of permanent botanicals (artificial flowers) or as cut-outs and were depicted on printed and woven textiles. Her use of flowers has been likened to classical dress and it is suggested that her engagement with flowers allowed the couturière to stray from a purist interpretation of modernity to one that could be called romantic. Chanel, most notably in the 1930s, fashioned her apparel with flowers; she dressed the hair with natural and artificial blooms; decorated the body with jewelry inspired by flowers and scented it with their essences.

1

Mary Van Kleek, Russell Sage
Foundation, *Artificial Flower Makers*,
New York: Russell Sage
Foundation, 1913; repr. Lightning
Source UK Ltd, 2019, p. 154.

2

Marcel Haedrich, *Coco Chanel:
Her Life, Her Secrets*, Boston:
Little, Brown, 1971, p. 34.

3

Vogue UK, 22 February 1939, p. 7.

4

Paul Morand, *The Allure of Chanel*,
London: Pushkin Press, 2008,
p. 48.

5

Vogue UK, 25 December 1929, p. 22.

6

Paul Morand, *The Allure of Chanel*,
p. 48.

7

Marcel Haedrich, *Coco Chanel*,
p. 125.

8

Vogue US, 1 March 1937, pp. 60–61.

9

Vogue UK, 25 December 1935.

10

Vogue US, 15 March 1938, p. 100.

11

Vogue UK, 6 July 1938, p. 50.

ill. 4 **Chanel gown,** *Excelsior Modes*,
**no. 23, Spring 1935, p. 33.
Palais Galliera, Paris.**

Afternoon dress, Spring–Summer
1930, white silk chiffon
with pale pink and brown print.
cat. 14

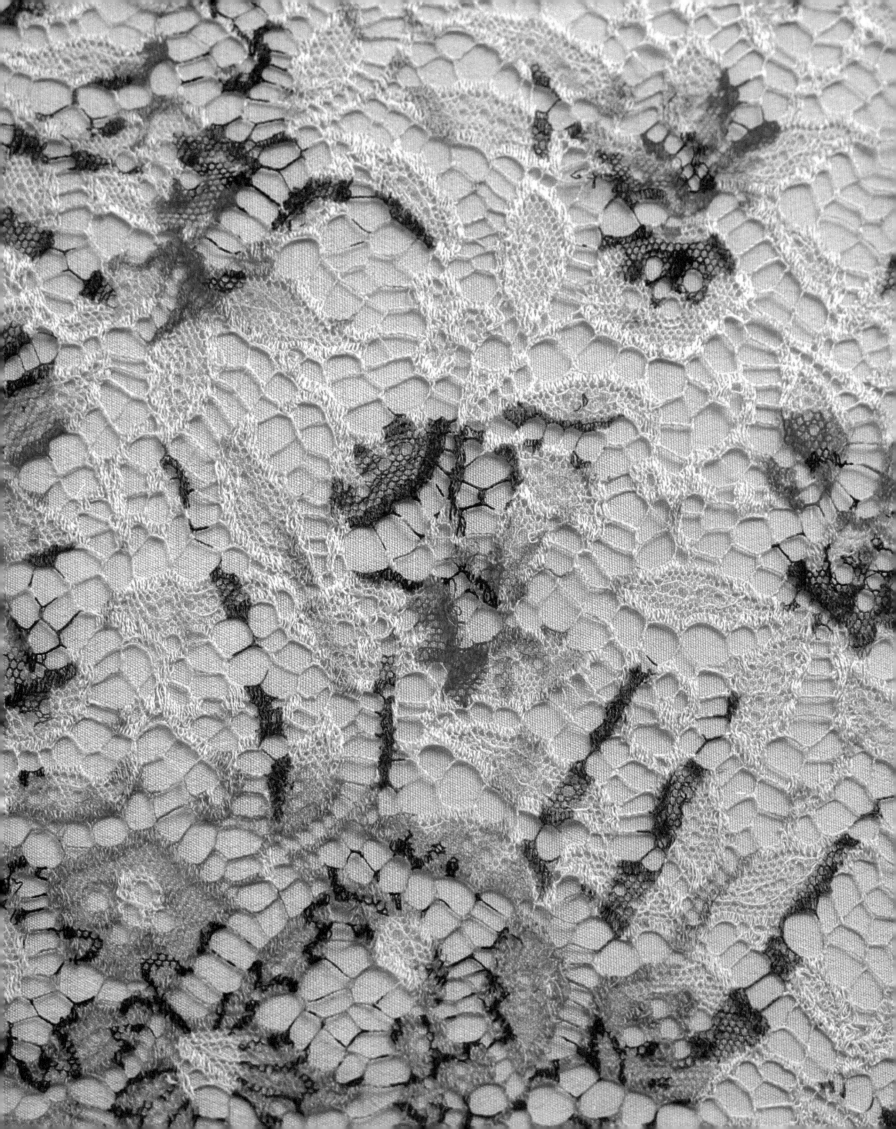

Previous pages

**Dress and scarf, Spring–Summer
1929, white silk lace
with multicoloured print,
white silk crêpe.**
cat. 12 (detail)

**Day ensemble with dress and coat,
1929, green wool,
silk chiffon with multicoloured
print, appliqué motifs.**
cat. 15

**Dress, 1935, ivory silk
organza with multicoloured print.**
cat. 13

Evening dress, Spring–Summer
1930, ivory silk chiffon with insets.
cat. 46

Ensemble with dress and cape,
between 1933 and 1935,
ivory silk crêpe with black print.
cat. 18

Dress, Spring–Summer 1930,
white broderie anglaise.
cat. 77

**Evening dress,
Autumn–Winter 1933–34,
ivory silk lace
with metallic gold thread,
rhinestones.**
cat. 78

**Evening dress,
Spring–Summer 1933,
black crêpe silk chiffon,
silk taffeta and lace.**
cat. 83

Evening dress, Autumn–Winter
1937–38, silk velvet, lace insets,
red silk tulle and taffeta.
cat. 84

Evening dress, between 1930 and 1935, black silk tulle embroidered with silver sequins and bugle beads.
cat. 42

Evening dress,
Autumn–Winter 1938–39,
midnight blue silk tulle
embroidered with midnight
blue sequins.
cat. 107

ill.¹ **Gabrielle Chanel, photograph by François Kollar, published in** *Harper's Bazaar*,
November 1937 (advertisement for Parfums Chanel).

Julie Deydier

A HOLISTIC VISION OF BEAUTY

THE 1920S: THE FIRST PERFUMES AND COSMETICS

Although Paul Poiret had founded the Parfums de Rosine perfumery in 1911, it was Gabrielle Chanel, in 1921, who became the first couturier to create her own perfume and name it after herself. Chanel N° 5 was innovative in several ways, making it one of the landmarks of the history of modern perfumery. Its name, its fragance, the radical simplicity of its bottle design, [cat. 47] and the sophistication and quality of the raw materials used all helped to turn it into an icon of the Roaring Twenties.

During this period, there were several dominant themes for the naming of perfumes, including orientalism (Le Minaret, Parfums de Rosine, 1913), and romance (Amour Amour, Jean Patou, 1926). By using a number as the name – the number of the chosen sample – Chanel broke away from these trends and entered a world of abstraction. She wanted to move beyond the naturalist and floral traditions of the 19th century, and offer women a perfume designed in the same way as a haute couture gown: 'A perfume, but an artificial perfume. I insist on artificiality, just as a dress is artificial, fabricated. I am a fashion artisan. I don't want rose or lily of the valley; I want a perfume that is a compound.'[1]

Inspired by this concept, the perfumer Ernest Beaux[2] created a composition that did more than simply reproduce a naturally occurring scent. N° 5 is immediately identifiable by its atypical fragrance, created by the high content of synthetic compounds known as aldehydes. This high aldehyde content – unusual for its day – brings a freshness to the floral notes and gives the perfume its 'abstract' quality.

The packaging of N° 5 – the bottle and its box – established the graphic identity for Chanel perfumes and beauty products. Chanel declared her intention 'to put everything into the perfume, and nothing into the presentation: a simple, straightforward bottle, the simplest label and box – no name, just a number.'[3] This radical aesthetic helped to define her unique visual signature, evoking both the style and the spirit of her designs: 'Chanel perfumes – as modern and young as a Chanel costume!'[4–ill. 3]

The sleek geometric bottle was square in shape, with a square stopper engraved with a double C set within a circle – the first time we see the Chanel monogram. It came in a box of white cardboard with black edging and the overall effect was striking, simple and timeless – a combination of clean lines, sharp contours and contrasting colours and materials.

In 1924, the design of the bottle was changed: it now had bevelled edges and the stopper was in the form of an eight-sided faceted gemstone, a shape inspired by the traditional 'emerald cut' used by jewelers. Although slight adjustments were made in later years to the proportions of the stopper, the label and the lettering, the overall look remained the same – and is the look that we still know today. The beauty of the packaging was widely acknowledged and in 1959 it was featured in an exhibition entitled 'The Package' at New York's Museum of Modern Art. The catalogue refers to 'the most sophisticated use of bold black lettering on a white ground', adding: 'Bounded by thin black borders, this package becomes elegant through understatement.'[5]

Chanel's perfumes and cosmetics followed the minimalist aesthetic of her fashion creations: a purse-sized perfume bottle in black glass, [cat. 50] for example, mirrored the simplicity and straight lines of the little black dress. This quest for perfection even extended to promotional items, as can be seen from a perfume card of the 1950s bearing the slogan 'The last refuge of distinction'.

This elegance – a blend of quality and simplicity – was epitomized by a nickel-chrome-plated travel case. Stripped of logos or lettering, its mirror-like surface reflected its immediate surroundings, combining discreet restraint with the very height of luxury and sophistication.

LIFESTYLE PRODUCTS AND TOP-TO-TOE BEAUTY

In 1906, Paul Poiret helped to liberate women from their corsets, starting a trend for comfort and freedom of movement. The Roaring Twenties brought a new kind of woman: the *garçonne* or flapper. She was slender, willowy and strong-limbed, sported a suntan and wore her hair cropped short, and Gabrielle Chanel – thanks to both her personal style and her designs – was one of her foremost embodiments. 'I cut my hair: it was me who changed the fashion, it was me who was in fashion',[6] she declared. 'Everyone laughed when they saw me dressed like that, but that was what made me successful. I didn't look like anyone else.'[7]

By creating an original fragrance with a distinctive scent signature, Gabrielle Chanel addressed the modern woman – the woman who embraced her femininity and affirmed her individuality through her perfume, makeup and appearance, perfume being as much a part of her self-created identity as fashion. 'Women wear the perfumes they are given! It's important to wear a perfume that you like, your *own* perfume', said Chanel. 'If I leave my jacket behind, people know it's mine.'[8]

The *garçonne* behaved in ways and adopted habits that had once been the sole preserve of men. She played sports and she drove automobiles. What's more, these developments went hand in hand, among the wealthier social classes, with the fashion for holidaying and weekends spent in the country or at the seaside – overturning the social convention that saw pale skin as desirable.

'I dress for myself. If I don't wear it, I don't make it,'[9] said Chanel, and the same was true of her skincare and makeup ranges, created in response to the needs of women's changing lifestyles, both her own and those of her clients. Thus, from 1927, a range of skincare products was offered, including massage oils fragranced with jasmine and tuberose, and Sport face cream and face powder (1928), also available in a travel version.

Changing lifestyles also had an influence on makeup. Formerly, obvious makeup was worn only by actresses and demi-mondaines, but now the *garçonne* happily changed her face at will, reddening her lips and accentuating her eyes. In 1924, Chanel began selling compact products that enabled women to reapply makeup wherever they were – lipsticks, rouges and face powders, some of them even scented with Chanel Nº 5.[cat. 57] In 1932, the 'Chanel for summer' collection featured three products to suit the growing trend for sun-bronzed skin: a powder, an oil and a liquid in the Tan range.

Chanel breathed her vision of the modern woman into everything that she created – fashions, fragrances and beauty products. She saw her perfume as central to that vision: 'It's the most important thing,'[10] she insisted. Every day, when she left her rooms at the Paris Ritz, Chanel Nº 5 was sprayed in the stairwell and in the couture salons at 31, rue Cambon, so that the place where she designed and sold her creations carried her signature fragrance from the moment she stepped through the door.

Although invisible, perfume and beauty products are essential to a woman's look and style: not only do they complete her outfit, they serve to affirm and to inspire self-confidence via self-care.[11] So thought Gabrielle Chanel, who approached beauty as a whole and treated the two areas associated with the body – beauty and fashion – in a holistic and dynamic way. Chanel chose to represent the spirit of Nº 5 herself,[ill.1] appearing in an advertisement published in several US women's magazines in November and December 1937 – just as she had chosen to wear her own designs on the promenade at Deauville with her aunt Adrienne and her sister Antoinette in 1913.

The ad features a portrait of Chanel taken in her apartment at the Ritz Paris by photographer François Kollar in 1937. The text beneath the image reads: 'Madame Gabrielle Chanel is above all an artist in living. Her dresses, her perfumes, are created with a faultless instinct for drama. Her Perfume Nº 5 is like the soft music that underlies the playing of a love scene. It kindles the imagination, indelibly fixes the scene in the memories of the players.'

Chanel's later perfumes were more classical – Gardénia (1925), for example, named after a flower, and Cuir de Russie (1927) and Sycomore (1930), whose names evoke real substances but also the exoticism fashionable at the time. The most striking example of this was her Bois des Îles range (1928),[cat. 54] with both its name and the luxurious cedarwood boxes symbolizing distant horizons – a fashion trend also reflected in the Paris Colonial Exposition of 1931.

FROM THE 1950S TO 1971: A NEW KIND OF FEMININITY

The Maison Chanel closed its doors between 1939 and 1954, but its perfumes, beauty products and accessories continued to be sold during those years. It was in April 1952, during Chanel's absence from the media spotlight, that Marilyn Monroe made her famous claim about Nº 5 in an interview with *Life* magazine. She refers to another interview in which her response to a somewhat indiscreet question had been censored: 'What do you wear to bed?' Marilyn had been asked, to which she gave the reply 'I only wear Chanel Nº 5.' In 1960, she repeated the anecdote to Georges Belmont, then the editor-in-chief of *Marie Claire*.[12] Reiterating her original reply, she projected a femininity that was perhaps somewhat at odds with the *garçonne* style of the 1920s but echoed Gabrielle Chanel's own statement about the fragrance: 'Yes, that's what I wanted, a perfume such as has never before been made. A woman's perfume with a woman's scent.'[13]

Aside from Marilyn's comments, which contributed enormously to the popularity of the perfume, there are several photographs[14] illustrating the actress's fondness for Nº 5. The most iconic of these was taken by Ed Feingersh in March 1955 and bears the caption: 'Actress Marilyn Monroe gets ready to go see the play *Cat On A Hot Tin Roof*, playfully applying her makeup and Chanel Nº 5 perfume.'[ill.2]

A new Chanel woman was taking shape, quite different from her 1920s counterpart. The Nº 5 eau de toilette bottle appeared in several films, including Louis Malle's *The Lovers* (1958), starring Jeanne Moreau (1958), and Luchino Visconti's 'The Job', one of the stories from *Boccaccio '70* (1962), in which we see Romy Schneider getting dressed and putting on perfume – a sign of luxury, but also the mark of a woman, affirming her identity, femininity and sensuality.

In 1955, the year after her comeback, Gabrielle Chanel created her iconic quilted 2.55 bag, and her first fragrance for men, Pour Monsieur – an elegant, classic and distinguished fragrance based on fresh notes of cypress. She launched a whole range of

Pour Monsieur products, as evidenced by an advertisement from 1958: 'For men who seek perfection... Chanel's Pour Monsieur products, eau de cologne, soap, aftershave, moisturizer.'[15]

A new and more extensive skincare range was developed to accompany the new makeup lines. The most striking element was the new luxury lipstick case. The rectangular case with its rounded edges was totally novel and went on to serve as a blueprint for the packaging of many other fragrance and beauty products that Chanel was to release in the future. The iconic design continues to look utterly contemporary, while the colours of 'these emphatic reds, in black lacquer, with a ring of gold ... the hallmark of uncontested distinction'[16] set the style for Chanel makeup packaging that has lasted to the present day. In 1970, Henri Robert and Gabrielle Chanel created the couturière's final perfume, Chanel N° 19. The number represented her birthday (she was born on 19 August 1883) and – perhaps as a deliberate decision to come full circle – the bottle was the same as the one used for Chanel N° 5. In *Vogue* US, Chanel N° 19 was described as a 'new number on the world's most famous bottle'.[17]

Gabrielle Chanel was responsible for inventing a new style of femininity, which owed as much to who she was as to her creations. She offered women not just adornments but the means both visible (clothes, accessories, makeup) and invisible (perfumes, cosmetics) to express a new kind of womanhood, free from social constraints and traditional prejudices.

ill. 2 **Marilyn Monroe applying Chanel N° 5 at the Ambassador Hotel, New York, 24 March 1955. Photograph by Ed Feingersh.**

1
Pierre Galante, *Mademoiselle Chanel*, Chicago: Henry Regnery Company, 1973, pp. 67–68.

2
Ernest Beaux (1881–1961), the perfumer-creator of Chanel N° 5 in 1921, and technical director of the Société des Parfums Chanel between 1924 and 1954.

3
Interview with M. Pleneau, director of Maison Rallet, recorded by Henri Robert in 'Souvenirs d'un parfumeur', lecture given to the Académie d'Osmologie et de Dermatologie, Paris, 8 November 1977; quoted by Élisabeth de Feydeau, *Les Parfums. Histoire, anthologie, dictionnaire*, Paris: Robert Laffont, 'Bouquins', 2011, pp. 583–585. Henri Robert (1899–1987) was Chanel's in-house perfumer from 1953 to 1978.

4
Advertisement for Chanel Perfumes, published in the *New York Times* on 11 December 1928.

5
Mildred Constantine and Arthur Drexler, *The Package*, exhibition catalogue, New York: Museum of Modern Art, 1959, p. 19.

6
Interview with Jacques Chazot for the TV series *Dim Dam Dom*, directed by Guy Job, 1969.

7
Marcel Haedrich, *Coco Chanel*, Paris: Éditions Belfond, 1987, p. 54.

8
Claude Delay, *Chanel solitaire*, Paris: Éditions Gallimard, 1983, p. 31.

9
Interview with Jacques Chazot, 1969.

10
Interview with Jacques Chazot, 1969.

11
'The figure is more important than the face, and more important than the figure is the means by which you keep it.' From Djuna Barnes, 'Nothing Amuses Coco Chanel After Midnight', September 1931; reprinted in *Interviews*, Los Angeles: Sun & Moon Press, 1985.

12
Georges Belmont, 'Marilyn Monroe et son mari confient à *Marie Claire* ce qu'ils n'ont jamais dit', *Marie Claire*, no. 72, October 1960, pp. 45–57, 236, 238.

13
Pierre Galante, *Mademoiselle Chanel*, 1973, p. 74.

14
See Sidney Skolsky, 'I love Marilyn', *Modern Screen*, June 1953, photographs by Bob Beerman.

15
Advertisement for Chanel Pour Monsieur, in *Adam, la revue de l'homme*, year 34, no. 245, February/March 1958, p. 34.

16
Edwige Bouttier, 'Carnet de beauté', *L'Art et la mode*, June/July/August 1954, p. 90.

17
'Announcing a new number on the world's most famous bottle', advertisement for Chanel N° 19, in *Vogue* US, October 1972, pp. 17–19.

ill. 3 **US advertisement for Chanel Perfumes, published in the** *New York Times*, **11 December 1928.**

Bois des Îles fragrance, 1928,
cedarwood, paper, black paper,
black wax seal, glass,
black cotton cord.
cat. 54

Chanel N° 5 purse bottle, c. 1930,
black glass, silver-plated metal,
beige jersey, cardboard, paper.
cat. 50

Blusher compact, 1924, enamelled
metal, mirror, fabric powder puff.
cat. 56

Lipstick, 1929, enamelled metal.

Loose powder scented
with N° 5 perfume, c. 1930,
cardboard, paper.
cat. 57

N° 5 perfume bottle, 1921,
glass, black cotton cord,
black wax seal, printed paper.
cat. 47

ill.1 **Gabrielle Chanel with her dog Gigot at the Villa La Pausa, Roquebrune, 1930.**
Photograph Granger Archives.

Caroline Evans

CHANEL: THE NEW WOMAN AS DANDY

Look at the image of Chanel in her mid-twenties at a racecourse in the south of France in 1907 or 1908.[ill. 2] She looks chic and *sportive*, in a man's coat and tie, topped with a small, neat boater of her own making. Her stance, too, reveals her mastery of masculine insouciance, in two quintessentially male gestures. Her hands are thrust deep into her coat pockets, her binoculars slung casually across her chest. Both are signs of effrontery, in a period in which women's social and economic dependence on men was symbolized by their fashionable outfits at the races. Everything in Chanel's appearance sets her apart from the other women racegoers, with their ornate hats and elaborate fashions, women whose appearance was defined by their relationship to men, be they husbands, lovers or fathers. Chanel, who at this time was a kept woman living in an unconventional household, differentiated herself from those women by, paradoxically, wearing men's clothing as a form of social incognito: the tie of her lover, Étienne Balsan, and an overcoat belonging to his friend Baron Foy. 'Before becoming a brand, Chanel was an adventuress', wrote Lilou Marquand, her assistant in later life.[1] From her twenties, if not earlier, Chanel developed a unique form of dandyism as social masquerade that never left her: the possibility of both seeming to be what she was not, and not being what she seemed. Ellen Moers has described how the 19th-century dandy was displaced in the early 20th century by the New Woman, a lady with 'a cigarette, a bicycle and a will of her own'.[2] Yet there were underlying continuities between the two. Both in her social mobility and in her panache, Chanel had much in common with the

English dandy George 'Beau' Brummell, who used elegance, wit and a degree of bravado to navigate the aristocratic circles to which he was not born. In his book on Brummell, the 19th-century writer Jules Barbey d'Aurevilly pinpointed the dandy's essential gender ambiguity in ways that anticipated Chanel's debut in French society half a century later. Barbey described the dandies of the Second Empire as 'hermaphrodites of History' and 'twofold and multiple natures, of an undecided intellectual sex'.[3] To equate Chanel's dandyism with cross-dressing *tout court*, however, would be fundamentally to misconstrue the facts: the point is not that Chanel wore men's clothes but, rather, that she understood their modernity, and was able throughout her life to re-gender all clothing in a way that put into question the essential nature of both masculinity and femininity.

Like Chanel, the first writers on dandyism treated gender as a serious business: Moers reminds us that Barbey 'makes dandyism available as an intellectual pose'.[4] In Chanel's hands, it became the pose of a professional woman in the modernist period. As she explained to Paul Morand after the Second World War: 'The enclosure before 1914! When I went to the races, I would never have thought that I was witnessing the death of luxury, the passing of the 19th century, the end of an era .... That is why I was born, that is why I have endured, that is why the outfit I wore at the races in 1913 can still be worn in 1946, because the new social conditions are still those that led me to clothe them.'[5]

She lived the rhetorical and polemical possibilities of fashion. At the races before 1914, Chanel had admired a woman with a metal arm as 'the height of elegance'.[6] In this view, the prosthetic body can become a stylish accessory to a self that is always under construction: volatile, mutable, protean. Chanel understood the power of the transaction between the organic and the inorganic, alongside the techniques of what Barbey called 'a science of manners and attitudes'.[7] Her relaxed disengagement was the product of a stringent bodily discipline. Barbey describes 'those minds which speak to the body by the body',[8] and in this respect, Chanel's lifelong mobilization of the triumvirate of gesture, pose and personality was eloquent. The photograph from 1907 seems prophetic: Chanel has her eyes firmly fixed on the future as much as on the racecourse.

A photograph from 1925 shows her on the deck of the Duke of Westminster's yacht, the *Flying Cloud*.[ill. 3] Though the clothes are ostensibly more feminine, Chanel's pose and short hair display a very modern tomboyish grace for a 40-year-old woman. Fifteen years after the racecourse picture, in a world transformed by war and revolution, Chanel was now a successful designer and businesswoman who had made her early reputation by pioneering sportswear for women. In 1916, her ankle-skimming beige shirtwaist dresses had 'with one stroke ... annihilated the centuries-old gesture so many men had breathlessly awaited as a woman prepared to mount a step: the discreet lifting of the skirt. A certain form of femininity was ending,' recorded Edmonde Charles-Roux.

Chanel 'was an absolutely new woman, a woman whose dress was without allusion'.[9] Here was where her modernism and her dandyism intersected. Rhonda Garelick argues that Chanel was the pivot between 19th-century dandyism and the late 20th-century cult of celebrity.[10] Her simple designs were imbricated both with her complex personality and with her signature style: it was an incendiary catalyst for the modern woman. Like the 19th-century English dandies who adapted country hunting dress for formal society, Chanel created sportswear in 'poor' fabrics for a fashionable elite. In the *Flying Cloud* image, she wears it with her customary élan. Witness her underplayed nonchalance and relaxed, modern pose as she sits ramrod straight with crossed legs. As she said, 'All the articulation of the body is in the back; *all movements stem from the back*.'[11] And as Barbey noted, dandyism is 'a manner of existing'[12] rather than a way of dressing. Chanel trained her models to move in her style, and her blueprint for her customers was her own self. Beyond merely dressing a woman, she wanted to form her person, her style and even her way of thinking; to make her 'walk straight, her chin up, her shoulders forward, her hips tilted, like those of a horserider ... Ready to run or to cross her legs.'[13] For, in Barbey's words, 'For Dandies, as for women, to *seem* is to be.'[14]

Aged 54, she was photographed at the Venice Lido, dressed as an androgynous twin to her male companion, albeit accessorized with a bandeau turban and costume jewelry.[ill. 4] She holds a lit cigarette between thumb and two fingers, palm upwards; it's a masculine smoking gesture mirrored by the way the man, Serge Lifar, holds his cigarette. Lifar, future director of the Paris Opéra, had danced the role of a gigolo in *Le Train Bleu* in 1924, a ballet for which Chanel had designed the costumes, putting the gigolos in up-to-the-minute swimsuits. It was from Serge Lifar that she learned all her ideas about movement, according to Lilou Marquand.[15] The fashion editor Bettina Ballard, who modelled for Chanel in the 1920s, wrote: 'She has invented that famous Chanel stance that looks relaxed as a cat, and has an impertinent chic; one foot forward, hips forward, shoulders down, one hand in a pocket and the other gesticulating.'[16] In this photograph, Chanel propels the 1920s flapper pose into the 1930s, through the angle of her hips, the casually held cigarette (wrist upturned), and the performative, gestural stance. Her left arm thrown loosely around Lifar's shoulders, she stands *contrapposto*, her relaxed elegance an invocation of Barbey's aphorism that Dandyism is a way of being that is 'made up entirely of shades'.[17]

As if to confirm Charles Baudelaire's characterization in 1863 of fashion as the art of the ephemeral, and his description of modernity as 'the transitory, the fugitive, the contingent',[18] another photograph captures Chanel and the artist Salvador Dalí in a brief moment of casual intimacy.[ill. 5] His dark silhouette forms an elegant counterfoil as he watches her attentively, but it is her brightly lit figure which draws the eye. Appropriating masculine details into women's fashion, Chanel's outfit blurs the line between the two, as does her attitude. Not for her, the traditional feminine pose of waiting for a man to light her cigarette. Instead she lights her own. Dandyism is in the details: the cane, the snuff box and the eye glass are accessories made to be handled, in minimal gestures that contain a wealth of meaning, wrote Olga Vainshtein.[19] She describes Brummell's poised performance, 'snapping the [snuff] box open with a deft click of the thumb' and taking care to show to the best advantage his gold ring, his pocket handkerchief, and his shirt cuff. Here Chanel updates the gesture, holding the cigarette case so as to complement her softly tailored tweed jacket, cuffs turned back, the camellia worn like a man's buttonhole on the lapel, necklaces that recall a fob chain, the bracelet like a broad cuff. In a photograph that lingers on the fine details of her accessories, the great Dalí himself becomes just another accessory alongside the fact of Chanel's stylish self-absorption.

After an interregnum of over 15 years, Chanel made her Paris comeback in 1954. A photograph[ill. 6] shows her in 1965, aged 82, when she spent her days shuttling between her home at the Ritz and the *maison* in the rue Cambon. There she worked – and talked – incessantly, spinning tales of her life in ever-changing narratives. 'He became desperately elegant,'[20] wrote Barbey of the aging Brummell. Chanel too detested old age. 'Mademoiselle refused to see herself age. She wore the same suits and even put makeup on her hands. Nothing was allowed to blemish her image, her allure, her scent,'[21] wrote Lilou Marquand, who saw her every day in the final years of her life.

What does life offer the aging dandy, especially a female one? Is the concept of the elderly woman dandy even viable, in a world that puts a high premium on a woman's youth? Even the dandy cannot hold old age at bay, however hard she tries. But although the attempt is bound to fail, there is another kind of dandyism in Chanel's compulsive reinvention of her past that makes the story ever-young, in the manner of Oscar Wilde's Dorian Gray. Every day as Chanel went down the stairs at the rue Cambon, she retouched the portrait of herself by Marion Pike that hung on the staircase, using a stick of red lipstick.[22] Just as she retouched her portrait, she retouched her past through incessant retelling, and her past changed from day to day. But where does retelling stop, and lying begin? Throughout her life, Chanel told lies about her origins. Her compulsive lying was an extension of her masquerade, or perhaps indistinguishable from it. The lying was, wrote Marquand, part of her charm, like her brusqueness; by the time she was old, her lies had aged with her until they had become her truth. Where does the truth of Dorian Gray lie, then: in the portrait or in the man? Wilde's novel ends badly for the protagonist, and in its denouement, the book becomes a moral reprimand. Chanel's dandyism, by contrast, became something more ambitious in her final years, turning more ambiguous and ambivalent: it revealed the truth of the lie. Chanel's end, like her beginning, was elusive, and rooted in her own telling. 'When were you invented, Mademoiselle?' asked Marquand. 'All the time,' came the reply.[23]

ill. 2 **Gabrielle Chanel at a racecourse in the south of France, c. 1907–8. Patrimoine de CHANEL collection.**

ill. 3 **Gabrielle Chanel on the deck of the** *Flying Cloud*, **1925.**

ill. 4 **Gabrielle Chanel and Serge Lifar at the Lido, Venice, 1937, with dedication from Chanel to Lifar. Photograph by Jean Moral. Patrimoine de CHANEL collection.**

ill. 5 **Gabrielle Chanel and Salvador Dalí, 1930s.**

ill. 6 **Gabrielle Chanel in 1965. Photograph by Hatami.**

1

Lilou Marquand, *Chanel m'a dit*, Paris: Éditions Jean-Claude Lattès, 1990, p. 7.

2

Ellen Moers, *The Dandy: Brummell to Beerbohm*, Lincoln: University of Nebraska Press, 1960, p. 283.

3

Jules-Amédée Barbey d'Aurevilly, *Of Dandyism and of George Brummell* (1879), trans. Douglas Ainslie, London: J.M. Dent, 1897, p. 141.

4

Ellen Moers, *The Dandy*, p. 263. See also Jessica R. Feldman, *Gender on the Divide: The Dandy in Modernist Literature*, Ithaca: Cornell University Press, 1993.

5

Paul Morand, *The Allure of Chanel*, trans. Euan Cameron, London: Pushkin Press, 2013.

6

Paul Morand, *The Allure of Chanel*, 2013.

7

Barbey d'Aurevilly, *Of Dandyism and of George Brummell*, p. 46.

8

Barbey d'Aurevilly, *Of Dandyism and of George Brummell*, p. 32.

9

Edmonde Charles-Roux, *Chanel: Her Life, Her World, and the Woman Behind the Legend She Herself Created*, London: MacLehose Press, 1976, pp. 168–169.

10

Rhonda K. Garelick, 'The Layered Look: Coco Chanel and Contagious Celebrity' in Susan Fillin-Yeh (ed.), *Dandies: Fashion and Finesse in Art and Culture*, New York: New York University Press, 2001, pp. 35–58.

11

Paul Morand, *The Allure of Chanel*, 2013.

12

Barbey d'Aurevilly, *Of Dandyism and of George Brummell*, p. 22.

13

Lilou Marquand, *Chanel m'a dit*, pp. 37, 72 and 104.

14

Barbey d'Aurevilly, *Of Dandyism and of George Brummell*, p. 102, n. 1.

15

Lilou Marquand, *Chanel m'a dit*, p. 104.

16

Bettina Ballard, *In My Fashion*, New York: David McKay, 1960, p. 55.

17

Barbey d'Aurevilly, *Of Dandyism and of George Brummell*, pp. 18–19.

18

Charles Baudelaire, 'Le Peintre de la vie moderne' (1863), in *Oeuvres complètes de Charles Baudelaire*, vol. III, Paris: Calmann Lévy, 1885, p. 68.

19

Olga Vainshtein, 'Walking the Turtles: Minimalism in European dandy culture in the nineteenth century', *Fashion, Style & Popular Culture*, 4 (1), 2017, p. 90. See also Olga Vainshtein, 'Dandyism, visual games and the strategies of representation', in *The Men's Fashion Reader*, eds. Peter McNeil and Vicki Karaminas, Oxford: Berg, 2009, pp. 84–108.

20

Barbey d'Aurevilly, *Of Dandyism and of George Brummell*, p. 129, n. 1.

21

Lilou Marquand, *Chanel m'a dit*, p. 158.

22

Lilou Marquand, *Chanel m'a dit*, pp. 38 and 85.

23

Lilou Marquand, *Chanel m'a dit*, p. 63.

Ensemble with dress and jacket,
Spring–Summer 1926,
Ivory silk toile, black silk taffeta.
cat. 32

Jacket, between 1928 and 1930,
beige chiné wool jersey,
multicoloured jacquard knit,
beige silk crêpe.
cat. 21

Day ensemble with dress and coat,
c. 1927–28, silk serge with black
and white print, black silk crêpe.
cat. 33

Dress, Autumn–Winter 1962–63,
black wool, white cotton piqué,
gilded metal.
cat. 151

Evening dress,
Autumn–Winter 1933–34,
black rayon,
ivory silk organza.
cat. 39

**Day ensemble with waistcoat,
jacket and skirt, 1928,
white cotton muslin with
blue grey and black print.**
cat. 10

**Coat, Autumn–Winter 1933–34,
chiné wool tweed in ivory and
plum, green Galalith.**
cat. 20

**Day ensemble with dress, jacket
and belt, between 1928 and 1930,
multicoloured figured silk velvet,
chiffon lining, quilted écru raw silk,
metal and coloured glass.**
cat. 26

**Suit with jacket, skirt and top,
c. 1928, multicoloured jersey,
plain yellow jersey.**
cat. 22

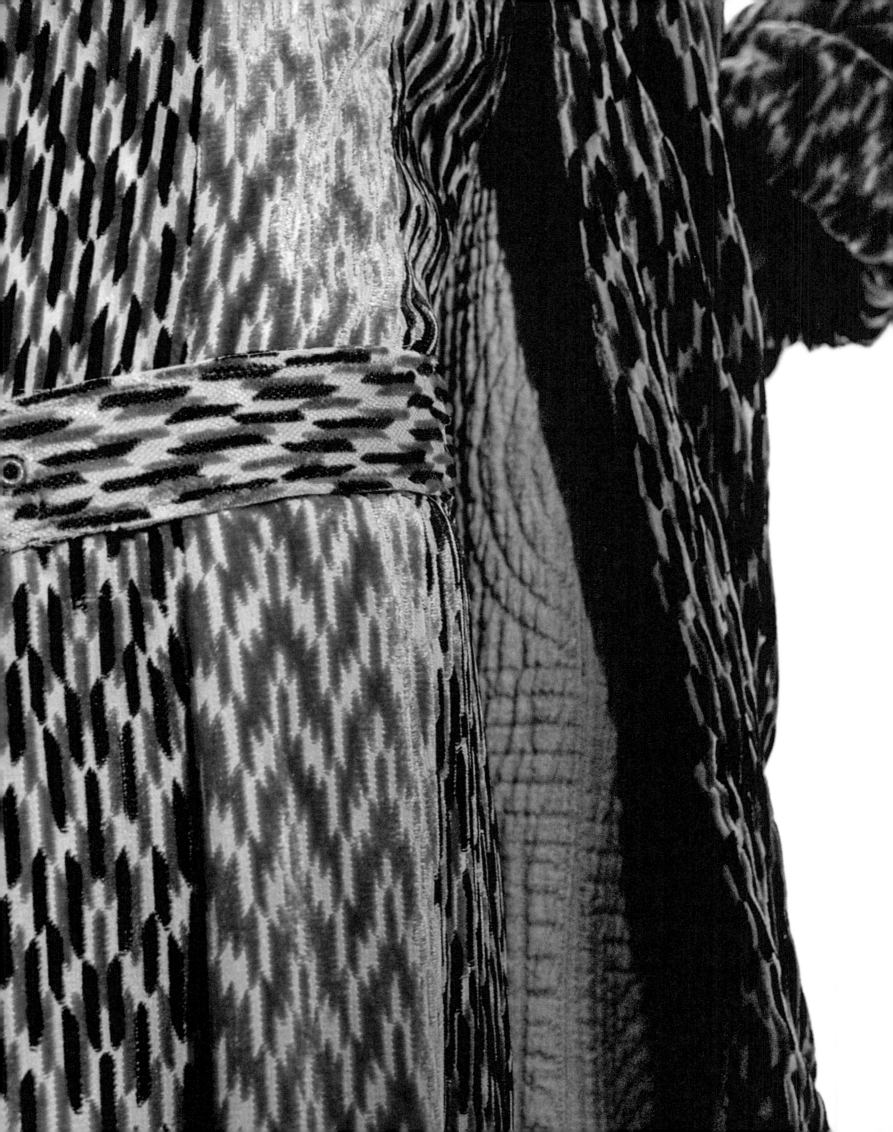

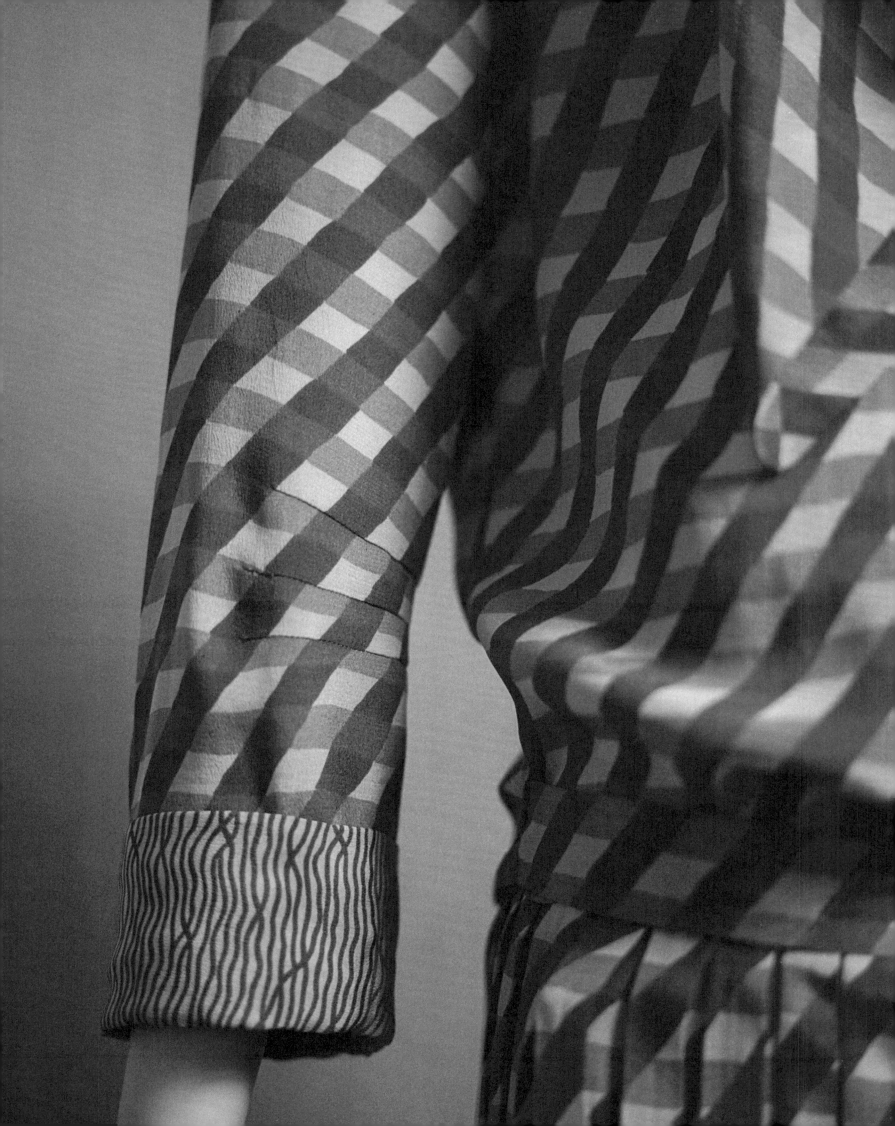

**Day dress, between 1926
and 1928, ivory crêpe de chine
with russet print.**
cat. 27

**Clutch bag, 1928, ivory silk crêpe
with multicoloured print by Tissus
Chanel, chrome-plated steel.**
cat. 29

**Dress, between 1930 and 1939,
printed ivory surah
with black repeat motif.**
cat. 9

'Comète' brooch from the 'Bijoux de Diamants' collection, 1932,
platinum, old-cut diamonds.
cat. 117.

Marie-Laure Gutton

'BIJOUX DE DIAMANTS': THE GLITTERING TRIUMPH OF GABRIELLE CHANEL

'Mademoiselle Chanel has seen fit to give women back their jewels of earlier times – while adapting them to the demands and the trends of an age she knows better than anyone.'[1] This was how, on 26 October 1932, the newspaper *L'Intransigeant* made its surprise announcement regarding the society and charity event of the season – Gabrielle Chanel's 'Bijoux de Diamants' exhibition. The attitude that Chanel had previously exhibited towards jewelry in no way anticipated this sudden interest in diamonds, which took the form of a dazzling collection that attracted fashionable Paris like a magnet. The exhibition was a major media event, reported in more than 250 articles in both the French and the international press, but what were Chanel's reasons for conceiving a collection that was worlds away from the costume jewelry she had always championed?

OPULENCE AND CHARITY COMBINED

The exhibition, described by the press as one of 'the most remarkable artistic events witnessed in Paris',[2] was held between 7 and 19 November 1932, not at the Chanel boutique, but at the couturière's own private residence, at 29, rue du Faubourg-Saint-Honoré. The opulent surroundings of the Hôtel de Rohan-Montbazon, built in 1719, provided the most glorious setting for the jewelry.[ill.1] The tall windows looking out over the French-style gardens and their fountain, the elegant Coromandel screens and mirrors and

polished chairs combined to create 'a "climate" that showed off the marvellous jewels to particular advantage'.[3] Abandoning the conventional shop window approach, in which individual pieces of jewelry are displayed like works of art, dissociated from a woman's body, Chanel chose a more innovative way of presenting the jewels, by digging out some old wax busts from the early years of the century (possibly the work of Pierre Imans). Placed on black marble columns inside tall glass showcases for protection, these long-lashed mannequins were carefully made up and draped in black moiré, offering a perfect foil for the jewels, which nestled in their natural hair or glittered on their waxen décolletés. The pieces intended for afternoon wear were displayed on fur hats and capes.

This profusion of luxury was, in addition, combined with 'a profane pleasure – the pleasure of giving to charity',[4] since the admission fees[5] were donated to two well-known charitable foundations, the Société de la Charité Maternelle de Paris, whose patron was the Princesse de Poix, and the Assistance Privée à la Classe Moyenne, presided over by Maurice Donnay of the Académie Française. The charity aspect of the event gave journalists an added incentive to report on the exhibition and to encourage their readers to go along. The exhibition was a success and, whether out of friendship with Chanel or a sense of charity, interest in her art or a love of diamonds, a number of high-profile figures attended, especially for the two private viewings: the press launch on Saturday, 5 November, and the following Sunday, the day dedicated to the 'beau monde'.[6] Princess Aspasia of Greece, the British ambassador Lord Tyrrell, Prince and Princess Jean-Louis de Faucigny-Lucinge, the Princesse de Broglie, the Duchesse de Gramont, the Baronne Édouard de Rothschild, Pablo Picasso, Jean Cocteau, and José María and Misia Sert all filed through Chanel's salons, admiring the couturière's glittering creations under the watchful eye of policemen and security guards – a massive presence that prompted the illustrator Sem to wittily remark: 'There are too many policemen here for my liking... I don't have a good feeling about it. I'm worried someone might steal my wallet!'[7]

A NEW VISION OF JEWELRY

'I want a piece of jewelry to be like a ribbon on a woman's fingers. My pieces are supple. They can be taken apart and reassembled. For grand gala evenings, the idea is to wear the entire creation. For more modest soirées, the main part and the larger elements can all be removed. The parure can be dismantled and individual motifs can be used on a hat or a fur coat. A parure is therefore no longer a static, fixed thing. Life transforms it and it must meet life's demands.'[8] In describing her conception of a piece of jewelry, Chanel was echoing the principles that also underpinned her couture collections. It must be modular and transformable; it must be suitably adapted to circumstances and a woman's life. Jewelry is always an integral element of 'the idea of the woman and of her dress. It is because the dresses change that my jewelry changes.'[9]

The settings needed to be discreet. To achieve this, Chanel opted for platinum, a relatively new material (platinum hallmarking was only introduced in 1912) whose suppleness and malleability enabled the creation of subtle, light, articulated settings.[10] These allowed the diamonds – which 'represent the greatest value in the smallest volume'[11] – to take centre stage, and used only medium-sized stones, which retained their impact. Fringes of gems shimmered on foreheads and wrists; stars replaced buttons and clips. Tiaras, rings, bracelets and necklaces wrapped around the body as delicately as lengths of fabric, taking the subtle forms of ribbons, feathers, bows, stars, sunbursts and comets. [cat. 117] The inspiration for this collection apparently came from a summer night in 1931, when Chanel saw the Champs-Élysées, with all its advertising hoardings, glittering under a starry sky.[12] The 'Plume' brooch particularly appealed to the Comtesse Marie-Laure de Noailles, who wore it in the pages of *Vogue* France in June 1933.[13] – ill. 3 This piece is an excellent example of the adaptability of Chanel's jewelry designs, since it can be worn on the shoulder, at the waist, on a hat, or pinned in the hair, tiara-style.

Just as with couture, Chanel produced no sketches. Instead she entrusted this crucial stage of the design process to several draughtsmen, including Paul Iribe (1883–1935), who became a close friend.[14] One example is Iribe's gouache design [ill. 4] for a necklace of graduated diamonds, decorated with a diamond tassel. [ill. 2] This collection seems to have also given Iribe the opportunity to execute some of his own designs from some years earlier. The iconic 'Comète' necklace, a key piece in the exhibition, was apparently derived from a sketch that Iribe published in his album *Choix*[15] in 1930, but was adapted to fit Chanel's specifications: loathing clasps of any sort, she transformed the choker into a flexible necklace that curved around the wearer's throat. The aesthetic of these pieces of jewelry and their themed focus are evidence of the close ties between the two artists and perfectly illustrate the concepts previously explored by Iribe in *Choix* and *Défense du Luxe*,[16] in which he criticizes modern geometric jewelry. Chanel for her part affirmed: 'My jewelry designs have moved away from those rebuses – too literary to be visually pleasing – that the Cubist style attempted to popularize. I look for motifs that show off to best advantage the sparkle of a diamond: star, cross, graduated waterfall and big sun-drenched cabochons.'[17]

A NECESSARY JUSTIFICATION

This wealth of diamonds raised an obvious question: why did the woman once regarded as the 'queen of costume jewelry'[18] commit to such a project? Some kind of justification seemed necessary and Chanel thought the best way to explain her position was to ask Jean Cocteau to write a statement putting forth a reasoned argument.[19] Passages from Cocteau's text were reproduced in the foreword to the exhibition catalogue and were also echoed in the interviews that Chanel granted to the press. 'In my profession, any means is legitimate, as long as it serves the true spirit of fashion', she said. 'I started to design costume jewelry because I felt that it was refreshingly free of arrogance, in a period that tended towards ostentatious displays of luxury. But considerations of this kind disappear in a time of financial crisis, when an instinctive desire for authenticity in all things begins to emerge, restoring the true value to an amusing trinket.'[20]

The economic repercussions of the Wall Street Crash of 1929 therefore appear to explain Chanel's change of heart. On one hand, 'real' jewelry represented a solid financial investment, in contrast to 'paste jewelry that quickly loses its appeal, is regularly swapped for something else and has zero market value'.[21] Chanel's *haute joaillerie*, moreover, was helping the jewelry workshops, which had been obliged to lay off workers, to extricate themselves from the economic mire. Like haute couture, jewelry was badly affected by the crisis, whose causes were – in the view of Georges Fouquet, President of the Chambre Syndicale de la Bijouterie, de la Joaillerie et de l'Orfèvrerie – excessive taxation,[22] the high cost of living and the shift towards decorative austerity in art, leading to many French workers losing their jobs.[23] This unemployment affected ninety per cent of workers in the jewelry sector. Denouncing the poor economic climate, Chanel explained that – while not seeking to compete with Parisian *bijoutiers* – she wished 'to reinvigorate a very French art that was threatening to stagnate during the crisis'.[24] She said nothing, however, about the provenance of the diamonds or the manufacture of the jewelry itself, so the collection continues to be shrouded in a degree of mystery.

THE FRENCH JEWELRY TRADE STRIKES BACK: THE 'CHANEL AFFAIR'

The early 1930s saw the price of diamonds artificially inflated thanks to a situation where gems were drip-fed on to the market. While some people were sceptical about how long this phenomenon would last, others started putting strategies in place to protect their future. It was in this context that the directors of the UK-based Diamond Corporation Limited (formerly the De Beers Syndicate) sought to relaunch the fashion for diamonds in their purest form by entering into a collaboration with Chanel, a couturière of international renown who 'did six months before the others what everyone dreamed of doing'.[25] To this end, they entrusted her with more than twenty million francs' worth of diamonds in order to produce a series of sumptuous parures. Chanel commissioned two Parisian jewelry workshops, Lemeunier and Rhudart,[26] to make the pieces, based on the sketches. Everything seems to have been organized with great discretion, without the knowledge of the Chambre Syndicale de la Joaillerie, which only learned about the upcoming exhibition from an article in *L'Intransigeant* on 26 October 1932.[27] The initial

ill.1 **Princesse de Faucigny-Lucinge, Madame Ralli and Baron de Gunzburg at the 'Bijoux de Diamants' exhibition. Photograph by André Kertész, published in** *Vogue* **France, January 1933.**

ill. 2 **Diamond jewelry set, 1932. Photograph by Albert Harlingue.**

141

article in *L'Intransigeant* on 26 October 1932.[27] The initial surprise gave way to anger, with the jewelers of the Place Vendôme expressing outrage that, as Georges Fouquet put it, 'the English diamond merchants, while they may not have seen fit to approach their fellow jewelers back home, should have approached a French couturière rather than the Corporation des Joailliers Parisiens'.[28] 'It is indeed regrettable that the English consortium failed to communicate with our association through the official channels,' continued Fouquet: the Chambre Syndicale would then have been in a position to organize the event by calling upon the services of a number of French firms. All of this was a pretext to criticize Chanel's designs, which, it was said, 'offer nothing new in terms of ideas or formulas, either in the shapes, the lines, or the designs, or even in the use of new materials'.[29] What is more, according to Fouquet, championing a style of jewelry that utilized invisible settings was damaging to French workshops, since it emphasized the gems themselves and not the technical craftsmanship involved.

Paul Iribe, as the Maison Chanel's representative, was invited to a meeting with the jewelers Chaumet, Cartier, Van Cleef, Mellerio, Mauboussin and Radius on 3 November, in order to offer an explanation. At the end of the meeting, Iribe was given a note in which it was stipulated 'that the jewelry must not be sold, that it must be dismantled after the exhibitions, under the direction of the Chambre Syndicale and that visitors must be told that the designs can be made by their accredited jewelers'.[30] They also demanded a share of the sales resulting from the exhibition, to be put towards the work of the Chambre Syndicale. The next day, Chanel – who was particularly irritated by an article in *Candide*[31] reproaching her for favouring English-made textiles to the detriment of French manufacturers – declared her rejection of all their demands. Citing ill health, she asked Iribe to show members of the Chambre Syndicale around the exhibition, on 5 November. Fouquet, in a report written on 12 November, encouraged his colleagues 'not to give any weight to conversations, negotiations, discussions and transactions', in an attempt to calm the situation and perhaps to avoid antagonizing the Diamond Corporation.

The exhibition was a runaway success in Paris, and was also expected to attract a large number of visitors when it moved, as was planned, to London and then Rome, under the patronage of the Marchioness of Londonderry and Princess Colonna, respectively. However, the Diamond Corporation found itself facing exorbitant customs duties, which led to the other exhibitions being postponed and then, apparently, cancelled, since there are no known records relating to these events. The diamonds were probably removed from their settings and only two identifiable pieces from the collection exist today: a 'Comète' brooch conserved by the Maison Chanel,[cat. 117] and the 'Plume' brooch formerly owned by Marie-Laure de Noailles. Later, Gabrielle Chanel would offer her clients other jewelry designs, made notably by Robert Goossens, but she would never again stage an event on the same glittering scale as the 'Bijoux de Diamants' exhibition.[32]

1
A. de Gobert, 'Le luxe de Paris contre le chômage', *L'Intransigeant*, 26 October 1932, p. 2.

2
'Les bijoux Chanel', *L'Officiel de la Couture et de la Mode*, December 1932, p. 28.

3
'Bijoux de Diamants', *Vogue* France, January 1933, p. 25.

4
'Bijoux de Diamants', *Vogue* France, January 1933, p. 25.

5
The price of admission was 20 francs.

6
'Des diamants chez Chanel', *Candide*, 10 November 1932, p. 7.

7
'Des diamants chez Chanel', *Candide*, 10 November 1932, p. 7.

8
'Bijoux de demain', *L'Intransigeant*, 8 November 1932, p. 6.

9
'Bijoux de demain', *L'Intransigeant*, 8 November 1932, p. 6.

10
Laurence Mouillefarine and Véronique Ristelhueber (eds.), *Raymond Templier: Le bijou moderne*, Paris: Norma Éditions, 2005, p. 14.

11
Bijoux de Diamants créés par Chanel, Montrouge: Draeger Frères, 1932.

12
'Un essai de rénovation dans l'art de la parure', *L'Illustration*, 12 November 1932, p. 361.

13
Vogue France, June 1933, p. 17.

14
Letter from Léon Bailly (editor of the newspaper *L'Intransigeant*) to Maurice Donnay of the Académie Française, Paris, 8 October 1932. Patrimoine de CHANEL collection.

15
Paul Iribe, *Choix*, Montrouge: Éditions Iribe/Draeger Frères, 1930.

16
Paul Iribe, *Défense du luxe*, Montrouge: Draeger Frères, 1932.

17
'Le luxe de Paris contre la misère', *La Femme de France*, 25 December 1932, p. 14.

18
Charlotte de Faucigny-Lucinge, 'On lance le bijou vrai', *Marianne*, 30 November 1932, p. 6.

19
'Préface', Jean Cocteau manuscript, 1932. Bibliothèque Historique de la Ville de Paris, cote 2-MS-FS-05-0082.

20
Bijoux de Diamants créés par Chanel, 1932.

21
Jean Cocteau manuscript, 1932, p. 2.

22
Notably the import tax on precious stones.

23
See Hector Ghilini, 'Le Bijou et la haute couture – Deux de nos industries, dites de luxe, les plus atteintes par la crise', *L'Intransigeant*, 7 December 1932, p. 5.

24
'Un essai de rénovation dans l'art de la parure', 1932.

25
Marcel Astruc, 'Est-ce le boom du diamant?', *Les Annales*, 18 November 1932.

26
'Affaire Chanel', Note of the Chambre Syndicale de la Joaillerie dated 4 November 1932. Copy conserved in the archives of the Haute École de Joaillerie de Paris.

27
A. de Gobart, 'Le luxe de Paris contre le chômage', p. 1.

28
Report by Georges Fouquet to the members of the Chambre Syndicale de la Joaillerie, 12 November 1932, p. 2. Copy conserved in the archives of the Haute École de Joaillerie de Paris.

29
Report by Georges Fouquet, p. 3.

30
'Affaire Chanel', 4 November 1932.

31
'Étrange propagande', *Candide*, 3 November 1932, p. 2.

32
Thanks to Garance Salaün for her assistance with research.

ill. 3 **Marie-Laure de Noailles.
Photograph by George
Hoyningen-Huene, published
in** *Vogue* **France, June 1933.**

ill. 4 **Necklace design
by Paul Iribe, 1932.
Guillaume Villemot collection.**

ill.1 **Gabrielle Chanel, photograph by Mark Shaw
published in** *Life***, August 1957.**

Véronique Belloir

THE CHANEL SUIT: THE SHAPE OF FREEDOM

The concept of comfort, although formerly alien to women's fashion, attracted a following, although critics judged the style to be too austere and masculine and therefore unflattering. In the 1910s, the tailored suit was almost always made of wool, in neutral colours: greys, beiges, pale browns or a greenish tone known as 'pea soup fog'. It was a city outfit, worn for morning walks, sports or travelling; in the afternoon it was mostly reserved for the racetrack. It was promoted for its practicality, although it was still worn with a corset, and while the skirt did not touch the ground, apparently leaving the feet free, its close fit sacrificed true freedom of movement to the demands of fashion. The skirt was complemented by a long, wasp-waisted jacket in the same fabric. Broad Directoire-style lapels opened to reveal a high-necked boned bodice or a fitted waistcoat, often with a lace or pleated tulle jabot frothing out at the top.

From the start of her career, Chanel fought against the idea that clothing should be subject to the whims of fashion, as well as rejecting the rigid and stereotypical expression of femininity. It was goodbye to complicated drapery, unwieldy trains, outdated ideas, frills and furbelows, and excess of all kinds; goodbye to convoluted cuts, restrictive forms and asymmetrical outlines. Her credo could be summed up as: 'Subtle elegance – nothing superfluous, nothing artificial, nothing useless, lacking in point or purpose … based on deduction, deliberation, logic, reason, elegant solutions to a problem.'[2]

'It could be said that Chanel rarely,
if ever, varies her line, and that
is quite rightly her source of strength.'
– *Vogue*, 1 April 1921

BALANCING FUNCTION AND FORM

When the Maison Chanel reopened in 1954, the first collections received a cool reception from the Paris press. In a world still marked by the spirit of the New Look and characterized by the revival of a silhouette that glorified traditional femininity, the extreme simplicity of her designs was seen as a lack of innovation, and the Chanel suit did not attract attention. It proved, nevertheless, 'that a formula can evolve, renew itself, and even astonish, while remaining strictly faithful to an unchanged style'.[1]

On the cutting edge of fashion and keen to flout convention, Gabrielle Chanel designed whatever she pleased and always thought in terms of practicality as well as style. She pared things back, rejected ornamentation, which she claimed 'destroyed the line',[3] sought balance and simplicity, conferred lightness and, prompted perhaps by her early intuition, created a sense of freedom, right at the moment when, after experimenting with a different way of dressing during the Great War, women were beginning to feel freedom was exactly what they needed. To Chanel, who designed directly on the body rather than sketching, 'fashion does not exist only in dresses; fashion is in the air, it is borne on the wind, you can sense it, you can breathe it, it's in the sky and on the highway, it's everywhere, it has to do with ideas, with social mores, with events.'[4]

TAILORED SUITS FOR WOMEN

When Gabrielle Chanel started out in the fashion world, the tailored suit, or 'costume', had already found its way into women's wardrobes. This two-piece outfit, originating in England and associated primarily with sports and other outdoor activities, first appeared in the 1850s, when it was exclusively made to measure by gentlemen's tailors. The British tailoring firm of John Redfern helped to popularize the fashion in France, but it was not until the mid-1880s that French firms, such as Old England, and a handful of couturières began making two-piece suits for women, which were advertised as 'comfortable'.

Although the Chanel suit of 1954 continued to reflect some of the principles that had made Chanel's work so successful and distinctive, more so than any of her other designs it seemed like a culmination, almost a manifesto.[5] More than ever, its form and elegance were rooted in the quality of the chosen fabrics; it respected the body's anatomy, was designed to move and was ruled by a spirit of naturalness that was diametrically opposed to the sophisticated fashions of the post-war period. While these principles were unique within the world of fashion, similar ideas were embraced by leading architects and designers, including Robert Mallet-Stevens, Eileen Gray, Jean-Michel Frank, Le Corbusier, Pierre Chareau and Charlotte Perriand. Like them, Chanel was looking for the right balance between function and form, rejecting superfluous detail and appropriating techniques and materials not traditionally associated with her field. After all, this was the woman who said: 'As for me... I sell clothes, objects.'[6]

The Chanel suit showed evidence of careful attention to every detail. And if it is true that 'designers are not, strictly speaking, the people responsible for bringing about progress, but they are the ones who give it form,'[7] Chanel was certainly one such designer.

SPECIALIST TECHNIQUES

In 1958, *Elle* began to showcase the uniqueness of the Chanel suit. Created by women for women, the weekly magazine revealed, step by step, the secrets of how a 'little Chanel suit' was made, and even offered its readers a pattern. While it was certainly inspired by its masculine counterpart, the Chanel suit retained only the overall concept of that garment[8] and a few of its practical aspects. The feminine version was elegant, suitable for contemporary lifestyles, wearable throughout the day and also by women of all ages. Designed to be comfortable, it nevertheless respected the concept of femininity. In its classic form, the suit comprised a jacket with either two or four pockets, a skirt, and a blouse, sometimes with a tie neck or cufflinks at the wrists. There were numerous variants on the basic design, which could be teamed with *marinière* tops, dresses and coats in matching fabrics and with matching linings. 'No two are the same,' commented *Vogue*. 'What unifies them is not the fact of being made from a mould or a standard pattern. It's a unity of style.'[9] And while the suit was originally designed for daytime, Chanel also produced versions in shimmering fabrics for cocktail and evening wear. *Elle* recorded that the range 'retains the casual morning look, but the lustrous fabrics add a dressy note'.[10]

These ensembles were, as one might expect, created by the company's tailoring ateliers. However, the techniques and materials chosen by Chanel differed somewhat from those most frequently used by the ateliers, which traditionally made structured garments. The suit jacket was more like a cardigan of sorts; it was light and supple because it had no interfacing. Its cut – a complex piece of geometry but almost indetectable because it merged with the fabric itself – gave structure to the overall lines while preserving the flexibility of the fabric. The front of the jacket had no bust darts; instead it was made up of four pieces with shoulder darts, creating a gentle tapering effect that accentuated the figure: 'The idea: to avoid disrupting the natural lines of the body and of the fabric.'[11] Two side panels – known as *petits côtés* – defined the silhouette, gently moulding the waist and slimming the hips without restricting either, and allowing for comfortable movement.

In the 1930s, Chanel came up with 'a new way of making up a sleeve which leaves everything else free

ill. 2 **Gabrielle Chanel in 1962.**
Photograph by Douglas Kirkland.

ill. 3 **Jean Cazaubon, known as 'Monsieur Jean', head of the Tailoring atelier, on the staircase of the couture salons, 31, rue Cambon, Paris, 1960. Photograph by Giancarlo Botti.**

ill. 4 *Dorothy + Little Bara*, **Paris,
1960. Photograph
by William Klein, published
in *Vogue* France, October 1960.**

when the arms are in movement'.[12] Its width was governed by that of the *petit côté*, and the armholes were very high, allowing the arms to move freely without disturbing the rest of the jacket. The sleeve was also curved for greater comfort and always finished a little above the wrist in order to show off the wearer's hands. If the cuffs had vents, they were given buttons and could be left open, a detail that evoked the dress codes of elegant gentlemen: at that time, only made-to-measure suits had real buttonholes at the cuffs, and deliberately leaving the last button undone was a sign of social distinction.

The back of the jacket was made up of two pieces with a centre seam and was intentionally allowed to hang: 'It's the back that takes the strain. ...All the articulation of the body is in the back; *all movements stem from the back.*'[13] If the jacket had a collar, instead of being made of multiple layers of fabric and lining, the collar was simply lined and finished with a picot edge – a rolled edge with herringbone overstitching – in woollen yarn to create a pleasingly rounded effect. The collar was never placed too close to the neck, in order to visually lengthen it and prevent any tightness.

Another element borrowed from the male wardrobe, flap pockets, safari pockets or simple patch pockets were useful and practical – somewhere to put your hands. Whether there were two or four, the pockets added to the overall symmetry of shapes and proportions, and played a key role in the graphic arrangement of braiding and buttons, which provided a form of punctuation.

Skirts, whose 'stitched and lightly ironed panels make walking easy',[14] were generally made up of four pieces. Either straight, wrap or pleated, they were only slightly flared and flattened the wearer's hips, while responding to her movements. Dipping slightly at the back and reaching just below the knee, they showed off the legs to best advantage. The belt, made from grosgrain and fabric-lined to keep it thin and flexible, rested on the hip bones rather than encircling the waist. Finally, the zip was never placed at the side, but always at the back, to avoid disrupting the line of the skirt.

LUXURY AND COMFORT

The choice of fabric was crucial to the Chanel suit. Whether wool, silk or a blend of fibres, every fabric had to be comfortable. Chanel's preference was for something soft and supple – ranging from jersey, one of her long-standing favourites, to shantung, a natural, raw silk with a very fluid quality, and a range of wools. Of course, Chanel suits are most indelibly associated with tweed. Traditionally woven in Scotland, this sturdy, rather rugged-looking fabric was formerly used for country clothing before being embraced by women's fashion in the 1920s. Its use gave a garment a sporty look.

During the 1950s, Chanel opted for classic plain or chiné tweeds, but also lighter, softer, downier versions, in textured, bouclé or mottled wool, sometimes combined with chenille, ribbon yarn or shiny metallic threads. She called upon the services of many specialist wool manufacturers, including Lesur, Moreau, Dormeuil and Daumas-Maury, but also obtained fabrics from less conventional sources. In 1959, Malhia Kent, a law student and total newcomer to the field who was passionate about weaving, began producing, exclusively for Chanel, handwoven tweeds and trims that were as soft as knitwear. For her Spring collection in 1963, Chanel chose fabrics handwoven by textile designer Bernat Klein, who had just begun selling his textiles in Paris. Based in Scotland, this instinctive colourist favoured mohair, which gave greater depth to his highly decorative tweeds. Shades of white – chalk, ecru, nougat, ivory, parchment – and black may have been one of her trademarks, but Chanel also used a great many other shades: navy, of course, but also reds, pinks (from bold to pale), and gold.

For evening suits, figured and cloqué silks and glittering lamé were principally sourced from the firms of Bucol and Abraham. Artificial fibres, including nylon, Crylor, Rhodia and Lurex, were often blended with natural silks for greater lightness and ease of maintenance.

PERFECTION, INSIDE AND OUT

The Chanel suit did not have a lining in the traditional sense. Instead, its underlayer was an integral part of the jacket and skirt. It was created using a carefully developed process that was similar to quilting, closely following and consolidating the cut of the garment. The two layers were fixed together with vertical rows of stitching, positioned approximately four centimetres apart and stopping a few centimetres from the edge. On the inside, tiny, invisible stitches – known as *points perdus* – secured the hem. And as a final touch of sophistication, exclusive to the Chanel ateliers, the buttonholes were hand-embroidered on the right side and then bound on the inside to create a sort of inward-facing carbon copy. The chosen lining fabrics – twill, soft and silky pongee, light and airy silk gauze – added a touch of luxury without being over-ostentatious. Whether self-coloured, tone-on-tone, contrasting or printed, the fabric used for this unobtrusive part of the garment sometimes reappeared as edging for the pockets, on the lapels and cuffs, or in the form of a skirt belt.

The lining fabric could also be used to make a matching top, creating a unified look. Chanel was the only designer to adopt this approach, examples of which abound in her creations from the 1920s onwards: 'When the blouse has a tie neck, the jacket lining is in the same fabric, a harmonious arrangement often favoured by Chanel.'[15] There was another practical and at the same time stylish feature inside the jacket: a gilt chain sewn into the hem ensured that the fabric hung straight and fell back into place when the wearer moved. It was also a discreet trademark that Chanel initiates knew to look out for.

'Each suit holds the secrets of Chanel luxury', *Vogue* asserted. 'And that luxury is all about details.'[16] The Chanel suit would not be quite the same without the famous trim in a contrasting colour that made it so strikingly original. Braid, gimp, grosgrain ribbon and piping were used to trim jacket hems, pockets and cuffs and helped to structure the garment. The most complex and inventive of these trimmings were the work of the ineffable and self-taught Madame Pouzieux. Every piece of braid created on her farm near Montargis was utterly unique. Chanel also made use of the selvedges of the fabric from which the suit was cut. These narrow edges created by the weaving process, which often had a tighter weave and a slightly different colour from the rest of the fabric, are traditionally hidden behind seams so that the unsightly aspects of garment-making are concealed. By overturning this rule, Chanel demonstrated her innovative spirit. She made it the height of refinement to cut off the selvedge and use it as a trim, fixing it in place with overstitching.

As for buttons, they were also very important: 'Don't use any old buttons... it's a question of taste, and it's also a matter of taking a little trouble, but elegance demands it.'[17] Gilded, engraved, bearing a lion's head or a double C, or hand-painted to match the colours and pattern of a tweed, these little objects highlighted Chanel's perfectionism and her precise attention to detail.

When we think of a Chanel suit, we think of the simplicity – or apparent simplicity – of a design that has been created with such care that it withstands the test of time and never goes out of fashion. The Chanel suit is a vision of life, a way of being. As Chanel said to Marie-Hélène Arnaud, her favourite model, and her double: 'Your dresses must resemble the life you lead, your car, your work, your loves.'[18]

1

'Le manifeste Chanel', *Vogue* France, September 1958, p. 120.

2

Élisabeth Rombach, 'Le talent de Chanel vu par Sem', *Les Feuillets Sem*, no. 70, Association Sem, September 2014, p. 10 (from a handwritten note by Sem).

3

Claude Delay, *Chanel solitaire*, Paris: Gallimard, 1983, p. 55.

4

Paul Morand, *The Allure of Chanel*, trans. Euan Cameron, London: Pushkin Press, 2008, p. 145.

5

See 'Le manifeste Chanel', *Vogue* France, September 1958, p. 120.

6

L'Express, 11 August 1960, p. 18.

7

Olivier Assouly, 'Autour des enjeux de la qualification du design. Entretien avec Catherine Geel', Paris: Institut Français de la Mode, June 2010: https://www.ifmparis.fr/fr/recherche-academique/autour-des-enjeux-de-la-qualification-du-design

8

'The man's suit and the woman's suit by Chanel have one ideal in common: "distinction".' From Roland Barthes, 'Le match Chanel-Courrèges', *Marie Claire*, no. 181, September 1967, pp. 42–43; reprinted in Roland Barthes, *The Language of Fashion*, trans. Andy Stafford, London: Bloomsbury, 2013, pp. 99–103.

9

'La Française en uniforme', *Vogue* France, February 1962, p. 59.

10

'Le bon ton en tailleur du soir', *Elle*, 1 September 1961, p. 66.

11

'Chanel aujourd'hui', *Elle*, 17 November 1958, p. 50.

12

'Mademoiselle Chanel, la grande couturière de Paris', *Sud Magazine*, 15 November 1934, p. 36.

13

Paul Morand, *The Allure of Chanel*, pp. 48–49.

14

'Une démonstration d'élégance', *Vogue* France, March 1961, p. 221.

15

'Il y a harmonie entre toutes les collections', *Vogue* France, April 1921, p. 52.

16

'Bon sens luxueux. Chanel', *Vogue* France, September 1959, p. 136.

17

'C'est être merveilleuse avec le petit tailleur Chanel', *Elle*, 4 December 1959, p. 103.

18

'Elle chez Chanel', *Elle*, 17 February 1958, p. 30.

ill. 5 **Gabrielle Chanel in 1962. Photograph by Douglas Kirkland.**

ill. 6 **From left to right: The models Marie-Hélène Arnaud, Gisèle Franchomme, Paule Rizzo and Mimi d'Arcangues, Maison Chanel, 31, rue Cambon, Paris, 27 November 1958. Photograph by Bernard Lipnitzki.**

Overleaf

Suit, Autumn–Winter 1960–61,
ivory wool tweed, navy
and red fringed wool braid.
cat. 157

Suit, Autumn–Winter 1963–64,
ivory wool tweed, ivory
silk pongee, chiné braid in navy
and ivory wool, gilded metal.
cat. 163

Suit, Autumn–Winter 1960–61,
white wool by Burg, navy wool
braid, silk pongee, gilded metal.
cat. 162

Suit, Autumn–Winter 1964–65,
off-white tweed,
navy and red wool braid.
cat. 156

**Cardigan jacket and skirt ensemble,
Spring–Summer 1971,
ivory wool jersey with navy print,
gilded metal and navy Galalith.**
cat. 137

**Suit, Spring–Summer 1965,
white silk cloqué with navy print.**
cat. 138

Suit with jacket, blouse and skirt, Spring–Summer 1964, navy and white check tweed, white silk twill with navy print, gilded metal.
cat. 136

Previous pages

**Dress and coat ensemble,
Autumn–Winter 1965–66,
navy tweed, red wool, gilded metal.**
cat. 174

**Suit, Autumn–Winter 1965–66,
navy tweed, red silk cloqué,
navy Galalith, gilded metal.**
cat. 175

**Ensemble with dress
and coat, Spring–Summer 1963,
multicoloured mohair tweed,
raspberry silk twill with navy print.**
cat. 144

Previous pages

**Coat, Autumn–Winter 1961–62,
black silk cloqué,
white mink, gilded metal.**
cat. 146

**Tunic and skirt ensemble,
Spring–Summer 1960,
black silk crêpe with Lurex lamé,
black silk cord.**
cat. 326

**Pelisse coat, Autumn–Winter
1966–67, black wool with check
effect, clipped beaver fur,
black Galalith and gilded metal.**
cat. 147

Ensemble with coat, top and skirt,
Autumn–Winter 1965–66,
ivory and grey houndstooth wool,
white mink, ivory tweed,
gilded metal.
cat. 140

Previous pages

**Jacket and skirt suit,
Autumn–Winter 1961–62,
chiné tweed, black grosgrain,
écru and black twisted braid,
pink silk pongee.**
cat. 129

**Suit with jacket, top and skirt,
Spring–Summer 1964,
beige chiné tweed, beige
and pink wool braid,
sand-coloured shantung.**
cat. 131

Suit, Autumn–Winter 1965–66,
silver lamé, white mink,
gold metallic braid, ivory silk satin.
cat. 178

Dress and jacket ensemble, Autumn–Winter 1963–64, gold lamé cloqué by Bucol, sable, pink silk pongee.
cat. 179

ill.1 Gabrielle Chanel at the Ritz, Paris, 1938. Photograph by Boris Lipnitzki.

Marie-Laure Gutton

CHANEL ACCESSORIES: THE BUILDING BLOCKS OF STYLE

'Dressing with the correctness, the extreme rigour, I would even say the austerity that characterizes true Paris fashion, Gabrielle adds to her toilette that effective element of surprise, that touch of brilliance, that detail, that last word, without which no masterpiece is complete and no woman well-dressed.... She knows that accessories carry the mark of personality, the indefinable force that is pure love, and the anticipated loss of which makes death detestable.'[1] These lines, published in French *Vogue* in 1927, encapsulate Gabrielle Chanel's view of accessories, those fundamental elements which, in their various forms, accentuate and complete a woman's look, meet the demands of an active life and help to form our concept of style.

A PRAGMATIC VIEW OF ACCESSORIES

From her earliest days as a milliner in 1910, Gabrielle Chanel aspired to simplicity of form, practicality and comfort, seeking to eliminate physical constraints and increase freedom of movement. At a time when society women were wearing broad-brimmed capeline hats garnished with a multitude of feathers and flowers, Chanel turned her attention to the male wardrobe, and chose to focus on the boater, which sat neatly on the head and needed no artifice to keep it in place. Just as the couturière's modest origins were her justification for the austerity of her designs, the same was true of her hats: 'If I wore hats pulled down over my head, it was because the wind in the Auvergne might mess up my hair.'[2] She reduced their volume and got rid of excessive ornamentation.[cat. 2] Her success was soon reported in the press, with *Women's Wear Daily* lauding one of her creations in October 1912: a wine-coloured plush hat with a brim and a flat bow at the front.[3] The American press primarily focused attention on her 'sporty' designs, especially her jersey and ribbon hats, which were boaters or cloche-shaped and easy to wear. The boater continued to occupy an important place in Chanel's repertoire, especially after her comeback in 1954, with the rise of the two-piece suit. Its proportions changed, as did the materials used (straw or jersey), but it remained a constant; in 1967, it took the form of a 'black picador hat with a light veil shading the face and hair fastened at the nape of the neck.... It was in partnership with this hat that all Chanel suits were shown.'[4]

With hats as well as other accessories, such as gloves and bags, Chanel used colour coordination in a playful way. She was not the only couturière to do this, but she did it brilliantly, guided once again by the principles of simplification and rationalization. In 1932, for example, we read that 'velvet gloves coordinated to match the outfit are the great new innovation from Chanel'.[5] Similarly, for the summer of 1927 she offered her clients 'a "uniform" belt that can be worn with any dress, including evening gowns.'[6]

Two iconic designs, Chanel's 2.55 bag and her two-tone slingback shoes, are perfect examples of her quest for functionality and comfort. In the 1920s, Chanel began designing purses and clutch bags to accompany her outfits, often in matching fabrics, but it was not until 1955 that she launched her classic 2.55 bag.[cat. 125] This bag, available in jersey, silk velvet or lamb's leather to suit the time of day, was extremely distinctive – its rectangular shape, its flap, its stitched decoration that created a quilted look and its twist clasp, known as a 'Mademoiselle clasp' – yet at the same time it was eminently practical. Its strap, a chain with a strip of leather threaded through to prevent the metal from clinking, itself an iconic feature, allowed the wearer to carry it in her hand, over her arm or on her shoulder. Chanel explained how this particular feature came about: 'Tired of holding my bags in my hand and losing them, I added a strap and wore it over my shoulder.'[7] The interior was also designed to make life easy for women: the lining in red grosgrain or leather and the many pockets helped the owner find what she was looking for, especially her lipstick, for which there was a special compartment. The bag even came in three sizes designed to meet a range of different demands, depending on a woman's lifestyle.

To create the first two-tone shoes in 1957, Chanel approached, in turn, the shoemakers Casale, Jourdan, Mancini, Villon, and Massaro; it was the latter's design that she eventually decided to use. Chanel wanted a graphic look. The beige made the leg look longer and the black toe made the foot look smaller, while hiding scuff marks.[cat. 128] The elasticated slingback made it possible to slip the shoes off discreetly beneath the table, without struggling to get them back on again. 'With four pairs, I could go around the world,'[8] Chanel told Raymond Massaro, and there were in fact four versions of the shoe, for every occasion: black-toed for daytime and general wear, navy blue for summertime, brown for a 'sporty' look, and gold for evening. They were further proof that any accessory must be elegant, practical and adaptable. There was one element, however, that appeared to contradict this pragmatic vision: Chanel's lavish and ubiquitous jewels.

A WEALTH OF JEWELS

From the 1920s onwards, jewelry was a key component of the Chanel look, and the couturière introduced her own costume jewelry range[ill. 4] in around 1924.[9] Paul Morand, in *The Allure of Chanel*, records her own personal thoughts on the matter: 'Expensive jewelry does not improve the woman who wears it any more than costly fabrics woven with precious materials do; if she looks plain, she will remain so. The point of jewelry is to pay respect to those for whom, and at whose homes, one wears it. I readily wear a lot of jewelry because, on me, it always looks artificial. The mania to want to dazzle disgusts me; jewelry is not meant to arouse envy; still less astonishment. It should remain an ornament and an amusement.'[10] In a spirit of iconoclasm, Chanel playfully combined real and fake gemstones, wearing the two indiscriminately, often together, exhibiting no qualms about combining glass and precious stones in a single piece. As an example of this mixing and matching, the pendant brooch[cat. 289] worn by the couturière in numerous photographs, and almost certainly based on a 19th-century design, is decorated with old-cut diamonds and a real emerald, alongside imitation rubies and emeralds.

This 'love of fakery',[11] as the press sometimes termed it, demonstrated Chanel's eagerness to challenge conventions, in particular those of the aristocracy and the bourgeoisie, who flaunted their pearls and precious stones as if they were badges of social status. A piece of costume jewelry gave Chanel licence to be creative in the way that she wanted, allowing her to experiment with colours and materials. Although she removed the mystique from fine jewelry, she did not reject it: Chanel herself wore pearls and precious stones and offered her clients genuine gemstones. The brooches[cats. 197, 198] from the 1930s belonging to Diana Vreeland (1903–89), editor of American *Vogue*,[ill. 3] are good examples. Encrusted with cabochon sapphires, rubies, emeralds, citrines, tourmalines and aquamarines, they demonstrate Chanel's love of coloured stones, which she boldly combined. They also echoed her love of abundance and profusion, which was reflected in the way that she wore jewelry and encouraged others to do so. She would layer strings of pearls and sautoirs over high necklines, adding bracelets, brooches and earrings, always to elegant effect. Often, bracelets and brooches were worn in pairs. These 'sunshine jewels',[12] which might relieve the austerity of a very simple outfit or accentuate the sumptuousness of lamé, figured or printed fabrics, could also be worn in different ways. A brooch could be fastened to the cuff of a jacket sleeve,[13] positioned on the shoulder,[14] or the hip, or perched on the crown of a hat.[15] Chanel's love of jewelry was also reflected in the way that she made use of the technique of *trompe-l'œil* throughout her career. In 1925, a day dress adorned with an embroidered sautoir was published in American *Vogue*,[16] and on 20 September 1933, the firm of Tissus Chanel registered seventeen designs for fabric prints,[17] three of which featured imitation beading, made up of cut gemstones alternating with cabochons, or rows of irregular cabochons. Chanel continued to use the theme of optical illusions right up to her final collection, creating a dress design in Bucol's 'A-Tell' black crêpe, printed with rows of necklace motifs.[18]

When the choice of jewelry was more discreet, it was left to gilded chain belts[cat. 278] and buttons decorated with Chanel's favourite symbols to add a touch of sparkle that structured a garment and relieved its uniformity, particularly in the case of two-piece suits. The buttons were usually made by Desrues, François Hugo or Robert Goossens, and gave the feel of a military uniform, especially when applied in double rows or used to garnish a cuff.[19] They are indisputably a key feature of the Chanel style.

HALLMARKS OF THE CHANEL STYLE

Jewelry offered Gabrielle Chanel a rich outlet for creative expression and helped to set the house style. The use of pearls was one of the most obvious 'Chanelisms'.[20] They first appeared in 1924, in the form of a sautoir, in the pages of French *Vogue*,[21] and, thirty years later, according to the same magazine, pearls were still the Chanel trademark: 'There are pearl years, just as there are champagne years. *Vogue* predicts that 1958 will be a famous pearl vintage. Thanks to whom? Chanel. With her sense of "what women of today require", she has necklaces cascading down the front of simple bodices and transforms the most modest dress into a treasure trove.'[22] Pearls also nestled in Chanel's famous 'Nest' earrings and adorned her Renaissance-inspired necklaces and the clip brooches[cats. 298, 299, 300] which, from 1960 onwards, could be used to fasten a suit jacket or hold a scarf in place.

Chanel loved vintage jewelry and in 1924 she asked Comte Étienne de Beaumont (1883–1956) to make her first pieces of costume jewelry. The resulting collection included colourful crucifixes and long gold sautoirs. Chanel later entrusted the production of her jewelry line to Fulco di Verdura (1898–1978),[23] who would take inspiration from the medieval and Renaissance collections at the Louvre, the Talisman of Charlemagne in Dresden, and his own Mediterranean origins. Their collaboration gave rise to a piece that has since become iconic, a cuff bracelet embellished with a Maltese cross in coloured stones. The two artists can be seen giving the bracelet close attention in a series of photographs taken by Boris Lipnitzki in 1937.[ill. 6] It was in the pieces made by jeweler and goldsmith Robert Goossens (1927–2016),[24]

ill. 2 **Gabrielle Chanel in 1957.**
Photograph by Mark Shaw.

ill. 3 **Diana Vreeland in the 1930s.**
Photograph by
George Hoyningen-Huene.

ill. 4 **Window display at the Chanel**
boutique at 31, rue Cambon, 1939.
Photograph by Roger Schall.

ill. 5 **Mademoiselle Chanel
with the '2.55' bag in 1957.
Photograph by Mike de Dulmen.**

ill. 6 **Fulco di Verdura
and Gabrielle Chanel
in the haute couture salons
at 31, rue Cambon, 1937.
Photograph by Boris Lipnitzki.**

however, that the influence of history found its supreme form of expression. Goossens began working for Chanel in 1961, drawing his inspiration from Venice, Byzantium, Persia and the Celts, and creating 'barbarian' jewelry that emulated the shapes, materials and *cloisonné* settings of antique pieces. He made crosses in rock crystal [cats. 250, 251] and turquoise, and eagle-shaped brooches [cat. 235] reminiscent of 6th-century Visigoth fibula brooches, and borrowed their openwork metal mounts studded with faceted gemstones from Renaissance jewelry. [cat. 255] Chanel and Goossens shared pieces and visited museums together, including the Château de Chantilly, [25] where they studied the jewelry depicted in paintings, with Dürer, Holbein and Paolo Veronese all providing fuel for their imaginations. As well as drawing on antique jewelry for inspiration, Goossens created a few replica pieces, beginning with a Byzantine reliquary cross, [cat. 234] which was given to Chanel by Hélène Lazareff, [cat. 233] and a Syrian bracelet dating from the 2nd century, [cat. 282] found in the Yakhmur necropolis and now conserved in the Louvre.

From the Byzantine to the baroque, via the ornamental styles of ancient Egypt, everything could become a source of creative inspiration – for example, Mughal Indian influences were evident in the coloured droplet necklaces of the late 1930s. [cat. 207] These exotic and historical roots give a certain timelessness to these pieces, which do not reflect the dominant styles of the period. However, Chanel's Art Deco jewelry of the 1920s – long sautoirs composed of geometric stones – was much more representative of its times. Similarly, her necklaces and brooches of enamelled metal with floral and plant motifs, made by Gripoix in the 1930s, [cats. 215, 216] reflect the romanticism of the period, which was also echoed in the couturière's textile designs.

A defining characteristic of Chanel accessories is the use and reuse of symbols – signs of the Zodiac (especially Chanel's own sign of Leo, the lion), [cat. 281] ears of wheat (sign of prosperity and fertility), stars, suns, crosses, camellias, and more – as well as the use of symbolic materials – such as rock crystal, used in the decor of the couturière's rue Cambon apartment, and to which she attributed protective powers – and decorative elements (chains, medallions, etc.). All of these emblems of the Chanel style speak to us today. 'She excels in fine details, letting her whims and fancy and imagination shine through, yet cautiously controlling them when it comes to the fundamentals, as Gabrielle is too classical in her tastes to allow anything that would disturb the purity of her lines,' wrote Princess Bibesco. [26] Chanel cleverly succeeded in setting her own rules of style, marrying the brilliance of her jewelry with the chic, comfort and functionality of her other accessories. These accompaniments are inseparable from her clothing designs and have become true fashion icons in their own right, instantly recognizable and impossible to ignore.

1

Princess Bibesco, 'Gabrielle ou le génie de l'accessoire', *Vogue* France, December 1927, p. 29.

2

Paul Morand, *The Allure of Chanel*, trans. Euan Cameron, London: Pushkin Press, 2008, p. 45.

3

Women's Wear Daily, 1 October 1912, p. 5.

4

Vogue France, September 1967, p. 215.

5

Frivoline, 'L'art de la mode', *L'Art et la Mode*, 20 September 1932, p. 2.

6

Femina, April 1927, p. 40.

7

Claude Delay, *Chanel solitaire*, Paris: Gallimard, 1983, p. 275.

8

Interview with Raymond Massaro, 5 and 27 April 2006. Chanel estate.

9

See Florence Müller, *Les Paruriers de la haute couture*, exhibition catalogue, Grand-Hornu, Brussels: Mercator Fonds , 2006, p. 56.

10

Paul Morand, *The Allure of Chanel*, p. 122.

11

'La question des bijoux', *Femina*, February 1928, p. 36.

12

Marie Claire, no. 12, September 1955, p. 91.

13

See *L'Officiel de la Mode et de la Couture*, March 1955, p. 91.

14

See *Elle*, no. 1241, 29 September 1969, p. 88.

15

See *Elle*, no. 691, 23 March 1959, p. 62.

16

Vogue US, 15 May 1925, p. 80.

17

'17 designs for printing on fabric', Fabric Department, registration no. 15466, model nos. 4, 13 and 14. Archives de la Ville de Paris, shelf mark D12U10 176.

18

See *Vogue* France, March 1971, p. 164.

19

See *Vogue* France, September 1969, p. 31.

20

Marie Claire, no. 77, March 1961, p. 124.

21

Vogue France, November 1924, p. 27.

22

'Le point de vue de Vogue sur le temps des perles', *Vogue* France, December 1957, p. 61.

23

Fulco di Verdura's name appears in the staff register of the Maison Chanel from November 1933 to January 1934. The jeweler then moved to the USA, where he probably continued to work for Chanel.

24

Robert Goossens worked for Chanel from 1954 onwards through the Maison Degorce, and then in his own name after 1961.

25

Interview with Robert Goossens, 7 and 11 April 2006; Chanel estate.

26

Princess Bibesco, 'Gabrielle ou le génie de l'accessoire', p. 29.

'2.55' bag, between 1955 and 1971,
black-dyed quilted lamb's leather,
gilded metal, twist clasp.
cat. 125

Necklace, **CHANEL design made by Gripoix, Spring—Summer 1938,** gilded metal, translucent polychrome glass.
cat. 216

Brooch, CHANEL design
made by Gripoix, 1937,
gilded metal, translucent
and opaque polychrome glass.
cat. 215

Brooch, CHANEL design
made by Robert Goossens, 1960s,
vermeil, tourmaline.
cat. 235

Necklace and earrings,
Spring–Summer 1928,
silver, rock crystal.
cat. 194

Crucifix pendant, CHANEL design
made by Robert Goossens, 1960s,
yellow gold, rock crystal.
cat. 251

Pendant, CHANEL design made
by Robert Goossens, 1960s,
vermeil, rock crystal, tourmaline.
cat. 250

Brooch, CHANEL design
made by Robert Goossens,
between 1954 and 1974,
gilded bronze, tourmaline.
cat. 254

Brooch, CHANEL design
made by Robert Goossens,
between 1954 and 1974,
gilded bronze, tourmaline.
cat. 255

205

Previous pages

**Bracelet, CHANEL design made
by Robert Goossens, 1960s,
vermeil, polychrome glass.**
cat. 282

**Pendant, CHANEL design
made by Robert Goossens,
Autumn–Winter 1965–66,
gilded metal, red and green glass.**
cat. 239

**Pendant, CHANEL design made by
Robert Goossens, 1960s, yellow
gold, turquoise, tourmaline, pearls.**
cat. 248

Necklace, CHANEL design made
by Robert Goossens,
Autumn–Winter 1965–66,
gilded bronze.
cat. 280

Overleaf

**Necklace, CHANEL design
made by Robert Goossens,
Autumn–Winter 1969–70,
gilded metal, red and green
glass, imitation pearl.**
cat. 256

**Necklace, Autumn–Winter
1938–39, gilded metal,
polychrome glass, pearls.**
cat. 207

**Bracelet, CHANEL design
by François Hugo,
Spring–Summer 1938,
gilded metal, cut glass.**
cat. 206

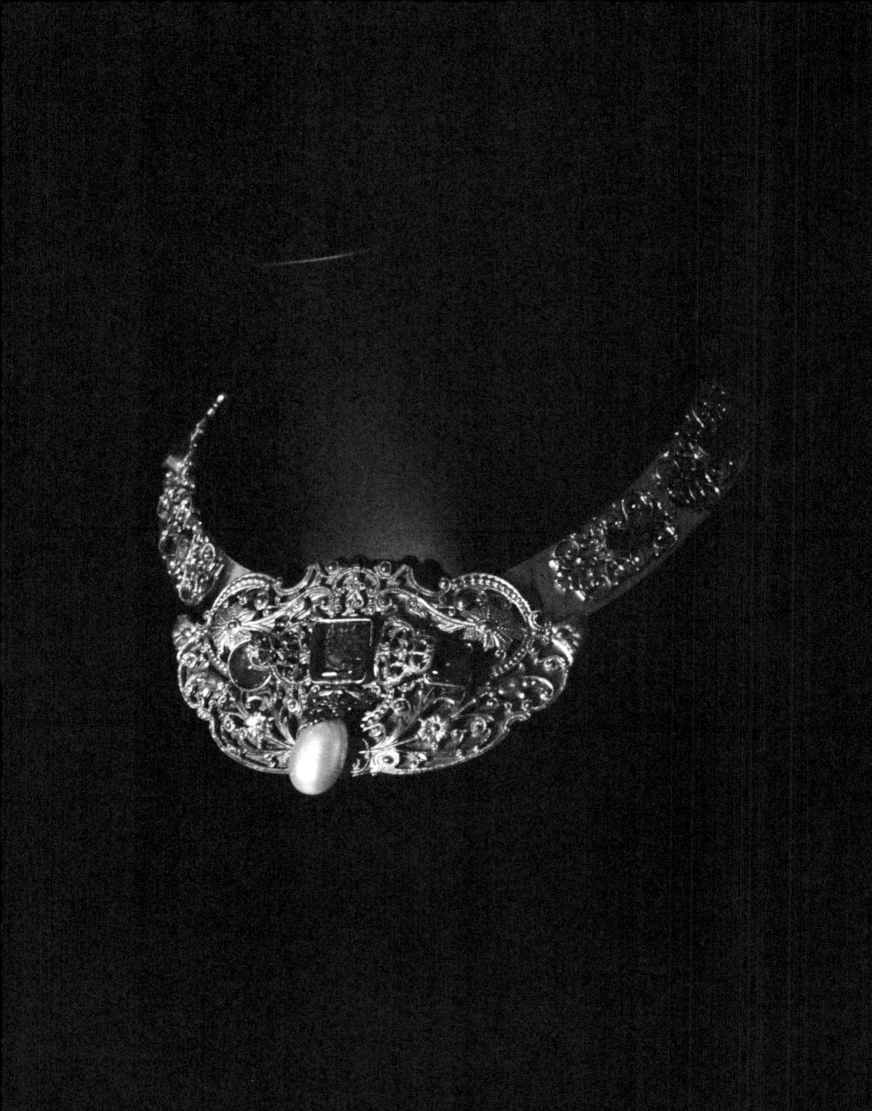

Previous pages

**Dress, Spring–Summer 1964,
black organza and cotton cloqué.**
cat. 324

**Brooch, CHANEL design
made by Robert Goossens,
Autumn–Winter 1961–62,
gilded metal, crystal, pearl.**
cat. 265

Dress
cat. 324

Brooch
cat. 265

**Formal dress,
Spring–Summer 1959,
black silk chiffon,
black silk satin ribbon.**
cat. 320

**Brooch, CHANEL design
made by Robert Goossens,
Spring–Summer 1959,
gilded metal, turquoise glass,
rhinestones.**
cat. 268

**Prototype for two-tone shoe,
CHANEL design made
by Massaro, c. 1961, beige kidskin,
black silk satin.**
cat. 128

ill.1 Gabrielle Chanel in New York, 1931. Photograph by George Rinhart.

Alexandra Palmer

CHANEL: THE AMERICAN WAY

Gabrielle Chanel 'reigned over Paris for twenty years, vanished for fifteen years, then reappeared because she was bored. And this winter [1965] everyone is imitating her designs.'[1] Cecil Beaton said that she showed women how to 'take on an appearance which has since become the American working girl of today.'[2] So what was it about her clothes that most appealed to North American tastes? Chanel fashions were 'not spectacular in line or trimming, but most original', 'wearable', and always 'youthful'.[3] Seasonally there were 'no radical changes', making Chanel reliable and profitable for manufacturers with small, seasonal modifications. The Chanel 'atmosphere' was 'always the same but with enough newness and difference to make it difficult for her clients to deny themselves any new clothes'.[4] Nor did the clothes go out of fashion, as *Vogue* proved by publishing a picture of Mrs Harrison Williams in 1945, wearing a 1939 Chanel velvet suit.[5]

Chanel was first introduced to America through both originals and imitations of her millinery. By 1920, American *Vogue* declared that a 'woman of taste and distinction will have no difficulty in finding the costume to meet every need of the day at the Maison Chanel, and because of this avoidance of extremes, each model … suits an amazing variety of types.'[6] It was the 'ultra-modern' actress Ina Claire who helped launch the Chanel look in the USA.[7–ill. 5] She was the epitome of youthful sophistication, and the Chanel outfits she wore in the 1924 production of Henry Miller's play *Grounds for Divorce* were described as the 'smartest … of the season in any play' on Broadway. *Vogue* declared that the 'English herring-bone tweed'

dress was the "perfect expression of youthful chic,'[8] and examples could be found at Franklin Simon. A reproduction of the 'velveteen overblouse costume' was available at Bergdorf Goodman, and a cheaper imitation displayed in the windows of Best & Co. resulted in over half the stock being sold by 11 a.m.[9] A year later, New York debutantes were wearing a version for tea parties as Chanel's influence had created a 'ban' on 'everything that is not simple'.[10] By 1928, Chanel was recording annual sales over 10 million francs higher than her Paris competitors, due to her sales to US manufacturers and speciality shops.[11] Chanel's style relied on details that she reprised throughout her career.[12] Her cardigan-style, open 'air-conditioned' jackets that were so influential in the 1950s and 60s, were based on her earlier 'very short jackets that make these suits so young'.[13] In 1914 she had designed tops, sweaters and even coats that you had to dive into, as they slipped on over the head, and dresses that opened in front,[ill. 3] making dressing speedy and easily accomplished alone, without the help of servants.[14] She repeatedly used simple trims as style features, placing 'octave upon octave of buttons down the front' of a simple black dress, and designed fashions that allowed one to 'trot around town the whole day long'.[15] Her look, said to be based around French simplicity,[ill.1] included the 'shortest of short skirts'[16] in 1910, but she refused to raise the hem high above the knee in the late 1960s, considering it ugly and inappropriate.

Chanel was possibly the most copied couturier of the 20th century.[17] She famously said she did not mind because imitations gave her free publicity, and stimulated her designs, stating: 'What they can never steal from me is the authenticity, the spirit of discovery, and the flawlessness of production that costs so much because it does not lie in the motor of a sewing machine, but in the hands and mind of a French seamstress.'[18] She condescendingly added that they also helped 'many poor couturières, devoid of imagination … to make a living with my models, at no detriment to myself!'[19] Gabrielle Chanel's views on copying flew in the face of the Chambre Syndicale de la Haute Couture, whose role was to facilitate access to the collections, legal sales, and to control illicit copying that principally came from US style-pirates who made the Paris couture originals obsolete and economically worthless. Chanel's acceptance of copying was practical and strategic. By 1935, her sales to American buyers were the third highest in Paris, after Molyneux and Vionnet, whose unit numbers were lower as their costs and revenues were higher.[20] Chanel focused on volume of sales with lower prices and earlier deliveries.[21]

Originals and imitations of Chanel generated enormous profits for North American stores and textile and clothing manufacturers in the interwar period, and again after her comeback in 1954.[22] *Vogue* US published an editorial describing the domino effect and profits a Chanel winning move could generate. The 'Chanel 142' dress was shown to press and buyers on a Monday in February 1926. By Friday night, the commercial orders had left the house and they arrived by boat in New York the following Thursday.

At the same time, examples of the dress made by the Maison Chanel itself were delivered to Paris clients and six New York clients received US-made custom copies based on the imported originals. Simultaneously, the dress was being reproduced and sold for $75.00 to 'Mrs Average Manhattan', and copies and copies of copies in various textiles sold in prices ranging from $25.00 to $49.50. Within months, the dress had been reproduced ten thousand times by one wholesaler and others had also made thousands. *Vogue* explained that the dress was 'so perfectly fitted to supply the demand of almost any woman who knows clothes, that nothing could kill her – not even little Mr Cheap and his copies.' It was a 'wonder' and the magazine listed its virtues: 'Simple. Sophisticated. Practical. Becoming to almost every one. Easy to copy; hard to spoil. In short, Chanel One-Forty-Two is almost the ideal dress.'[23] This is why *Vogue* had called the 'Model 817' dress a 'Ford' – 'the frock that all the world will wear'.[24]

However, Chanel understood the importance of exclusivity and explored a variety of ways to secure it. She had a new idea for matching accessories; gloves, leather scarves and handbags, and signed contracts to have them made in factories jointly operated by Chanut and Steinberger in Grenoble and Steinberger Bros. Block Corp. of New York, who oversaw US distribution.[25] Chanel was marketed differently in the US and France. Sales of scarves were important because 'when the American woman thinks of sweaters she also thinks of scarves,' and Chanel had made sweaters fashionable. American tourists were advised: 'The chic [Chanel] scarves which you see in New York … you will not find in Paris…. The tricolour scarf of Chanel which made such a hit in the season of 1928 … could be bought in any smart New York shop, but nowhere in Paris except at Chanel's at Chanel's prices!'[26]

Chanel aggressively created her own textiles, which gave authenticity to Chanel originals and to good imitations, as it was far more time-consuming and expensive to make textiles than fashions. She founded the Tissus Chanel brand in 1928, which incorporated the Tricots Chanel label, and sold yardage to large retail stores such as Galeries Lafayette, and around the world.[27] She signed manufacturing agreements with English, Irish and Scottish factories, much to the ire of the French textile industry, and founded Chanel Commission Export[28] to control US distribution and sales. Within three years, her textile profits increased 20 per cent.[29] Clearly, reproductions of Chanel fashions stimulated sales of Chanel textiles, and was in part why Chanel could afford to be so cavalier about her fashions being copied.

Just before Chanel closed in 1939, Americans considered her the 'Grande Mademoiselle of French dressmaking', the woman who had 'changed the face of the dressmaking industry. She designed clothes for smart women, which were as simply cut and as foolproof as if they had been made for workmen.'[30] Indeed, Chanel's comeback on 5 February 1954 may never have succeeded without the support of the American fashion press and markets that, again, enabled manufacturers to 'season after season [sell] Chanel-like styles … in increasing numbers at every price level'.[31] The first collection was seen by 'a silent audience', the jersey designs were described as having 'a shoddy, lifeless appearance' and Chanel was called a 'prisoner of the period she influenced so strongly'.[32] The French had not forgotten her actions against the collective interests of Paris couture and French textile manufacturers.

But Bettina Ballard, American *Vogue*'s fashion editor, acted as a champion, saying that the news of Chanel reopening had been an important pre-collection influence, inspiring a casual look.[33] The March issue featured three Chanel ensembles that summed up what Americans looked for in Chanel designs and why they endured.[ill. 4] One suit 'represents everything Chanel has believed in all her life. Navy-blue wool Chanel jersey… two patch pockets; cuffs that button and unbutton to turn back; side-pleated skirt for walking ease; a launderable, tucked, white muslin blouse, with real cuffs and cuff-buttons, and with tabs buttoning onto the skirt, front and back, a young turn-down collar, and a young bow at the neck.'[34]

Carmel Snow, editor of *Harper's Bazaar*, engaged the interest of a manufacturer, likely the important firm of Davidow, which had done an excellent pre-war trade in imitations of Chanel.[35] Davidow's suits were said to be better than a Chanel; they were nearly as expensive, featured superb workmanship, and sold around 60,000 units annually.[36] By enlisting these powerful advocates, Chanel made the rest of the industry pay attention, including the largest couture buyer, Ohrbach's, nicknamed 'The Miracle on 34th Street', which sold 200 copies of a Chanel suit in a single day.[37]

Chanel said: 'I'm making clothes that will suit the woman of 20 and the woman of 40… My collection will not take age into consideration – it will be the young look.'[38] She was a goldmine for the North American textile and clothing industry and retailers because the Chanel look crossed all fashion markets nationally, reaching generations of mature women, Juniors, Misses and even 'subteens'.[39] In 1964, *Life* magazine called this success 'The Everywhereness of the Chanel Look'.[40]

4679.
Chanel

ill. 2 **Sketch, Chanel files, 1922–29.**
Fashion Institute
of Technology, New York.

Planche III. — ROBES DE JERSEY. — Modèles de Gabrielle Chanel *(fig. 146, 147 et 148)*

garni de galon ciré noir. Doublure
de satin ciré apparaissant au col.
Fig. 84. Robe de faille bleu foncé
lamée d'or. Dentelle d'or au corsage.
Traîne de tulle noir, alourdie de
dentelle d'or (Léroc).
Fig. 85. Robe de
mousseline de soie blan-
che bordée d'une large
dentelle d'argent posée
sur un ruban bleu, tu-
nique de Chantilly noir,
corsage de dentelle d'argent, ceinture de
ruban bleu-nattier (Bènre et Hennance).
Dentelle de Tableurr).
Fig. 86. Déshabillé de taffetas
glacé rose : ceinture et col en faille

d'un ton plus soutenu (Crésot).
Fig. 87. Robe de tulle, bordée de filet
ourlé d'un volant d'organdi : ceinture en
ruban de faille, de deux tons de bleu.
Ruban N° 565 de la Maison Blum.
Dentelle Myra de la
Maison Marescot.
Fig. 88. Robe de taf-
fetas tricolore sur un
dessous de Chantilly
blanc (Marescot), ruban
de velours noir. Tissu
N° 19116 A (Bianchini et Férier).
Fig. 89. Robe de Malines : ceinture
lamée blanc, or et argent : ruban bro-
ché. Dentelle Radium de la Maison
Marescot : ruban 2549 de la Maison

Blum : tissu de la Maison Bianchini
et Férier.
Fig. 90. Chapeau de faille grège,
plumes assorties (Lewis).
Fig. 91. Chapeau de paille anglaise
noire, calotte de satin bleu vif.
Motif noir et bleu (Lewis).
Fig. 92. Chapeau de satin gris-
argent orné sur le devant de deux
galons d'argent (Lewis).
Fig. 93. Grand canotier de taffetas
glacé amaranthe, garni de franges de soie du même
ton. Gros pavot de taffetas sur le devant (Lewis).
Fig. 94. Grand chapeau de taffetas vieux rose du
Barry, doublé de taffetas taupe. Motif en ruban
picot rose et taupe (Lewis).

ill. 3 **Jersey dresses**
by Gabrielle Chanel, *Les Élégances*
parisiennes, **May 1916, p. 15.**

223

ill. 4 'Paris Collections:
One Easy Lesson', *Vogue* US,
1 March 1954, p. 100.
Photograph by Henry Clarke.

ill. 5 'Ina Claire selects the newest
Chanel sports frocks in tweed
and velveteen', *Vogue* US, vol. 64,
no. 10, 15 November 1924, pp. 46–47.
Photographs by Edward Steichen.

46   *VOGUE*   *November 15*   47

PHOTOGRAPHS ON THESE TWO PAGES POSED BY INA CLAIRE

Chanel, to whom all the well-dressed world looks for the epitome of smart simplicity, sponsored the shirt and jumper, or vareuse, type of frock as newly smart in her opening collection this season. This sports model of English herring-bone tweed in tan and white is a perfect expression of youthful chic

Ina Claire, who is now playing in the very successful comedy, "Grounds for Divorce," chose these three attractive models from Chanel's collection. The tweed dress above is worn with a heavy brown belt, a beige felt hat, and beige gauntlets, slightly large. Copies of this model may be had from Franklin Simon

The newest thing in sports frocks, this season, is the flat back and the circular front. These two versions—the morning dress at the left and the sports dress at the right—show, in different views, exactly the effect which is smart at the moment. The morning dress is in beige crêpe Elizabeth

One of Chanel's most successful sports models is in sapphire blue velveteen—a material this designer is featuring—and is made with the new circular fulness at the front, leaving ample freedom for sports activity, and the correctly flat back. Copies of this dress may be had from Bergdorf Goodman

INA CLAIRE SELECTS THE NEWEST CHANEL   SPORTS FROCKS IN TWEED AND VELVETEEN

224

1
Françoise Giroud, '"Backstage at Paris" Fashion Drama', in Jeannette A. Jarnow & Beatrice Judelle, *Inside the Fashion Business*, New York, London & Sydney: John Wiley & Sons, 1965, p. 108.

2
Cecil Beaton, *The Glass of Fashion*, New York: Doubleday, 1954, p. 162.

3
'Flaring as opposed to bouffant silhouette…', *Women's Wear*, 23 September 1919, p. 20; 'Fashion: Chanel keeps the secret of eternal youth', *Vogue* US, 15 October 1924, pp. 66–69.

4
Marie Lyons, 'Atmosphere in dress: dressing the hand', *Harper's Bazaar*, October 1923, pp. 71–76.'

5
'Good fashions never die…', *Vogue* US, 15 March 1945, p. 113.

6
'Chanel maintains the normal lines of the figure', *Vogue* US, 15 October 1920, p. 50.

7
Cecil Beaton, *The Glass of Fashion*, p. 163; quoted by Ernestine Carter, *The Magic Names of Fashion*, London: Weidenfeld & Nicolson, 1980, p. 59.

8
Eleanor Gunn, '"Grounds for Divorce" introduces best gowns of season…', *Women's Wear*, 25 September 1924, p. 3; 'Ina Claire selects the newest Chanel sports frocks in tweed and velveteen', *Vogue* US, 15 November 1924, p. 46.

9
'Exploitation of stage costumes a retail venture…', *Women's Wear*, 22 October 1924, p. 26. 'Best & Co. display Chanel velvet model as worn by Ina Claire', *Women's Wear*, 22 October 1924, p. 30; 'Ina Claire selects…', *Vogue* US, 15 November 1924, p. 47.

10
'Vogue's eye view: of the mode', *Vogue* US, 1 February 1925, p. 35.

11
See B. J. Perkins, 'Chanel trade reported above all other couturiers', *Women's Wear Daily*, 13 August 1928, p. 4; B. J. Perkins, 'Chanel opposed on copying theory', *Women's Wear Daily*, 15 March 1935, p. 6.

12
On the subject of Chanel's return to the USA, see Alexandra Palmer, 'Chanel: American as apple pie', in *The Chanel Legend*, exhibition catalogue, Mettingen: Draiflessen Collection, 2013, pp. 170–181.

13
'Paris: Lanvin-Castillo: flyaway jackets', *Vogue* US, 15 March 1957, p. 86; 'Chanel's famous city-country suits', *Vogue* US, 15 April 1931, p. 83; Bernadine Morris, 'They all tried that Chanel copy', *New York Times*, 3 October 1970, FS18.

14
See De Lange, 'Novelties in Deauville shops…', *Women's Wear*, 27 July 1914, p. 1; 'Coats go to three lengths to prove themselves in fashion', *Vogue* US, 1 September 1915, p. 58; 'The new Parisienne, hoopless and in furs', *Vogue* US, 15 July 1916, p. 38.

15
'French recordings', *Vogue* US, 1 October 1934, p. 60; 'New lines from Paris', *Vogue* US, 15 October 1935, p. 131.

16
'Paris not influenced by American standards: Chanel models', *Women's Wear Daily*, 11 August 1919, p. 5.

17
From the early 1970s onwards, the Maison Chanel protected its designs and fought against piracy.

18
Gabrielle Chanel, 'Éloge du plagiat', *Marianne*, 15 February 1933, p. 8.

19
'Mlle. Chanel tells Baron de Meyer her opinions on good taste', *Harper's Bazaar*, February 1923, p. 30.

20
See B. J. Perkins, 'Differ on which house got most US Orders', *Women's Wear Daily*, 12 March 1935, p. 4.

21
See B. J. Perkins, 'Chanel opposed on copying theory', p. 6.

22
See 'Chanel suit-Fords', *Vogue* US, 15 October 1961, pp. 78–83; 'The Chanel influence – the suit American women won't give up', pp. 152–155.

23
'Fashion: Chanel 142: The tale of a Paris model', *Vogue* US, 1 April 1927, pp. 88, 156, 158.

24
'The debut of the Winter mode', *Vogue* US, 1 October 1926, p. 69.

25
See 'Plan Chanel bags, scarfs to match gloves…', *Women's Wear Daily*, 5 July 1929, SII1, SII23.

26
Therese and Louise Bonney, *A Shopping Guide to Paris*, New York: Robert M. McBride & Co., 1929, p. 89.

27
See B. J. Perkins, 'Chanel opposed on copying theory', p. 6; B. J. Perkins, 'Chanel organizes own commissionnaire firm', *Women's Wear Daily*, 26 July 1928, p. 1; B. J. Perkins, 'Tissus Chanel sending first collection here', *Women's Wear Daily*, 4 March 1930, p. 1; 'Chanel launching distinct fabric firm', *Women's Wear Daily*, 12 March 1928, p. 1; B. J. Perkins, 'Chanel confines certain cloths to Galeries Lafayette', *Women's Wear Daily*, 25 March 1931, p. 1.

28
See 'Chanel launching distinct fabric firm', *Women's Wear Daily*, 12 March 1928, p. 1; 'Chanel to design group of British fabrics', *Women's Wear Daily*, 28 March 1932, SII4; B. J. Perkins, 'Tissus Chanel sending first collection here', *Women's Wear Daily*, 4 March 1930, p. 1; 'Chanel to open office for sale of fabrics here', *Women's Wear Daily*, 6 April 1931, p. 32; 'Chanel fabrics to be shown here Tues.', *Women's Wear Daily*, 28 August 1931, p. 4.

29
See B. J. Perkins, 'Chanel's aims to show London and Paris can collaborate to advantage', *Women's Wear Daily*, 5 May 1932, p. 2, 24.

30
'The big ten', *Harper's Bazaar*, October 1934, p. 148.

31
Bernard Roshco, *The Rag Race*, New York: Funk & Wagnalls, 1963, p. 181.

32
Célia Bertin, *Paris haute couture*, Paris: Hachette, 1956, pp. 170–171.

33
See 'Chanel's casuals mark style trend', *New York Times*, 13 March 1954, p. 12.

34
'Paris Collections', *Vogue* US, 1 March 1954, pp. 100–4.

35
See A. Palmer, 'Chanel: American as apple pie', p. 172.

36
See 'American collections for Fall', *New York Times*, 27 May 1959, p. 30.

37
See Marilyn Hoffman, 'Meet Manhattan', in J. A. Jarnow & B. Judelle, *Inside the Fashion Business*, p. 113.

38
'Chanel's collection for all ages', *Women's Wear Daily*, 18 January 1954, p. 3.

39
'Smart fashions are available now – Chanel influence', *Tobe Report*, 12 December 1963, p. 26; 'Chanel still reigns', *Tobe Report*, 17 October 1963, pp. 43–46; 'Juniors Chanel', *Tobe Report*, 12 December 1963, p. 9.

40
Life, 14 February 1964, pp. 94, 97.

Suit, between 1927 and 1929,
chiné wool tweed in
écru and brown, beige Galalith.
cat. 19

Ensemble with sleeveless
blouse, skirt and belt,
Spring–Summer 1927, ivory silk.
cat. 8

Coat, Spring–Summer 1954,
ivory wool and silk
crêpe, mother of pearl.
cat. 167

Previous pages

**Dress, 1939, white cotton
organdy embroidered
with white silk thread.**
cat. 81

**Coat, Spring–Summer 1954,
ivory wool and silk
crêpe, mother of pearl.**
cat. 167

Suit, Spring–Summer 1961,
oatmeal tweed, red grosgrain
with navy braid, gilded metal.
cat. 158

Suit, Spring–Summer 1961,
oatmeal chiné tweed,
red grosgrain with navy braid,
gilded metal.
cat. 159

ill. 1 **Gabrielle Chanel and Suzy Parker in 1959. Photograph by Richard Avedon**

Sylvie Lécallier

GABRIELLE CHANEL AND HER DOUBLES

As the role of the fashion designer became codified in the early years of the 20th century, image became increasingly important to the way fashion operated. The innovative Paul Poiret was the first to create a close link between his artistic collaborations and the creative processes and identity of his fashion house, and to make use of the media as a modern and elite form of communication. For women in the fashion industry, their own personalities became a key element in their business strategies, and demonstrated differing degrees of willingness to engage with the process of identification. Recognizing that they themselves were the best advertisements for their own creations, Paquin, Chéruit, Lucile, Madame Agnès, Alix, Schiaparelli and Chanel were all famed for their skill at representing their own work, both in the media and within society itself. In the 1920s and 1930s, Elsa Schiaparelli and Gabrielle Chanel – who moved in the same artistic and aristocratic circles – not only collaborated with celebrities but were regularly seen wearing their own creations, and often the most spectacular examples in Schiaparelli's case. This visual rivalry can be seen in a number of striking portraits by Man Ray, François Kollar and Adolph de Meyer.

In the 1910s, Gabrielle Chanel made her Paris debut in hats she had designed herself. She was her own first model, appearing at the races in her latest styles – a strategy that contributed to her success and drew attention to her most recognizable physical characteristics, making them indissociably linked with her creative style. 'By 1909 Gabrielle Chanel had developed into this beauty with the heavy dark hair, the small turned-up nose, the marvellous profile – a young woman who was just now beginning to make a name for herself,'[1] wrote Edmonde Charles-Roux. In 1910, two portraits by Félix were published in Comœdia Illustré, [ill.1 p. 43] with the caption: 'Gabrielle Chanel's exquisite profile shows to advantage two designs from a truly impeccable range.'[2] In 1923, we see the couturière again, in a delicate portrait by Vladimir Rehbinder, Vogue's first studio director in Paris, who photographed her wearing jewelry and a hat with the added caption: 'Gabrielle Chanel, whose designs are as youthful and chic as herself'.[3] The match between the milliner, couturière and model and her own creations was a perfect one. In 1937, François Kollar took a number of photographs of Gabrielle Chanel at the Ritz. His portrait of her leaning on the mantelpiece, first published in Harper's Bazaar[4] in September, would also appear – rather unusually – in an advertisement for Chanel N° 5 perfume in the November issue of the magazine.[ill.1 p. 98] In fact, Chanel rarely used images of herself in direct advertising. Unlike the couturières Elsa Schiaparelli[5] and Madame Agnès,[6] who specialized in incorporating their advertising into a careful strategy of self-promotion that highlighted their uniqueness and originality, Chanel developed her own unique and effective tactic of 'doubling', based on an approach she had used from the start and pursued throughout her career.

In the early 20th century, models were sometimes sent to the races in pairs, dressed in completely identical outfits. By creating a double image of a particular design, a couturier could increase its visual and commercial effectiveness: its immediate impact at the racecourse, when the models were first seen, was boosted by the later publicity impact when the photograph was published in the press.[7] Gabrielle Chanel was familiar with this tactic from her days at the races with Étienne Balsan and adopted it for herself. She walked along the seafront at Deauville,[ill. 5] accompanied by her aunt Adrienne dressed in an identical outfit. Her younger sister Antoinette also acted as a model, both she and Adrienne serving as Gabrielle's first living advertisements in the milliner's bid to conquer Deauville. As well as duplicating the outfit, Chanel also chose women who looked like her. One of Balsan's close circle of friends was Gabrielle Dorziat, a 'second and brilliant Gabrielle',[8] and from 1912 Dorziat posed regularly for Les Modes in Chanel's creations. The first mention of Chanel's name in the magazine was accompanied by a photograph of the actress; a close connection was therefore forged not only between the two young women, but also between the actress and the brand. The singer Marthe Davelli took up the baton in 1920: 'Chanel's best friend and her double'[9] was always dressed in Chanel, from head to toe, and the pair cultivated the resemblance by adopting similar haircuts and wearing similar outfits.

From the 1920s on, this concept of doubling was reflected in terms of body type too. Chanel was tiny and relatively flat-chested. Her chosen models were extremely slim, like her, at a time when slimness as an ideal was becoming established. Chanel banished curves, prominent breasts and over-defined hips. Where necessary, she was willing to transform a model's body so that it conformed as closely as possible to her own, as later testimonies confirm: 'Sometimes, the living models selected by Mademoiselle had big busts. Mademoiselle, in an effort to flatten the chest (she was keen to replicate her personal silhouette), would have a corset made in cotton tulle with a lining; the corset was stiffened with whalebone and flesh coloured. The model for whom the corset was destined was obliged to wear it for every presentation in front of Mademoiselle.'[10] Using simple forms of physical modification, such as haircuts and makeup, Chanel shaped her models in her own image in an almost ritualistic way. In 1926, all the models wore a little chignon identical to Chanel's.[11] Similarly, in 1935 we read: 'Her dark hair was held flat with more grosgrain ribbon that she tied in a bow on top. Her mannequins wore their hair bows at the nape of their necks, George Washington fashion.'[12] In 1954, although now in her seventies, Chanel still looked like a schoolgirl, with her fringe and the little bow in her hair. But the tradition continued: 'Chanel continued to cut her models' hair – and her own, as part of the ritual of every new couture collection.'[13]

From the 1910s onwards, photographs show the couturière sticking her hands casually into the pockets of her jersey suits. Hand on hip was another signature look. Bettina Ballard, fashion editor of American Vogue, remembered her first visit to the rue Cambon, in 1935: 'She was small and built like a boy,' she wrote, 'her check-fronted vest sweater was hung with pearls, which I assumed were real, and she had a very special stance – hips forward, stomach in, shoulders relaxed, one foot forward, one hand plunged deep in her skirt pocket and the other gesticulating angrily.'[14] Sitting cross-legged, with a cigarette in her hand, she demonstrated just how comfortable her outfits were. Sometimes she would lean against a table or a desk, slightly off kilter, in a masculine stance typical of the 1930s.[ills. 2, 3] Chanel would adopt these physical poses throughout her life, and they defined her just as much as the clothes she wore – and they were imitated, too. In her cabine, newcomers would be given lessons in posture prior to the fashion shows: one foot forward, stomach pulled in, chin raised and hand in pocket. Numerous photographs show models more or less spontaneously making the same gestures as soon as they are wearing Chanel, and photographers would subconsciously encourage them to adopt the same iconic poses.

Within the walls of her couture house, the instantly recognizable Chanel style was also accentuated via a different kind of repetition. When fashion shows were held there, the models sometimes walked down the staircase, its mirrors creating a kaleidoscopic effect, reminiscent of chronophotography.[ill. 5 p. 290] These repeating images formed a kind of modernist vision of fashion and the female body.

Since it married so well with her philosophy and business strategy, Chanel also encouraged this doubling process beyond the walls of the rue Cambon. While most of the leading fashion designers in the 1920s were striving to protect themselves against piracy, Chanel, for her part, was delighted to see so many of her designs being imitated by major department stores. She regarded imitation as a form of flattery and encouraged her clients to identify with her: 'Dressed in her suits, her clients had a look almost identical to Mademoiselle's own, and from this came the birth of the Chanel style: known worldwide, easy to recognize, unique, timeless.'[15]

The year 1954 was something of a renaissance for Chanel, an expert in the art of self-reinvention and a woman who simply refused to grow old. Hired to help with the reopening of the Maison Chanel, Marie-Hélène Arnaud was the Gabrielle Chanel of the prewar years reborn: 'In Marie-Hélène ... Chanel found her star, her double and the memory of herself at twenty.'[16] In the March 1954 issue of French Vogue, a photograph by Henry Clarke advertised the comeback: 'The frontispiece showed Marie-Hélène Arnaud, a completely unknown mannequin whom Chanel had created in her own image, leaning against the wall in a navy jersey suit with her hands plunged deep in her pockets, her tucked white lawn blouse buttoned onto the easy skirt under her loose open jacket, her navy cuffs rolled back to show the white ones, and a navy straw sailor with ribbon streamers on the back of her head.'[17] Mademoiselle's youthful and irresistible double, Marie-Hélène Arnaud was her favourite model, one who inspired her work and showed it off to perfection. All eyes were on her when she strode down the catwalk, and her dresses were the first to be shown. In 1958, Elle magazine invented a modern-sounding Anglicism to describe the new face of Chanel: 'la Chanel girl'.[18] A full-length portrait of Gabrielle Chanel and Marie-Hélène Arnaud in the salon at 31, rue Cambon carries the caption: 'Marie-Hélène has unconsciously caught the Chanel bug; she has become the No. 1 Chanel girl. Her auburn hair is now black, her eyes shine more brightly. ...She has adopted Chanel's gestures, the way she puts her hands in her pockets, slips gold necklaces under her collar, positions a little bow on top of her head and wears Polish boots when it's cold'.[19] The expression 'Chanel girl' was utilized again a few months later in connection with Ludmila Tcherina and Françoise Sagan, described as 'No. 1 Chanel girls'[20] because they loved wearing Chanel. By extension, by 1960, all young women who dressed in the Chanel style were nicknamed 'Chanel girls'.[21]

Beyond these forms of self-duplication, Chanel also enjoyed seeing elegant society women disseminating her designs. We know how important it was to Gabrielle, at the start of her career, to stand out from the demi-mondaines by creating simple, austere outfits. The choice of models who made up her cabine reflected this preoccupation with distinction. By hiring models from aristocratic backgrounds in the 1920s, Chanel was very much of her time: indeed, a third of all models taken on by Paris haute couture firms were recruited from noble families who had fled the Russian Revolution. Adolph de Meyer, who was then a contributor to Harper's Bazaar, noted that Patou's models did not look like models at all but instead like the sort of high-society women one might meet at Cannes or Biarritz.[22] He was struck, nonetheless, by the quality of Chanel's cabine: 'I was impressed by the number of beautiful models chez Chanel. They look like women of high society. All are elegant, dressed in a youthful style, and give the

ill. 2 **Gabrielle Chanel in 1938.**
Photograph by François Kollar.

ill. 3 **Chanel suit in blue wool,**
photograph by Jean Moral,
published in *Harper's Bazaar*,
May 1936.

impression of having been well educated.'[23] When she returned to the fashion world in 1954, Chanel hired non-professional models, young women from good families, cultured and well educated, who would become the best possible worldwide ambassadors for her image. Marie-Hélène Arnaud and Suzy Parker were joined by Odile de Croÿ, Mimi d'Arcangues, Paule Rizzo, Ghislaine Arsac, Gisèle Franchomme, Claude de Leusse and Paule de Mérindol. While some of them played their own version of the chic Parisienne as reshaped by Chanel, Mimi d'Arcangues embodied Gabrielle Chanel's ideal vision of cosmopolitan elegance. Of Brazilian origin, born in Vienna, where her father was an ambassador, brought up in Chile, Turkey and France, she married Comte Guy d'Arcangues in 1955. Mimi joined the rue Cambon *cabine* in 1958 and took part in the successful showing of the Spring–Summer 1959 collection. *Vogue* commented at the time that the photographed garments 'are being modelled by young society women who form the most brilliant *cabine* we have seen in Paris this season'.[24]

Chanel often blurred the boundaries between the professional and the private spheres of her life. She was very fond of her models, regarding them simultaneously as models, clients and friends. She had great powers of persuasion, and she knew how to use them. As Bettina Ballard noted, she 'had, and still has, a strong proselyting instinct. She likes converting people to her way of thinking, dressing, and living.'[25] The emotional relationship she established with her models is illustrated by the examples of Marie-Hélène Arnaud and Suzy Parker. Parker was the face of Chanel N° 5 in the USA and she was also involved in Chanel's comeback in 1954. During her trip to Dallas in 1957, the couturière was accompanied by her friend, her best client and her most effective champion, Suzy Parker, who in ordinary life no longer wore anything but Chanel. She collected Chanel outfits and was very close to the couturière, who became godmother to her daughter in 1960. This physical and emotional closeness took the form of a kind of co-dependency, a mutual fascination between the young American and the Parisian couturière. 'Suzy for a while worshipped at Chanel's feet every afternoon at five, learned to stand like Chanel, imitate her gestures, and wear her clothes with ease, but never went so far as to cut off her long, glamorous red hair, which Chanel deplored,'[26] wrote Bettina Ballard. Chanel's relationship with her models could become almost smothering when the recipient of her attentions was as reserved as Marie-Hélène Arnaud, whose responses to Chanel were more passive: 'Marie-Hélène Arnaud loved Chanel in the way one loves one's creator. She was incapable of contradicting her, or even simply of answering her. She followed her everywhere like her shadow, without complaining. ...Mademoiselle loved her like a daughter, and that was enough for her.'[27] In a photograph of the two women dressed in the same suit, Chanel has her hand on the nape of Arnaud's neck, as if she were a young filly – a gesture both affectionate and proprietorial.[ill.5] The only way that Arnaud could break the spell was to leave, and she quit the Maison Chanel in the early 1960s. As for Suzy Parker, she returned to the States to pursue a career as an actress.

Filling the spaces left by her childhood, moulded in her own image in a ritualistic, methodical fashion throughout her career, Chanel's models were extensions of herself – in her couture house, in the street, in the press. In this way, Gabrielle Chanel produced multiple versions of herself, in an endless quest to keep her powers of enchantment alive.

ill. 4 **Gabrielle Chanel in front of her boutique in Deauville, 1913.**

ill. 5 **Gabrielle Chanel
and Marie-Hélène Arnaud
in September 1958.
Photograph by Roger Picherie.**

10

Palmer White, *Mademoiselle Chanel,
son style et son savoir-faire*,
June 1993, unpublished, part 1, p. 6.
Palmer White Archives,
Bibliothèque Forney, Paris.

11

'Bodies were styled identically, too:
in 1926 all the Chanel mannequins
wore their hair in a small
chignon identical to Chanel's.'
From 'And one more striking',
Vogue US, 15 February 1926, p. 81.

12

Bettina Ballard, *In My Fashion*,
New York: David McKay Company,
1960, p. 47.

13

Justine Picardie, *Chanel:
The Legend and the Life*,
London: Harper, 2013, p. 267.

14

Bettina Ballard, *In My Fashion*, p. 46.

15

Palmer White, *Mademoiselle Chanel*,
part 1, p. 1.

16

Elle, 17 February 1958, p. 29.

17

Bettina Ballard,
In My Fashion, pp. 57.

18

Elle, 17 February 1958, p. 29.

19

Elle, 17 February 1958, p. 30.

20

Elle, 14 November 1958, p. 57.

21

'Les *Chanel girls*, un air jeune à tout
âge', *Elle*, 2 September 1960, p. 36.

22

See Adolph de Meyer,
Harper's Bazaar, October 1927, p. 78.

23

Adolph de Meyer, *Harper's Bazaar*,
October 1925, pp. 99 and 190.

24

Vogue France, April 1959, p. 104.

25

Bettina Ballard, *In My Fashion*, p. 45.

26

Bettina Ballard, *In My Fashion*, p. 46.

27

Lilou Marquand, *Chanel m'a dit*,
Paris: Éditions Jean-Claude Lattès,
1990, p. 18.

1

Edmonde Charles-Roux,
*The World of Coco Chanel: Friends,
Fashion, Fame*, New York:
The Vendome Press; London:
Thames & Hudson, 2005, p. 62.

2

Comœdia Illustré, 1 October 1910,
pp. 28–29.

3

Vogue US, 15 May 1923, p. 41.

4

Harper's Bazaar,
15 September 1937, p. 92.

5

In May 1929, Elsa Schiaparelli
posed for the cover of *L'Officiel
de la Couture et de la Mode*.
In January 1931, she appeared
in the same magazine in an
advertisement for her couture
house. The tag line was her own:
'The modern dress for the
modern life. Elsa Schiaparelli'.

6

The celebrated milliner Madame
Agnès modelled her own
designs and was photographed
by her friend D'Ora.

7

A photograph of two models
wearing the same coat
and the same shoes, captioned
'The Chanel twins', appeared
in *Vogue* France, in September 1965,
pp. 190–191 (photograph by Hatami).

8

Edmonde Charles-Roux,
The World of Coco Chanel, p. 64.

9

Edmonde Charles-Roux,
The World of Coco Chanel, p. 170.

Overleaf

**Dress, Autumn–Winter 1924–25,
Black silk chiffon, black silk
crêpe embroidered with jet beads.**
cat. 35

**Dress, between 1917 and 1919,
silk tulle embroidered with glass
bugle beads, black crêpe
de chine, black beaded tassels.**
cat. 37

**Dress, Spring–Summer 1919,
Chantilly lace, black silk crêpe.**
cat. 36

Overleaf

Suit, Autumn–Winter 1964–65,
beige chiné tweed, gilded metal,
pink crêpe de chine.
cat. 130

Suit worn by Gabrielle Chanel,
Autumn–Winter 1958–59,
écru and brown chiné
tweed by Lesur, gilded metal.
cat. 121

Cocktail dress,
Spring–Summer 1959,
black lace by Dognin.
cat. 319

ill. 1 Jeanne Moreau and Gabrielle Chanel in the apartment at 31, rue Cambon, 1960.

Marion Langlois and Régis Robert

CHANEL AND THE CINEMA: THE RULES OF THE GAME

Gabrielle Chanel was born not long before the birth of cinema. She was only twelve years old when the Lumière brothers gave the first public demonstration of their Cinématographe in Paris in 1895, and the Parisian artistic milieu that she seemed destined to join was still a world away. Chanel's life was closely, if discreetly, connected with the growth of cinema as an artform. Moreover, her two most notable periods of cinematic collaboration occurred during two key decades in the history of cinema: the blossoming of talking pictures in the 1930s, and the birth of the French New Wave and *auteur* cinema in the early 1960s. Chanel's contributions to film raise the issue of continuity, and tell us something about the influence of fashion on cinema and vice versa. And if cinema and fashion had one thing in common it was – as Chanel intuited – the definition of identity.

The art of costume seems to have been intrinsically linked to Chanel's career path. Clients at her first milliner's shop included actresses Émilienne d'Alençon, Geneviève Vix and Gabrielle Dorziat, the latter of whom wore hats by Chanel on stage in 1912. The theatre acted as a shop window, contributing to the success of Chanel's designs. In the late 1920s, as a decade of artistic and intellectual ferment was drawing to a close, Chanel notably designed costumes for Serge Diaghilev's ballet *Le Train Bleu* and for several plays by her close friend Jean Cocteau. She was at the peak of her career, following the creation of her N° 5 perfume in 1921 and of the 'little black dress' in 1926,[ill. 4 p. 290] when Grand Duke Dmitri Pavlovich of Russia introduced Chanel to Samuel Goldwyn, who offered her a contract to work for United Artists in

Hollywood. In exchange for a vast sum of money, the movie mogul wanted Chanel to take on the role of costume designer for his forthcoming productions, and to overhaul the wardrobe of his stars. Before prematurely terminating the contract with Goldwyn, Chanel created gowns for three films released in 1931 and 1932: *Palmy Days* directed by A. Edward Sutherland, *The Greeks Had a Word for Them* by Lowell Sherman, and *Tonight or Never* by Mervyn LeRoy. It was Gloria Swanson who wore the magnificent gowns created for the latter film, and even the screen credit reflects the aura of luxury that Goldwyn wished to evoke: 'Miss Swanson's gowns designed and executed by Chanel of Paris'. In her autobiography, the actress described the requisite fittings in Paris, and the adjustments that Chanel was only reluctantly prepared to make: 'If Melvyn [Douglas] ever guessed that the woman in the love scenes with him was three months pregnant and bound into elastic underwear under all the Chanel finery, he never gave the slightest indication.'[1]

When Gabrielle Chanel travelled to the USA in April 1931, the press spoke of her vision of the art of movie costume design, which, while it was a specialized task, was also an excellent way of disseminating ideas, since it would mean designing 'clothes that will be seen in every small village of the world, in every city, in every country!' Chanel knew the difference between city fashion and screen fashion: on screen, an outfit had to convey a woman's character at a glance, but also had to adapt to her movements and gestures; it needed the photogenic quality that cinema demands, responding to the light. When 'designing fashion especially for cinema',[2] it was important that these clothes could stand the test of time.

In the 1930s, Chanel demonstrated how well she understood the character-enhancing aspect of film costumes. She was a great friend of Jean Renoir and her name appeared in the credits for *La Marseillaise* in 1938 ('Marie-Antoinette's dresses by Chanel') and *The Rules of the Game* in 1939 ('Dresses by Maison CHANEL'). For the latter film, she created no fewer than thirty-seven costumes,[3] including outfits worn by Nora Gregor, Mila Parély and Paulette Dubost: evening dresses, negligees and maids' uniforms, fur coats and a fur hat, and also the hunting outfits worn by the women at a key point in the film, giving them a masculine look, hands thrust deep in pockets.[ill. 3]

Chanel also made uncredited contributions to two other landmarks in the history of French cinema. One of them was Marcel Carné's *Le Quai des brumes* (1938), and led to this insightful anecdote recorded by producer and artistic advisor Denise Tual, which is also corroborated by Michèle Morgan's account: 'While I was trying to explain the style of the film, Mademoiselle Chanel grimaced in disgust. "A film like that doesn't need a dress," she said, "A raincoat and a beret, and that's it!" ...She had understood the tone of the film exactly and had identified its style: "a raincoat and a beret".[ill. 4] That was the mark of her genius.'[4] That genius was to have a lasting influence on French cinema. In the same year, in Jean Renoir's *La Bête humaine*, actress Simone Simon wore 'a simple and sensible little suit that befitted a person of modest means, with a white blouse, [and as the] sole extravagance ... a cheeky ostrich feather, perched on the front of her hat'.[5]

In 1960, while he was preparing to shoot *Last Year in Marienbad*, Alain Resnais did the rounds of the couture houses and fashion shows, accompanied by his assistant Jean Léon and his star Delphine Seyrig. Resnais chose the actress's outfits from Chanel's collection and her name once again appeared in the film credits ('Mademoiselle Seyrig's dresses... CHANEL'). Two of the gowns, one in black silk,[cat. 335] the other in gold lamé,[cat. 334] were donated by Seyrig to the Cinémathèque Française in the 1970s. The eminent French set designer Bernard Evein, then a costume designer, was responsible for the rest of the wardrobe for Seyrig's female character, known only as 'A'; his designs included negligees and a 1920s-style black cloak decorated with feathers. Records kept by Jean Léon and script supervisor Sylvette Baudrot document the selection of outfits, from Léon's early handwritten notes to Baudrot's final list, annotated during filming.[6] The dresses worn by 'A' play a major role in the complex narrative of the film: they serve as reference points for its fragmented chronology as well as reinforcing the film's black-and-white aesthetic. Sylvette Baudrot's shooting script, complete with numerous Polaroid shots, demonstrates the level of attention which she paid to the costumes and accessories to ensure the continuity of the story.[ill. 2] As a direct result of the film, the dresses worn by 'A' soon inspired what became known as the 'Marienbad style'.

The Maison Chanel closed at the start of the Second World War and reopened in 1954. By the early 1960s, the two-piece suit was enjoying considerable success, its modernity making it popular with Chanel's clientele. A great many actresses and celebrities wore it around town, including Jacqueline Kennedy, Grace Kelly, Anouk Aimée, Annie Girardot, and of course Jeanne Moreau,[ill. 1] who for five years wore nothing but Chanel after Peter Brook introduced her to the couturière in 1956. Spotted by the young Louis Malle while she was playing the role of Maggie – and wearing Chanel – in a stage production of *Cat on a Hot Tin Roof*, directed by Peter Brook, Moreau appeared in Malle's first two feature-length films: *Lift to the Scaffold* (1958) and *The Lovers* (1958), in which she wore a number of low-key outfits, as well as a classic little black dress. One particular skirt appears in these two films and in another that she shot six months later with Roger Vadim, *Les Liaisons dangereuses* (1959).

Then the influence was reversed and things came full circle: Gabrielle Chanel's creations found their way, quite naturally, from the streets to the screen as actresses were given a new freedom to dress as they chose. In a memorable early sequence in Jacques Demy's *The Umbrellas of Cherbourg* (1964), Catherine Deneuve wears a pink Chanel coat that came from her own wardrobe. In *Stolen Kisses* (1968), Delphine Seyrig, in a Chanel suit, played an elegant, cultured woman from a well-to-do background who seduces the young Antoine Doinel. The actress explained that François Truffaut had given her carte blanche to choose her own clothes.[7] It was now the case that a costume, rather than being designed especially for a film, was deliberately selected because it revealed and reflected the personality of the character being portrayed on screen.

The culmination of this trend saw movie heroines fully embracing the iconic feminine image that Chanel had developed and embodied over the years. In 1962, in *Éducation sentimentale* by Alexandre Astruc (credit: 'Dresses by Chanel'), the Chanel brand is referenced twice in the dialogue, right at the start of the film. The references may be no more than incidental from a narrative point of view, but they nevertheless bring Chanel into the diegetic universe of the film: the women's clothes have been designed by Chanel, and the characters flag up the fact. This is also the case with Pupe, played by Romy Schneider in Luchino Visconti's 'The Job', one of the three stories that made up the anthology *Boccaccio '70* (1962). Dressed entirely in Chanel, Pupe says of her own outfit: 'Chanel. It's old. I've had it a month now.'[ill. 5] Her three costumes occupy a key place in the narrative, since the character changes in front of our eyes and her clothes change with her. At Visconti's request, Chanel also transformed Romy Schneider herself, overhauling the actress's wardrobe and even her diet. She turned her from the 'apple-cheeked young Austrian' who had played the Empress Sissi into something very different – 'a real woman, sure of herself at last, elegant, sophisticated'.[8] The actress does more than simply wear Chanel: she internalizes her,[9] and this becomes the primary definition of her on-screen character.

Finally, we cannot talk about Gabrielle Chanel's connections with the world of cinema without mentioning her patronage, or at least the financial generosity the couturière extended to her artistic entourage. It was through Chanel that Visconti met Renoir in the mid-1930s. At around the same time, the Château de Corbère-Abères, which Chanel had bought for her nephew André Palasse, was offering a temporary home to the latter's brother-in-law, Robert Bresson, and his friend, the future set designer Pierre Charbonnier. It was therefore thanks to Chanel that Charbonnier was able to use Corbère to shoot *La Fortune enchantée* (1936), a partly animated experimental film. It was also to Robert Bresson that she entrusted the job of taking the magnificent photographs of her 'Bijoux de Diamants' jewelry collection in 1932. During the Second World War, Chanel provided clothing and supplies for Jean Marais's entire regiment. She came up with the stage name Anna Karina for the Danish-French actress Hanne Karin Bayer, and, as we saw earlier, she was instrumental in helping Romy Schneider to reinvent herself. These few examples illustrate the influence exerted by Gabrielle Chanel, who throughout her career wove bonds of friendship and formed artistic, financial and professional relationships with the world of cinema, where she occupied a pivotal role and on which she left her mark, a discreet but elegant legacy.

1

Gloria Swanson, *Swanson on Swanson: An Autobiography*, New York: Random House, 1980, p. 432.

2

Extracts from various interviews given by Chanel: Laura Blayney, 'Paris answers Hollywood', *Modern Picture*, vol. 46, no. 5, December 1933, p. 74; Laura Mount, 'Designs on Hollywood', *Collier's Weekly*, vol. 87, no. 14, 4 April 1931, p. 21; 'Mlle Chanel nous parle de la mode à l'écran', *Pour vous*, no. 127, 23 April 1931, p. 13.

3

Olivier Curchod, Christopher Faulkner, *La Règle du jeu*, scénario original de Jean Renoir, Paris: Nathan, 1999, p. 11.

4

Denise Tual, *Au cœur du temps*, Paris: Carrère, 1987, p. 191.

5

Denise Tual, *Au cœur du temps*, p. 193.

6

These records are conserved at the Cinémathèque Française. In conversation with the authors on 4 June 2019, Jean Léon confirmed these notes, which are published by François Thomas in *L'Atelier d'Alain Resnais*, Paris: Flammarion, 1989.

7

See 'The Lily in the Valley', *Sight and Sound*, Autumn 1969, p. 185.

8

Laurence Schifano, Luchino Visconti: *The Flames of Passion*, New York: Harper Collins, 1990, p. 330.

9

Laurence Schifano in conversation with the authors, 5 June 2019.

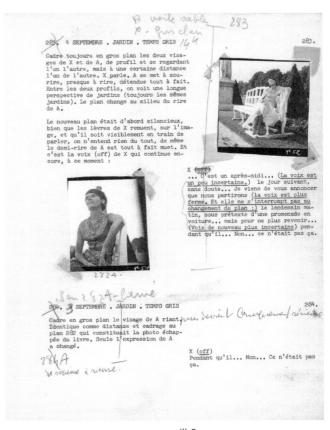

ill. 2 **Shooting script for** *Last Year in Marienbad* **by Alain Resnais, 1960. Photograph by Sylvette Baudrot. Cinémathèque Française collection.**

ill. 3 **Mila Parély in** *La Règle du Jeu* **by Jean Renoir, 1939. Photograph by Sam Lévin. Cinémathèque Française collection.**

ill. 4 **Michèle Morgan in** *Le Quai des brumes* **by Marcel Carné, 1938. Photograph by Roger Kahan. Cinémathèque Française collection.**

ill. 5 **Tomas Milian and Romy Schneider in** *Boccaccio '70* **by Luchino Visconti, 1962. Cinémathèque Française collection.**

Dress worn by Delphine Seyrig
in *Last Year in Marienbad*,
**Autumn–Winter 1960–61,
black silk chiffon.**
cat. 335

**Evening dress,
Spring–Summer 1955,
red silk chiffon,**
cat. 346

**Evening dress,
Autumn–Winter 1970–71,
red silk chiffon.**
cat. 345

Evening dress
cat. 346

Evening dress
cat. 345

**Dress, Autumn–Winter 1966–67,
black silk chiffon,
black lace appliqué.**
cat. 322

**Formal dress,
Spring–Summer 1960,
black silk chiffon and satin.**
cat. 318

**Cocktail dress,
Spring–Summer 1965,
black silk chiffon,
black silk satin ribbon.**
cat. 321

**Dress, Autumn–Winter 1969,
black silk chiffon
and fringing, gilded metal.**
cat. 323

Bolero and skirt ensemble,
Autumn–Winter 1963–64,
silk embroidered all over
with pearlized white sequins.
cat. 340

Evening dress,
Autumn–Winter 1965–66,
silk embroidered all over
with pearlized white sequins.
cat. 339

Dress, Spring–Summer 1971,
ivory figured organza, gold lamé.
cat. 336

Belt, CHANEL design
made by Robert Goossens,
Spring–Summer 1971,
gilded metal, green and red
glass, imitation pearls.
cat. 231

Evening dress,
Autumn–Winter 1967–68,
nylon netting, white silk chenille,
iridescent Lurex, ivory silk crêpe,
chiffon and charmeuse,
gilded metal, rhinestones
and mother of pearl.
cat. 338

CHANEL'S INTERIORS

'Our houses are our prisons;
let us learn how to liberate ourselves
in the way we arrange them.'[1]

The Chanel style is the personal style of Gabrielle Chanel. From the start, her clients bought clothes that the couturière originally designed for herself, adopting her poses and her gestures, attempting to change their silhouette to match hers. The Chanel style is based on intricate knowledge of the social mores and fashion codes of the time, a knowledge that it utilizes to free itself from such conventions, with a lightness, a casualness, that nonetheless operates within the context of rigorous classicism. Chanel wove a web of style that extends beyond fashion to encompass the whole art of living. The interiors where she lived and worked are key parts of a *Gesamtkunstwerk* – her life itself, which she conceived as a work of art. From 1922, the couturière's dresses were photographed in front of her Chinese lacquer screens – furnishings that contributed to her brand image, and which would become an integral part of her myth.[2]

Unlike Paul Poiret – whom she helped to push out of style – Gabrielle Chanel never launched an interior design or furnishings collection. Her fashion is nevertheless indissociably linked with the style of her homes. 'All my art', she said, 'has consisted of cutting away what others have added.'[3] Her concept for a garment or an interior was always based on a structure of the strictest simplicity, governed by notions of freedom and comfort – vital luxuries in Chanel's eyes. This was the basis for her vision of an updated form of classicism. With this rational and functional base in position, decorative elements could then be added. Accessories, furniture and objects were arranged sparingly, rejecting any kind of hierarchy between things that were costly and things that cost next to nothing: Chanel combined precious stones with costume jewelry, placed vermeil boxes alongside dried ears of corn, retouched the gilding on her lacquer screens herself,[ill.3] arranged bronze sculptures on the floor and treated objects worthy of a cabinet of wonders as if they were holiday souvenirs. Things possessed only the value she attributed to them. Objects of historical interest, symbols, keepsakes and pleasurable reminders, they were also sources of inspiration.

From her earliest interiors, such as the Paris apartment she shared with Arthur 'Boy' Capel in the avenue Gabriel in the latter half of the 1910s, which already featured Coromandel screens,[4] to her final residence in Switzerland, we find the same desire for isolation and protection. Chanel's grave, at the Bois-de-Vaux cemetery in Lausanne, contains echoes of the places where she lived: clipped yew hedges enclose the grave on three sides, like the patio at her villa in Roquebrune, and like the screens that surrounded her couch at the rue Cambon and lined many of the walls in the apartment. The gravestone – chosen by Chanel in preference to a slab, which, she said, would have prevented her ever being able to climb out – is decorated with a row of five lions' heads above a discreet Latin cross and resembles the headboard of a bed or the back of a couch. Here, once again, Chanel's love of symbols and lucky numbers linked to her own life takes precedence over references to the Catholic faith, to which she nevertheless claimed allegiance. A marble bench, positioned to the left of the grave, completes this open-air sitting room where the dead woman's friends and relatives could come and pay their respects. It must have been a select company, since – in a final gesture of exuberant misanthropy – Gabrielle Chanel took the trouble to acquire the two neighbouring plots, thus guaranteeing eternal peace for herself. This misanthropy reflected the final years of the couturière's life, when she dreaded solitude yet kept herself isolated.

The apartment at the Hôtel de Rohan-Montbazon, at 29, rue du Faubourg-Saint-Honoré, which Chanel rented until 1934, was the symbol of her success and the setting for a glittering life as a socialite. It was here, for the first time, that she made flamboyant use of mirrors to give the illusion of space and perhaps, also, reflect her own success.[ill.4] In the main living room, all that Chanel retained of the original wood panelling – painted in a shade of green she loathed – installed by the Comte de La Panouse in 1823 were the decorative structural elements: the pilasters and the mirror surrounds above the fireplaces. Previous owners had faithfully preserved the apartment in its entirety, and in all its undeniable aristocratic glory, the better to affirm their newly acquired wealth and position. Chanel, on the other hand, spent considerable sums acquiring the largest mirrors available, whose presence would be almost forgotten amid the visual interplay of infinite reflections, dominated by a monumental chandelier hung with antique rock crystal pendants. By modernizing the splendour of the Louis XIV style, Chanel succeeded in making it very much her own.

Did she seek advice from José María Sert on the redecoration carried out by Maison Jansen? Nobody can be absolutely certain. Whatever the truth of the matter, she made similar use of mirrors at her couture house, covering the walls with them, floor to ceiling, in the salons and up the staircase. From 1928 onwards, articles describe the latter as one of Paris's most iconic venues.[5] Nowhere is there any mention of the name of the interior designer for the project, carried out at a time when many of the large couture houses were undergoing refurbishment and when Jean-Michel Frank was the uncontested master of this type of work. It might be reasonably supposed that, for the refurbishment of the Maison Chanel, its owner would once again have employed the services of Jansen and his team.

In 1932, when she opened the salons of her own home to exhibit her 'Bijoux de Diamants' collection, the doors were hidden by screens made of narrow strips of mirror, which diffracted the space in the same way as the famous mirrored staircase at the rue Cambon, scattering the light from the glittering gems. [ill.1 p.141] The effect irresistibly recalled interior designer Syrie Maugham's all-white room at her home in London's King's Road, between 1929 and 1930, one wall of which was entirely lined with a screen made of narrow mirrored panels. Mirrored walls and screens – also found in the salons of couturier Norman Hartnell in London in 1934 – were then the height of modernity, as were the beige and white shades favoured by Maugham and Jean-Michel Frank. Chanel may have been a couturière and not an interior designer, but the interiors she commissioned, oversaw and furnished were nevertheless among the most striking and influential projects of her time and, accordingly, the name of Gabrielle Chanel can be ranked alongside the great names of interior design.

It was at the Villa La Pausa in Roquebrune that Chanel demonstrated her aspirations and talents to the fullest. The building project, on a parcel of land acquired during a trip to the area in 1928,[6] began in 1929. Chanel called upon the services of the young Robert Streitz. A more established architect – although she had the resources to hire one – might not have followed her instructions quite so conscientiously and might have been tempted to add personal touches of his own.

There were demands right from the outset. The site Chanel chose for the house had spectacular views but, with its combination of rocks and clay soil, was particularly ill-suited to construction. As Streitz noted, 'She refused to listen to our objections, and we were obliged to build extraordinary foundations. Think of it, underneath the house there are supporting beams whose cross-section measures one metre!'[7] Chanel sent Streitz to measure the staircase at the Abbaye d'Aubazine – the convent where she had spent her childhood – and reproduced it as a double flight of stairs in the entrance hall at La Pausa. The convent architecture is also mirrored by the central courtyard, one side of which looks onto the surrounding countryside, while an arcade runs around the other three sides to create a sense of protection and calm. The five windows positioned above the front door serve as a reminder of the couturière's lucky number.

Another of Chanel's specifications was that only handmade round tiles should be used, and Streitz was obliged to scour the surrounding villages for them: 'We bought the old tiles for a king's ransom, replacing them with new ones,'[8] he recorded. The colours of the villa harmonized with its natural surroundings: grey walls and green shutters echoed the hues of the venerable olive trees that surrounded the property and which were carefully preserved – including those that grew in the middle of the paved walkway leading to the house. The shutters and door frames were deliberately distressed to make them look old and evoke a family house whose details tell the story of its owner's life and demonstrate her triumph over an unhappy childhood. To bring the project to fruition, Chanel made the kind of demands from Streitz that would have been worthy of a fairytale princess; but, far from holding this against her, the architect commented only on his client's intelligence and generosity.

It was indeed generosity that underpinned this autobiographical form of architecture. Every detail was planned with a view to ensuring the privacy and well-being of the many guests that Chanel received at La Pausa while dispensing the most glorious largesse. In France, the first photographs of La Pausa were published in Vogue in May 1930, reprinted from an article in US Vogue's March issue.[ill.5] It was certainly no coincidence that Chanel chose the top fashion magazine in which to show off La Pausa. Was it not a way of taking the style of her couture collections into the world of architecture – architecture characterized by austere and simple elegance? The few pieces of furniture she installed in the house were from Provence or Spain, or else English in origin. Dating back to the 16th and 17th centuries, these latter pieces probably originated from one of the Duke of Westminster's many properties. The woodwork was in limed or pickled oak, the walls were white, or beige in the bedrooms, and the matching curtains hung floor to ceiling – a novel idea that gave a room an air of lofty majesty.

The interior was clearly inspired, in a formal sense, by Jean-Michel Frank. Olivier Meslay and Martha MacLeod also note the influence of La Mimoseraie, the villa owned by Eugenia Errázuriz in Biarritz, in the combination of limed walls and terracotta floor tiles, and that of Eileen Gray in the modernist fittings of Chanel's private bathroom.[9]

The extreme restraint of Chanel's interior designs was regarded as the height of good taste. Chanel is said to have been delighted by the compliment from her friend Fulco di Verdura – who made a number of striking pieces of jewelry for her – when he commented: 'What genius to have spent all that money and for it not to show!'[10]

A few years later, while it had retained its overall simplicity of design, the villa had filled up with furniture and objects, as seen in Plaisir de France in 1935[ill.6] and French Vogue in July 1938 – evidence of a love of the neo-baroque of which Gabrielle Chanel was one of the foremost champions.

ill. 2 **Gabrielle Chanel in her bedroom at the Villa La Pausa, 1938. Photograph by Roger Schall.**

ill. 3 **The hands of Gabrielle Chanel, 1937. Photograph by François Kollar.**

275

The Coromandel screens had remained behind in Paris. But, in a personal reshaping of 17th-century style and philosophy that incorporated both decoration and her own maxims and aphorisms (inspired by those of Saint-Simon and La Rochefoucauld), Chanel appeared to hold court from her monumental bed – in the manner of the Grand Siècle – overhung by a large five-pointed star. [ill. 2]

With the exception of the gilding (more restrained here) and the lack of Chinese lacquerwork, the colour scheme at La Pausa was identical to the somewhat masculine colour scheme of Chanel's Paris residences: black, white and an infinite range of browns and beiges designed to set off the patina of book bindings and the soft glow of marble. The colours evoked Chanel's life, as did the objects and works of art with which she surrounded herself – and the more precious they were, the more casually she treated them. The suede couches with quilted cushions were the shade of wet sand at Deauville and Biarritz, the walls at the rue Cambon were the gold of harvested wheat, while in the eyes of some, the Villa Bel Respiro in Garches (1920), with its beige roughcast walls and black lacquer shutters, was the embodiment of mourning following the death of Boy Capel. Gabrielle Chanel's generosity was as proverbial as her acid tongue. On multiple occasions, a person would admire some precious object belonging to her and she would immediately give it to them. A handful of objects, however, remained with her till the end of her life. These are still in their original places in the apartment in the rue Cambon, [ill. 1] bearing witness to the personal style of a woman it is hard to imagine having vanished from the place for ever – a woman who combined the beige of roughcast with glossy black window blinds in the same way as the two-tone leather of a pair of pumps; who turned a quilted suede cushion into her 2.55 bag; who used the same warm, neutral and natural shades as the basis for her interiors and for the tweed fabrics of her suits. The glitter of the chandeliers and the vermeil boxes lit up her interiors in the same way that her jewelry enlivened her clothes, according to the mood of the moment.

ill. 4 **Gabrielle Chanel's grand salon
at the Hôtel de Rohan-Montbazon,
published in** Art et Industrie,
February 1931, p. 17.

1

Edmonde Charles-Roux,
*The World of Coco Chanel: Friends,
Fashion, Fame*, New York:
The Vendome Press; London:
Thames & Hudson, 2005, p. 377.

2

See 'Mme Jacques Porel portant
une robe Chanel', *Vogue* France,
1 September 1922, p. 17.

3

Cited by Pierre Galante,
Mademoiselle Chanel, Chicago:
Henry Regnery Company, 1973.

4

See Jean Leymarie, *Eternal Chanel*,
Paris: Éditions de La Martinière,
2010, p. 137.

5

See especially Sylvia Lyon,
'Chanel', *The Bystander*,
10 April 1929, p. 70.

6

Deeds for the purchase for two
pieces of land in Roquebrune-
Cap-Martin by Gabrielle Chanel,
drawn up by the firm of Albert
Casiglia, Menton, 29 November
and 28 December 1928.
Nice, Archives Départmentales
des Alpes Maritimes, legal archives.

7

Quoted by Pierre Galante,
Mademoiselle Chanel, p. 118.

8

Pierre Galante,
Mademoiselle Chanel, p. 119.

9

Olivier Meslay & Martha MacLeod,
*From Chanel to Reves: La Pausa
and Its Collections at the Dallas
Museum of Art*, Dallas:
Dallas Museum of Art, 2015, p. 12.

10

Quoted by Claude Delay,
Chanel solitaire, Paris: Gallimard,
1983, p. 170.

ill. 5 **Entrance hall and dining
room at the Villa La Pausa,
Roquebrune, published
in *Vogue* France, May 1930.**

ill. 6 **The drawing room
of the Villa La Pausa,
photograph published
in *Plaisir de France*, 1935.**

Previous pages

Necklace, CHANEL design
made by Robert Goossens, 1970s,
vermeil, rock crystal.
cat. 281

**Evening dress, Autumn–Winter
1918–19, black silk tulle
embroidered with steel sequins
and jet beads, gold lamé.**
cat. 41

**Dress and coat ensemble,
Spring–Summer 1962,
ivory tweed bouclette
and silk crêpe, gilded metal.**
cat. 166

A CHRONOLOGY OF GABRIELLE CHANEL

Note:
The life of Gabrielle Chanel has been the subject of a great many publications and several documentary films; here, we focus exclusively on Chanel's professional career and her contribution to the history of fashion.

1883

Gabrielle Chanel is born at the charity hospital in Saumur (Maine-et-Loire), on 19 August. Her family background is a humble one.

1903

She begins working as an assistant, alongside her aunt Adrienne, in a draper's shop in Moulins (Allier). 'À Sainte Marie', a branch of the Maison Grampayre store, sells lingerie, knitted fabrics and household linen.

1909

Chanel opens a milliner's shop at 160, boulevard Malesherbes in Paris, with the assistance of experienced milliner Lucienne Rabaté. Rabaté works as manager of the Maison Caroline Reboux from 1920 to 1956.

1910

The millinery boutique 'Chanel – Modes' opens in Paris at 21, rue Cambon. On 1 October, *Comœdia Illustré* publishes two portraits of Gabrielle Chanel wearing her own hat designs, and features her on its cover.

1912

French actress Gabrielle Dorziat appears in *Bel Ami* at the Théâtre du Vaudeville. The hats she wears on stage are designed by Chanel.
On 1 October, the popular US magazine *Women's Wear Daily* mentions Chanel's hats – the first such reference in the American press.

Chanel opens another milliner's shop in Deauville. She soon branches out, adding a sportswear range, including sailor-collar tops, jackets and blouses.

1913

On 9 October, *Women's Wear Daily* mentions Chanel's clothing designs for the first time; one of her coats, in corduroy, creates a sensation.

1915

During the war, Chanel opens her first couture house, in Biarritz, in a townhouse located opposite the casino. At the time, the Basque Coast attracts a rich cosmopolitan clientele.

1916

Gabrielle Chanel designs a collection of garments in knitted jersey, sourced from Rodier.
French actress Jane Renouardt, a star of the silent movie era, is filmed by Gaumont Pathé wearing a Chanel dress on the Champs-Élysées in Paris.
On 3 July, three jersey outfits designed by Chanel are featured in the monthly magazine *Les Élégances parisiennes*. ill. 2 p.25
On 7 October, *Women's Wear Daily* features its first Chanel design – a woollen suit with moleskin trim and a matching hat and muff in the same fur.

ill. 2 **Street facade of the Chanel couture house at 31, rue Cambon, Paris, 1936. Photograph by Les Frères Séeberger. Bibliothèque Nationale de France, Paris.**

ill. 3 **Dancers Lydia Sokolova and Leon Woizikowsky in** *Le Train Bleu*, **performed by Serge Diaghilev's Ballets Russes, November 1924. Libretto by Jean Cocteau, music by Darius Milhaud, choreography by Bronislava Nijinska, costumes by Gabrielle Chanel. Photograph by Sasha.**

1917

Actress Hilda May is photographed riding a motor scooter in a Chanel suit made of knitted jersey.

1918

Gabrielle Chanel opens a couture house at 31, rue Cambon, the iconic address that will forever be associated with her name.
For the first time, Chanel designs costumes for stage actresses: Cécile Sorel in *L'Abbé Constantin* and Charlotte Lysès in the comedy *La Dame de chambre* at the Théâtre de l'Athénée, Paris.

1921

The perfume Chanel N° 5 is created in Grasse with Ernest Beaux, a Russian-born French perfumer who was purveyor to the Russian court before working for Chanel.
The Sport atelier is set up: Gabrielle Chanel offers a range of simpler clothes for women who want to take part in outdoor activities such as riding, skiing, tennis and golf.
The double C monogram is used for the first time.

1922

The perfume Chanel N° 22 is created.
At the request of poet and playwright Jean Cocteau, Chanel designs costumes for his play *Antigone*. Notable among these is a long brown woollen cape worn by the heroine.ill. 2 p.63
The bottle design for Chanel N° 5 is registered with the Institut National de la Propriété Intellectuelle (INPI), the French trademark office.

On 28 December, INPI registers some of Chanel's fashion designs for the first time: three suits and eight dresses.

1923

Chanel buys the building at 29, rue Cambon.
A Chanel boutique opens in Cannes.

1924

Chanel meets Pierre and Paul Wertheimer. On 4 April, they enter into a partnership and form the Société des Parfums Chanel. The partnership is later punctuated by commercial disputes, which eventually come to an end when the Wertheimers buy the Maison Chanel in the 1950s.
Chanel creates her first makeup range.
In around 1924, Chanel opens a costume jewelry department in her Paris couture house. The jewelry is made by Comte Étienne de Beaumont.
She designs the costumes for the ballet *Le Train Bleu*, which has a libretto by Cocteau.

1925

The perfume Gardénia is launched.

1926

Chanel's 'little black dress' is nicknamed the 'Ford' dress by *Vogue* US.
In April, Chanel buys the building at 25, rue Cambon.
Chanel designs the costumes for Cocteau's one-act tragedy *Orphée*, staged at the Théâtre des Arts, Paris.

ill. 4 **Chanel dress, Model 817,
black crêpe de chine,** *Vogue* **US,
1 October 1926, p. 9.**

ill. 5 **Model on the Chanel staircase
at 31, rue Cambon, 1937.
Photograph by François Kollar,
commissioned by** *Harper's Bazaar.*
**Gift of François Kollar,
Médiathèque de l'Architecture
et du Patrimoine,
Charenton-le-Pont, France.**

1927

A Chanel couture house opens in London.
The perfume Cuir de Russie is launched.
In October, Chanel acquires the buildings at 23 and 27, rue Cambon.
Launch of the first Chanel skincare range, which includes 15 products.

1928

In March, in order to obtain exclusive high-quality fabrics, Chanel opens a textile factory in Asnières-sur-Seine, near Paris, under the brand name Tissus Chanel, incorporating Tricots Chanel.
The perfume Bois des Îles is launched.

1929

On 18 September, *Vogue* UK makes the first recorded mention of the famous mirrored staircase at 31, rue Cambon.
The Société Chanel appears in the City of Paris's Registry of Commerce. Gabrielle Chanel and her nephew André Marcel Palasse (son of her sister, Julia Berthe Chanel) are listed as the authorized signatories of the company.

1931

Chanel signs a contract worth a million dollars a year with American film producer Samuel Goldwyn. She is contracted to design costumes for his Hollywood films. She designs the gowns worn by Gloria Swanson in *Tonight or Never*, directed by Mervyn LeRoy.

1932

Launch of the 'Bijoux de Diamants' jewelry collection. It is exhibited from 7 to 19 November at Chanel's apartment at 29, rue du Faubourg-Saint-Honoré.

1933

Tissus Chanel is registered as a trademark. Paul Iribe, French poster artist and interior designer, is one of the designers for the company, run by his elder brother Dominique.

1936

During a general strike in France, Chanel workers go on strike and occupy the rue Cambon premises.

1937

Chanel designs the costumes for *Oedipus Rex*, adapted by Jean Cocteau from the tragedy by Sophocles and staged at the Théâtre Antoine, Paris.

1938

Chanel designs costumes for *La Marseillaise* (filmed in 1937) by film director and screenwriter Jean Renoir.

1939

Chanel designs costumes for Renoir's *La Règle du jeu*. When France declares war, on 3 September, the Maison Chanel closes its doors. The weavers are called up and the Tissus Chanel factory is forced to close; but the boutique selling perfumes and accessories (31, rue Cambon) remains open throughout the war.

ill. 6 **Stanley Marcus, head of the US department store chain Neiman Marcus, shakes hands with Gabrielle Chanel at the airport, after her visit to the new store in Dallas, Texas, 1957. Photograph by Shel Hershorn.**

ill. 7 **Three-piece Chanel suit in wool jersey with necklace, photograph by Henry Clarke, published in *Vogue* France, March 1958. Palais Galliera, Paris.**

1944

Gabrielle Chanel is arrested at the Ritz by the French Forces of the Interior because of her relationship with a German officer, Baron Hans Günther von Dincklage. She is released after a brief interrogation. For the next ten years, Chanel lives away from the world of fashion, dividing her time between Lausanne, Paris, and La Pausa (her villa on the French Côte d'Azur), with trips to Italy and the USA.

1952

On 7 April, *Life* magazine interviews Marilyn Monroe, who responds to the question 'What do you wear to bed?' with the answer 'I only wear Chanel N° 5.' An enduring legend is born.

1953

The couture house reopens after fourteen years.

1954

Chanel unveils her new couture collection on 5 February. She is seventy-one years old.
French jeweler Robert Goossens produces his first designs for the Maison Chanel, although he does not meet Gabrielle Chanel until 1957.
Chanel muse and model Marie-Hélène Arnaud poses in a Chanel suit for American photographer Henry Clarke, for *Vogue* magazine.[ill. 4 p. 224]

1955

In February, Chanel designs a quilted lamb's leather handbag with a chain shoulder strap, and names it the '2.55' bag.
Launch of Pour Monsieur, the first Chanel fragrance for men.

1956

Chanel designs Ingrid Bergman's costumes for the play *Tea and Sympathy* by Robert Anderson, staged at the Théâtre de Paris in December.

1957

The first two-tone shoe is produced by Chanel in collaboration with the shoemaker Massaro.
Chanel receives the Neiman Marcus Award for Distinguished Service in the Field of Fashion, an award created by American businessman Stanley Marcus, proprietor of luxury store Neiman Marcus in Dallas, and co-founder Carrie Marcus Neiman. Chanel is honoured as 'the most influential female designer of the 20th century'.

1958

Chanel dresses Jeanne Moreau in director Louis Malle's film *Lift to the Scaffold* (filmed in 1957).
She collaborates with Malle once again by designing costumes for *The Lovers*.

ill. 8 **Actress Romy Schneider being interviewed at the Cannes Film Festival, 10 May 1962. Photograph by Jean-Claude Pierdet.**

ill. 9 **Models heading for the Soviet Union to present the Chanel Autumn–Winter 1967–68 collection at the International Fashion Festival in Moscow, September 1967.**

1959

The Chanel Nº 5 bottle is featured in the exhibition 'The Package', held from September to November at the Museum of Modern Art (MoMA), New York.
On 4 December, *Elle* magazine publishes the pattern for the legendary Chanel suit.
Designer Malhia Kent designs her first tweed fabrics for Chanel.

1961

Chanel designs the costumes worn by French actress Delphine Seyrig in Alain Resnais's film *Last Year in Marienbad*.

1962

Actress Romy Schneider is dressed by Chanel for 'The Job' by Italian director Luchino Visconti, one of the three stories that make up the film *Boccaccio '70* (filmed in 1961).

1963

On 22 November, the day that US president John F. Kennedy is assassinated in Dallas, Jackie Kennedy wears a pink Chanel suit from the Autumn–Winter 1961 collection.

1967

The Chanel Autumn–Winter collection is shown at the Luzhniki Stadium in Moscow.

1968

Chanel dresses Delphine Seyrig again, this time in François Truffaut's *Stolen Kisses*.

1969

On 18 December, the musical *Coco* opens at the Mark Hellinger Theatre in New York. Katharine Hepburn plays the role of Gabrielle Chanel.

1971

On 10 January, Gabrielle Chanel dies in Paris, in her apartment at the Ritz. She is buried in Bois-de-Vaux Cemetery, in Lausanne. Her tomb is decorated with five stone lion's heads, which she designed herself.

LIST OF EXHIBITED WORKS

Corresponding to the exhibition 'Gabrielle Chanel. Manifeste de mode' at the Palais Galliera.

Note:

Except where otherwise stated, all exhibited works were designed by Gabrielle Chanel.

A suit is traditionally made up of a skirt and jacket. When this is not the case, the individual elements are listed.

Cat. 1 📖 p. 29
Loose blouse with sailor collar
Summer 1916
Ivory silk jersey
Paris, Patrimoine de CHANEL,
inv. HC.PE.1916.1

Cat. 2 📖 p. 21
Hat
Between 1913 and 1915
Black woven straw,
black silk satin ribbon
Paris, Musée des Arts Décoratifs,
gift of André Eichthal, inv. 28167C

Cat. 3
Libretto for *Le Train Bleu*
Jean Cocteau
1924
Leather, paper, ink
Paris, private collection

Cat. 4
Portrait of Gabrielle Chanel
Jean Cocteau
1937
Graphite pencil sketch
Paris, Centre Pompidou,
MNAM-CCI, inv. AM2019-273

Cat. 5
Handprint of Gabrielle Chanel
1939
Ink on paper
Paris, Patrimoine de CHANEL,
inv. AG.MAN.1

Cat. 6
'Coco Chanel, in her Deauville boutique, offers different hat designs to a customer already wearing one of her creations.'
Sem
1919
Lithograph with pochoir colouring
Paris, Palais Galliera, acquired
by the Ville de Paris, inv. 2018.47.2

Cat. 7 📖 pp. 30, 31
Dress and jacket ensemble
Between 1922 and 1928
Ivory silk jersey
Paris, Patrimoine de CHANEL,
inv. HC.INC.1922-1928.1

Cat. 8 📖 p. 229
Ensemble with sleeveless blouse, skirt and belt
Spring–Summer 1927
Ivory silk
Paris, Patrimoine de CHANEL,
inv. HC.PE.1927.2

Cat. 9 📖 p. 135
Dress
Betwen 1930 and 1939
Printed ivory surah over black knit
Paris, Patrimoine de CHANEL,
inv. HC.INC.1930-1939.14

Cat. 10 📖 pp. 122, 123
Day ensemble with waistcoat, jacket and skirt
1928
White cotton muslin with
blue grey and black print
Paris, Palais Galliera,
inv. 1968.55.38ABC

Cat. 11
'142' dress
1926
Blue silk crêpe
New York, Fashion Institute
of Technology, gift of Mrs Georges
Gudefin, inv. 80.13.3

Cat. 12 📖 p. 72
Dress and scarf
Spring–Summer 1929
White silk lace with multicoloured
print, white silk crêpe
Paris, Patrimoine de CHANEL,
inv. HC.PE.1929.1

Cat. 13 📖 p. 75
Dress
1935
Ivory silk organza with
multicoloured print
Paris, Patrimoine de CHANEL,
inv. HC.INC.1935.3

Cat. 14 📖 p. 71
Afternoon dress
Spring–Summer 1930
White silk chiffon with pale
pink and brown print
Paris, Palais Galliera, gift of
Mme Bertin, inv. 1968.40.108

Cat. 15 📖 p. 73
Day ensemble with dress and coat
1929
Green wool, silk chiffon
with multicoloured print,
appliqué motifs
Paris, Palais Galliera, gift
of Mme Bertin, inv. 1968.40.93AB

Cat. 16
Day ensemble with dress and coat
Between 1928 and 1930
Dark green wool, printed silk
chiffon in shades of green
Santiago de Chile, Fundación
Museo de la Moda de Chile,
inv. 2010.321.a-d

Cat. 17
Dress and scarf
c. 1930
Ivory crêpe de Chine
with black print
Paris, Palais Galliera, gift
of Mme Bertin, inv. 1968.40.91AB

Cat. 18 📖 p. 83
Ensemble with dress and cape
Between 1933 and 1935
Ivory silk crêpe with black print
Paris, Patrimoine de CHANEL,
inv. HC.INC.1933-1935.1

Cat. 19 📖 p. 227
Suit
Between 1927 and 1929
Chiné wool tweed in écru
and brown, beige Galalith
Paris, Patrimoine de CHANEL,
inv. HC.INC.1927-1929.1

Cat. 20 📖 p. 125
Coat
Autumn–Winter 1933–34
Chiné wool tweed in ivory
and plum, green Galalith
Paris, Patrimoine de CHANEL,
inv. HC.AH.1933.3

Cat. 21 📖 p. 115
Jacket
Between 1928 and 1930
Beige chiné wool jersey,
multicoloured jacquard knit,
beige silk crêpe
Paris, Palais Galliera, gift
of the heirs of Henry Viguier,
inv. 1968.55.36

Cat. 22 📖 p. 127
Suit with jacket, skirt and top
c. 1928
Multicoloured jersey,
plain yellow jersey
Paris, Musée des Arts Décoratifs,
gift of Solange Granet,
inv. 74-29-232ABC

Cat. 23
Day ensemble with dress and jacket
Between 1925 and 1929
Black wool jersey, black
and beige jacquard knit
Charlotte, North Carolina,
Mint Museum, inv. 1983.75.467A-C

Cat. 24
Clutch bag
Between 1920 and 1929
Multicoloured ribbed cotton knit,
steel, white overstitched leather
Paris, Musée des Arts Décoratifs,
inv. 2004.02.7

Cat. 25
Ensemble with dress and cape
Autumn–Winter 1935–36
Ivory wool muslin
with brown print, chestnut
buckskin, white cotton piqué
Paris, Palais Galliera,
gift of the heirs of Henry Viguier,
inv. 1968.55.39AB

Cat. 26 📖 pp. 128, 129
Day ensemble with dress, jacket and belt
Between 1928 and 1930
Multicoloured figured silk velvet,
chiffon lining, quilted écru raw silk,
metal and coloured glass
Paris, Patrimoine de CHANEL,
inv. HC.INC.1928-1930.5

Cat. 27 📖 pp. 130, 131
Day dress
Between 1926 and 1928
Ivory crêpe de chine
with russet print
Paris, Patrimoine de CHANEL,
inv. HC.PE.1926-1928.1

Cat. 28
Day dress
Between 1928 and 1930
Chestnut silk crêpe
Paris, Patrimoine de CHANEL,
inv. HC.INC.1928-1930.4

Cat. 29 📖 p. 133
Clutch bag
1928
Ivory silk crêpe with multicoloured
print by Tissus Chanel,
chrome-plated steel
Paris, Patrimoine de CHANEL,
inv. ACC.HC.INC.1928.2

Cat. 30
Muff
c. 1920
Russet silk velvet
Paris, Palais Galliera, gift
of Mme Charamis, inv. 1981.69.5

Cat. 31
Pair of gauntlet gloves
1933
Brown cotton velvet, russet suede
Paris, Patrimoine de CHANEL,
inv. HC.INC.1933.1

Cat. 32 📖 p. 113
Ensemble with dress and jacket
Spring–Summer 1926
Ivory silk toile, black silk taffeta
Paris, Patrimoine de CHANEL,
inv. HC.PE.1926-1927.1

Cat. 33 📖 p. 117
Day ensemble with dress and coat
c. 1927–28
Silk serge with black and white
print, black silk crêpe
Paris, Patrimoine de CHANEL,
inv. HC.INC.1927-1928.1

Cat. 34
Dress
Between 1920 and 1923
Black silk tulle embroidered
with black sequins and jet beads
Paris, Patrimoine de CHANEL,
inv. HC.INC.1920-1923.1

Cat. 35 📖 p. 244
Dress
Autumn–Winter 1924–25
Black silk chiffon, black silk crêpe
embroidered with jet beads
Paris, Patrimoine de CHANEL,
inv. HC.AH.1924.1

Cat. 36 📖 p. 243
Dress
Spring–Summer 1919
Chantilly lace, black silk crêpe
Paris, Patrimoine de CHANEL,
inv. HC.PE.1919.3

Cat. 37 📖 p. 245
Dress
Between 1917 and 1919
Silk tulle embroidered with glass
bugle beads, black crêpe
de chine, black beaded tassels
Paris, Patrimoine de CHANEL,
inv. HC.INC.1917-1919.1

Cat. 38
Dress
Spring–Summer 1926
Black silk crêpe embroidered
with black sequins
Paris, Patrimoine de CHANEL,
inv. HC.PE.1926.4

Cat. 39 📖 p. 121
Evening dress
Autumn–Winter 1933–34
Black rayon, ivory silk organza
Paris, Patrimoine de CHANEL,
inv. HC.AH.1933.2

Cat. 40 📖 p. 33
Evening dress
Autumn–Winter 1924–25
Gold lamé, gold lace embroidered
with gold cabochons
Paris, Palais Galliera, acquired
by the Ville de Paris, inv. 1983.126.1

Cat. 41 📖 pp. 286, 287
Evening dress
Autumn–Winter 1918–19
Black silk tulle embroidered
with steel sequins
and jet beads, gold lamé
Paris, Patrimoine de CHANEL,
inv. HC.AH.1918.2

Cat. 42 📖 p. 93
Evening dress
Between 1930 and 1935
Black silk tulle embroidered with
silver sequins and bugle beads
Paris, Patrimoine de CHANEL,
inv. HC.INC.1930-1935.9

Cat. 43
Evening dress
c. 1930–31
Cotton tulle embroidered
all over with gold sequins
Brussels, Musée de la Mode
et de la Dentelle,
inv. MMD C 82.14.03

Cat. 44 📖 pp. 50, 51
**Evening ensemble
with dress and jacket**
Autumn–Winter 1934–35
Ivory Moroccan crêpe,
silk tulle embroidered
all over with copper sequins
Paris, Patrimoine de CHANEL,
inv. HC.AH.1934.1

Cat. 45 📖 p. 79
Ensemble with dress and jacket
c. 1930–31
Ivory silk satin
Paris, Patrimoine de CHANEL,
inv. HC.INC.1930-1931.4

Cat. 46 📖 p. 81
Evening dress
Spring–Summer 1930
Ivory silk chiffon with insets
Paris, Patrimoine de CHANEL,
inv. HC.PE. 1930.3

Cat. 47 📖 p. 105
N° 5 perfume bottle
1921
Glass, black cotton cord,
black wax seal, printed paper
Paris, Patrimoine de CHANEL,
inv. C.1.643

Cat. 48
**Sales catalogue for
Parfums Chanel**
1924
Paper, black grosgrain,
white cotton cord
Paris, Patrimoine de CHANEL,
inv. C.T.206

Cat. 49
**Advertisement for Chanel
Perfumes on sale at Bonwit
Teller & Co., published
in the** New York Times
16 December 1924
Printed paper
Paris, Patrimoine de CHANEL,
Paris, inv. DOC.PPB.C.1052

Cat. 50 📖 p. 103
Chanel N° 5 purse bottle
c. 1930
Black glass, silver-plated metal,
beige jersey, cardboard, paper
Paris, Patrimoine de CHANEL,
inv. C.5.174

Cat. 51
Travel case for N° 5
1921
Nickel chrome
Paris, Patrimoine de CHANEL,
inv. C.1.680a

Cat. 52
Travel soap case
c. 1930
Black Bakelite, soap
Paris, Patrimoine de CHANEL,
inv. C.10.12b

Cat. 53
**Box for Cuir de Russie
travel spray**
1936
Undyed leather, suede, glass,
fabric, paper, silver-plated metal
Paris, Patrimoine de CHANEL,
inv. C.9.130a

Cat. 54 📖 p. 102
Bois des Îles fragrance
1928
Cedarwood, paper,
black paper, black wax seal,
glass, black cotton cord
Paris, Patrimoine de CHANEL,
inv. C.1.751a

Cat. 55
Lipstick scented with N° 5 perfume
c. 1930
Enamelled metal
Paris, Patrimoine de CHANEL,
inv. C.7.294

Cat. 56 📖 p. 103
Blusher compact
1924
Enamelled metal, mirror,
fabric powder puff
Paris, Patrimoine de CHANEL,
inv. C.11.112

Cat. 57 📖 p. 103
**Loose powder scented
with N° 5 perfume**
c. 1930
Cardboard, paper
Paris, Patrimoine de CHANEL,
inv. C.16.429

Cat. 58 📖 p. 102
Powder box
c. 1930
Glass, enamelled metal,
cardboard, paper, powder puff
Paris, Patrimoine de CHANEL,
inv. C.16.228/236

Cat. 59
**Powder from the Tan
range of sun products**
Summer 1932
Black enamelled metal,
metal, glass, paper
Paris, Patrimoine de CHANEL,
inv. C.1.796

Cat. 60
**Liquid from the Tan
range of sun products**
Summer 1932
Glass, black Bakelite, paper
Paris, Patrimoine de CHANEL,
inv. C.1.804

Cat. 61
**Oil from the Tan range
of sun products**
Summer 1932
Glass, black Bakelite,
printed paper
Paris, Patrimoine de CHANEL,
inv. C.1.799

Cat. 62
Beauty cream
Between 1930 and 1939
White Opaline, black Bakelite,
cardboard, paper
Paris, Patrimoine de CHANEL,
inv. C.2.904

Cat. 63
Beauty cream
Between 1930 and 1939
Metal, black Bakelite, cardboard
Paris, Patrimoine de CHANEL,
inv. C.8.14

Cat. 64
Beauty cream
1935
Painted metal, black Bakelite, card
Paris, Patrimoine de CHANEL,
inv. C.8.14

Cat. 65
Oil of jasmine
Between 1930 and 1939
Glass, leather, black cotton cord,
black wax seal, cardboard, paper
Paris, Patrimoine de CHANEL,
inv. C.1.787

Cat. 66
Beauty milk
Between 1930 and 1939
Glass, white leather, black cotton
cord, black wax seal, paper
Paris, Patrimoine de CHANEL,
inv. C.1.790

Cat. 67
Lotion with fruit
Between 1930 and 1939
Glass, black glass, paper
Paris, Patrimoine de CHANEL,
inv. C.1.788

Cat. 68
N° 5 extract
Between 1950 and 1959
Glass, black cotton cord,
black wax seal, cardboard, paper
Paris, Patrimoine de CHANEL,
inv. C.1.579

Cat. 69
N° 5 eau de toilette
Between 1947 and 1967
Glass, black Bakelite,
printed paper
Paris, Patrimoine de CHANEL,
inv. C.1.3314

Cat. 70
N° 5 eau de cologne
Between 1950 and 1959
Glass, black Bakelite,
cardboard, printed paper
Paris, Patrimoine de CHANEL,
inv. C.1.3313

Cat. 71
N° 5 lotion
c. 1950
Glass, black Bakelite,
printed paper
Paris, Patrimoine de CHANEL,
inv. C.1.650

Cat. 72
Brillantine scented with N° 5
c. 1950
Glass, black Bakelite,
printed paper, cardboard
Paris, Patrimoine de CHANEL,
inv. C.1.662a

Cat. 73
N° 5 sun oil
Between 1957 and 1959
Glass, black Bakelite,
printed paper
Paris, Patrimoine de CHANEL,
inv. C.1.663a

Cat. 74
Evening dress
Spring–Summer 1939
Cotton voile with multicoloured
print, dyed pink ostrich feather
Sydney, Museum of Applied Arts
and Sciences, inv. 96/386/8

Cat. 75
Evening dress
Spring–Summer 1931
Beige lace, ivory silk crêpe,
metal, blue glass
Paris, Palais Galliera, gift
of the heirs of Henry Viguier,
inv. 1968.55.23ABC

Cat. 76
Evening dress
1930
Cotton muslin, white lace inlay
Paris, Palais Galliera, gift
of Mme Bertin, inv. 1968.40.94

Cat. 77 📖 p. 85
Dress
Spring–Summer 1930
White broderie anglaise
Paris, Palais Galliera, gift
of Mme Bertin, inv. 1968.40.113AB

Cat. 78 📖 pp. 86, 87
Evening dress
Autumn–Winter 1933–34
Ivory silk lace with metallic
gold thread, rhinestones
Paris, Patrimoine de CHANEL,
inv. HC.AH.1933.1

Cat. 79
Evening dress
Autumn–Winter 1930–31
Ivory charmeuse,
Alençon lace inlay
New York, Fashion Institute
of Technology, gift of Mrs Hill
Montague III, inv. 77.133.2

Cat. 80
Dress
Spring–Summer 1936
Beige lace
New York, Hamish Bowles
collection

Cat. 81 📖 pp. 230, 231
Dress
1939
White cotton organdy
embroidered with white silk thread
Paris, Patrimoine de CHANEL,
inv. HC.INC.1939.1

Cat. 82
Evening dress
1938
Black silk tulle and lace,
flesh-tone silk chiffon
Paris, Palais Galliera, gift
of Mrs Julian Allen, inv. 1972.35.1

Cat. 83 📖 p. 89
Evening dress
Spring–Summer 1933
Black crêpe silk chiffon,
silk taffeta and lace
Paris, Patrimoine de CHANEL,
inv. HC.PE.1933.1

Cat. 84 📖 p. 91
Evening dress
Autumn–Winter 1937–38
Silk velvet, lace insets,
red silk tulle and taffeta
Paris, Patrimoine de CHANEL,
inv. HC.AH.1937.1

Cat. 85 📖 p. 97
Evening dress
c. 1938
Black silk tulle, black silk
satin ribbon appliqué
Paris, Musée des Arts Décoratifs,
gift of Joëlle Despas in memory
of her mother, Isabelle Despas,
inv. 52834

Cat. 86 📖 p. 77
Dress
Spring–Summer 1930
Pale green silk tulle
Paris, Patrimoine de CHANEL,
inv. HC.PE.1930.4

Cat. 87
Fan
Spring–Summer 1928
Bakelite and cotton organdy
in pale green
Paris, Patrimoine de CHANEL,
inv. ACC.HC.PE.1928.1

Cat. 88
Fashion illustration
Christian Bérard
Autumn–Winter 1937–38
Watercolour and Indian ink
on paper
Paris, Palais Galliera, gift
of Antonio Cánovas del Castillo,
inv. 1985.182.345

Cat. 89
Fashion illustration
Christian Bérard
Autumn–Winter 1937–38
Watercolour and Indian ink
on paper
Paris, Palais Galliera, gift
of Antonio Cánovas del Castillo,
inv. 1985.182.346

Cat. 90
Fashion illustration
Christian Bérard
Autumn–Winter 1937–38
Watercolour and Indian ink
on paper
Paris, Palais Galliera, gift
of Antonio Cánovas del Castillo,
inv. 1985.182.347

Cat. 91
Fashion illustration
Christian Bérard
Autumn–Winter 1937–38
Watercolour and Indian ink
on paper
Paris, Palais Galliera, gift
of Antonio Cánovas del Castillo,
inv. 1985.182.348

Cat. 92
Fashion illustration
Christian Bérard
Autumn–Winter 1937–38
Watercolour and Indian ink
on paper
Paris, Palais Galliera, gift
of Antonio Cánovas del Castillo,
inv. 1985.182.349

Cat. 93
Coat
Autumn–Winter 1918–19
Black silk satin, brown fur
(probably beaver)
Paris, Patrimoine de CHANEL,
inv. HC.AH.1918.1

Cat. 94
Coat
1920
Black silk satin, brown fur
(unknown)
Paris, Patrimoine de CHANEL,
inv. HC.INC.1920.2

Cat. 95
Cape
c. 1930
Black silk velvet
Paris, Palais Galliera, gift
of Francisca Truel and Lalo Barron,
inv. 2019.44.1

Cat. 96
Evening coat
c. 1934–35
Midnight blue cotton velvet
Paris, Patrimoine de CHANEL,
inv. HC.INC.1934-1935.1

Cat. 97 📖 pp. 136, 137
Coat
Autumn–Winter 1937–38
Red cotton velvet
Paris, Patrimoine de CHANEL,
inv. HC.AH.1937.1

Cat. 98
Dress
c. 1922–23
Black silk crêpe embroidered
with jet beads
Paris, Patrimoine de CHANEL,
inv. HC.INC.1922-1923.1

Cat. 99
Dress
1922
Black silk chiffon embroidered
with jet beads
Paris, Patrimoine de CHANEL,
inv. HC.PE.1922.1

Cat. 100 📖 p. 37
Dress
1923
Figured black wool with silver
thread, black silk pongee
Paris, Palais Galliera, gift of Mme
Louis Nouguier, inv. 1961.71.4AB

Cat. 101 📖 pp. 34, 35
Coat
Autumn–Winter 1922–23
Black wool with chain stitch
embroidery in multicoloured
silk and gold thread,
modern fur, brown silk satin
Paris, Patrimoine de CHANEL,
inv. HC.AH.1922.1

Cat. 102
Evening dress
1939
Midnight blue silk tulle
embroidered with silver sequins,
blue silk crêpe
San Francisco, Fine Arts Museums
of San Francisco, gift of
Mrs C.H. Russell inv. 1983.63.13a-d

Cat. 103
Evening dress
Autumn–Winter 1938–39
Black silk tulle embroidered
with black sequins
Paris, Patrimoine de CHANEL,
inv. HC.AH.1938.1

Cat. 104 📖 pp. 46, 47
Evening dress
Autumn–Winter 1929–30
Blue silk tulle embroidered
with fancy blue sequins
Paris, Patrimoine de CHANEL,
inv. HC.AH.1929.5

Cat. 105 📖 p. 46
Evening dress
Autumn–Winter 1929–30
Pink silk tulle embroidered
with pink sequins
Paris, Patrimoine de CHANEL,
inv. HC.AH.1929.4

Cat. 106 📖 p. 53
Beret
c. 1935
Black nylon and cellophane
Paris, Palais Galliera, gift of Comte
Henri de Beaumont, inv. 1986.114.11

Cat. 107 📖 p. 95
Evening dress
Autumn–Winter 1938–39
Midnight blue silk tulle
embroidered with midnight
blue sequins
Paris, Musée des Arts Décoratifs,
gift of Joëlle Despas in memory
of her mother, Isabelle Despas,
inv. 52832

Cat. 108
Ensemble with trousers,
top and jacket,
worn by Diana Vreeland
Autumn–Winter 1937–38
Tulle embroidered all over with
black sequins, ivory silk chiffon,
ivory silk lace, mother of pearl
London, Victoria & Albert Museum,
gift of Diana Vreeland, inv. T.88
to B-19742

Cat. 109
Cape
c. 1925
Red silk chiffon and velvet,
swan feather dyed red
Marseille, Château Borély –
Musée des Arts Décoratifs,
de la Faïence et de la Mode,
inv. D1991.7.2

Cat. 110 📖 p. 39
Cape
Spring–Summer 1925
Ivory silk crêpe,
white rooster feathers
Paris, Patrimoine de CHANEL,
inv. HC.PE.1925.1

Cat. 111 📖 p. 39
Cape
Spring–Summer 1925
Black silk crêpe, black
rooster feathers
Paris, Patrimoine de CHANEL,
inv. HC.PE.1925.2

Cat. 112 📖 p. 41
Evening dress
Autumn–Winter 1926–27
Midnight blue crêpe georgette,
silk fringing dyed in graduating
shades of blue
Paris, Patrimoine de CHANEL,
inv. HC.AH.1926.4

Cat. 113 📖 p. 41
Evening dress
Spring–Summer 1927
Ivory silk fringing and crêpe
Paris, Patrimoine de CHANEL,
inv. HC.PE.1927.1

Cat. 114 📖 p. 45
Short evening dress
1927
Black silk crêpe embroidered
with white glass beads
Paris, Patrimoine de CHANEL,
inv. HC.INC.1927.2

Cat. 115 📖 pp. 42, 43
Short evening dress
Autumn–Winter 1927–28
Blue silk crêpe embroidered
with blue glass beads
Paris, Patrimoine de CHANEL,
inv. HC.AH.1927.1

Cat. 116 📖 p. 49
Evening dress
1923
Navy crêpe de chine embroidered
with navy sequins, midnight blue
pongee, royal blue crêpe georgette
Paris, Palais Galliera, gift of
Mme Louis Nouguier, inv. 1961.71.5.

Cat. 117 📖 p. 138
'Comète' brooch
'Bijoux de Diamants' collection
1932
Platinum, old-cut diamonds
Paris, Patrimoine de CHANEL,
inv. JOA.4.1932.3

Cat. 118
'Bijoux de Diamants' catalogue
1932
Paper
Paris, Patrimoine de CHANEL,
inv. DOC.JOA.4

Cat. 119
Case
1932
Midnight blue silk velvet
Paris, Patrimoine de CHANEL,
inv. JOA.4.1932.3

Cat. 120
Handwritten text for
the 'Bijoux de Diamants' exhibition
Jean Cocteau
1932
Paper
Bibliothèque Historique
de la Ville de Paris

Cat. 121 📖 p. 249
Suit worn by Gabrielle Chanel
Autumn–Winter 1958–59
Écru and brown chiné tweed
by Lesur, gilded metal
Paris, Patrimoine de CHANEL,
inv. HC.AH.1958.1

Cat. 122
Suit and blouse worn
by Gabrielle Chanel
c. 1966
Beige tweed, navy silk gauze
Marseille, Château Borély –
Musée des Arts Décoratifs,
de la Faïence et de la Mode,
inv. MADM 890110a

Cat. 123
Coat and hat worn
by Gabrielle Chanel
Before 1961, altered in 1961–62
Brown mink
Marseille, Château Borély –
Musée des Arts Décoratifs,
de la Faïence et de la Mode,
inv. MADM89011d

Cat. 124
Pyjama suit worn
by Gabrielle Chanel
1954
Ivory silk
Marseille, Château Borély –
Musée des Arts Décoratifs,
de la Faïence et de la Mode,
inv. MADM890113c

Cat. 125 📖 p. 191
'2.55' bag
Between 1955 and 1971
Black-dyed quilted lamb's leather,
gilded metal, twist clasp
Paris, Patrimoine de CHANEL,
inv. ACC.HC.INC.1954-1971.3

Cat. 126
'2.55' bag
Between 1955 and 1971
Quilted silk velvet, black grosgrain,
gilded metal
Paris, Patrimoine de CHANEL,
inv. ACC.HC.INC.1955-1971.11

Cat. 127
'2.55' bag
Between 1955 and 1971
Quilted dyed black lamb's leather,
gilded metal, twist clasp
Paris, Patrimoine de CHANEL,
inv. ACC.HC.INC.1955-1971.1

Cat. 128 📖 p. 219
Prototype for two-tone shoe,
CHANEL design made by Massaro
c. 1961
Beige kidskin, black silk satin
Paris, Patrimoine de CHANEL,
inv. ACC.HC.INC.1960-1962.1

Cat. 129 📖 pp. 176, 177
Jacket and skirt suit
with modern blouse
Autumn–Winter 1961–62
Chiné tweed, black grosgrain,
écru and black twisted braid,
pink silk pongee
Paris, Patrimoine de CHANEL,
inv. HC.AH.1961.14

Cat. 130 📖 p. 248
Suit
Autumn–Winter 1964–65
Beige chiné tweed, gilded metal,
pink crêpe de chine
Paris, Patrimoine de CHANEL,
inv. HC.AH.1964.3

Cat. 131 📖 p. 179
Suit with jacket, top and skirt
Spring–Summer 1964
Beige chiné tweed, beige
and pink wool braid,
sand-coloured shantung
Paris, Palais Galliera, acquired by
the Ville de Paris, inv. 1989.2.30AB

Cat. 132
Suit
Autumn–Winter 1958–59
Chestnut and white chiné tweed
by Lesur, gilded metal
Paris, Patrimoine de CHANEL,
inv. HC.AH.1958.3

Cat. 133
Suit with jacket, blouse and skirt
1962
Ivory shantung, navy grosgrain
Hasselt (Belgium), Modemuseum,
inv. 2011.049

Cat. 134
Suit
Spring–Summer 1962
Beige tweed, black silk braid
Paris, Patrimoine de CHANEL,
inv.HC.PE.1962.1

Cat. 135
Suit worn by Princess
Grace of Monaco
c. 1960
Beige and plum tweed,
gilded metal
Monaco, Prince's Palace, inv. 13410

Cat. 136 📖 p. 159
Suit with jacket, blouse and skirt
Spring–Summer 1964
Navy and white check tweed,
white silk twill with navy print,
gilded metal
Paris, Palais Galliera, gift
of the Société de l'Histoire
du Costume, inv. 1975.33.3ABC

Cat. 137 📖 pp. 154, 155
Cardigan jacket and skirt ensemble
Spring–Summer 1971
Ivory wool jersey with navy print, gilded metal and navy Galalith
Paris, Patrimoine de CHANEL, inv. HC.PE.1971.10

Cat. 138 📖 p. 157
Suit
Spring–Summer 1965
White silk cloqué with navy print
Paris, Palais Galliera, acquired by the Ville de Paris, inv. 1991.68.3AB

Cat. 139
Suit with jacket, skirt, shirt and tie
Spring–Summer 1969
Navy and white checked wool, white cotton poplin, black silk
Paris, Patrimoine de CHANEL, inv. HC.PE.1969.4

Cat. 140 📖 p. 175
Ensemble with coat, top and skirt
Autumn–Winter 1965–66
Ivory and grey houndstooth wool, white mink, ivory tweed, gilded metal
Paris, Palais Galliera, acquired by the Ville de Paris, inv. 1990.12.3ABC

Cat. 141
Coat
Autumn–Winter 1970–71
Ivory and pale grey checked wool, fur, gilded metal
Paris, Palais Galliera, gift of Mme Dagousset, inv. 1998.227.2

Cat. 142
Pelisse coat
Autumn–Winter 1961–62
Grey chiné wool tweed, undyed shearling
Paris, Patrimoine de CHANEL, inv. HC.AH.1961.6

Cat. 143
Day ensemble
1929
Sand-coloured tweed, silk chiffon with multicoloured print
New York, Metropolitan Museum of Art, gift of the Isabel Shults Fund, inv. 1984.31a-c

Cat. 144 📖 p. 167
Ensemble with dress and coat
Spring–Summer 1963
Multicoloured mohair tweed, raspberry silk twill with navy print
Paris, Palais Galliera, acquired by the Ville de Paris, inv. 1990.12.4A-E

Cat. 145 📖 p. 163
Dress and coat ensemble
Spring–Summer 1962
Raspberry quilted silk taffeta and wool, gilded metal
Paris, Palais Galliera, acquired by the Ville de Paris, inv. 1989.2.31A-F

Cat. 146 📖 pp. 168, 169
Coat
Autumn–Winter 1961–62
Black silk cloqué, white mink, gilded metal
Paris, Palais Galliera, gift of Jeanne Guillard-Kirsteller, inv. 1995.95.5

Cat. 147 📖 p. 173
Pelisse coat
Autumn–Winter 1966–67
Black wool with check effect, clipped beaver fur, black Galalith and gilded metal
Paris, Palais Galliera, gift of Mme Dagousset, inv. 1998.227.1

Cat. 148
Short jacket and pleated skirt ensemble
Spring–Summer 1962
Black grain de poudre, ivory surah
Paris, Patrimoine de CHANEL, inv. HC.PE.1962.7

Cat. 149
Suit
Autumn–Winter 1970–71
Black patterned jersey by Marescot, gilded metal
Paris, Patrimoine de CHANEL, inv. HC.AH.1970.10

Cat. 150
Suit
Autumn–Winter 1962–63
Black silk velvet, black silk satin ribbons, gilded metal
Paris, Patrimoine de CHANEL, inv. HC.AH.1962.5

Cat. 151 📖 p. 118
Dress
Autumn–Winter 1962–63
Black wool, white cotton piqué, gilded metal
Paris, Palais Galliera, gift of the Comité de Développement et de Promotion de l'Habillement, inv. 1989.86.3A-D

Cat. 152
Suit with jacket, skirt and belt
1929
Navy wool jersey
New York, Metropolitan Museum of Art, gift of Mrs David Acheson, inv. 1984.154.1a-c

Cat. 153
Ensemble with jacket, top and skirt
1927
Black and ivory charmeuse
New York, Metropolitan Museum of Art, acquired by the New York Historical Society, inv. 1984.29ABC

Cat. 154
Suit worn by Lauren Bacall
c. 1958
Black wool, black silk gimp, white surah
New York, Metropolitan Museum of Art, gift of Lauren Bacall, inv. 2009.300.7625a-g

Cat. 155
Ensemble with dress and coat
1956
Ivory surah with black print, black wool crêpe, black lamb's leather
New York, Metropolitan Museum of Art, gift of H. Gregory Thomas, inv. 2009.300.261A-C

Cat. 156 📖 p. 151
Suit
Autumn–Winter 1964–65
Off-white tweed, navy and red wool braid
Paris, Patrimoine de CHANEL, inv. HC.AH.1964.12

Cat. 157 📖 p. 152
Suit
Autumn–Winter 1960–61
Ivory wool tweed, navy and red fringed wool braid
Paris, Patrimoine de CHANEL, inv. HC.AH.1960.6

Cat. 158 📖 p. 235
Suit
Spring–Summer 1961
Oatmeal tweed, red grosgrain with navy braid, gilded metal
Paris, Patrimoine de CHANEL, inv. HC.PE.1961.8

Cat. 159 📖 p. 235
Suit
Spring–Summer 1961
Oatmeal chiné tweed, red grosgrain with navy braid, gilded metal
Paris, Patrimoine de CHANEL, inv. HC.PE.1961.3

Cat. 160
Suit with jacket, top and skirt worn by Princess Paola of Belgium
1961
Oatmeal tweed, fuchsia grosgrain with navy braid
Antwerp, MoMu, inv. T06/1101ABC

Cat. 161
Coat and belt
c. 1964
Ivory wool, navy and pink wool braid
Max Mara Archives

Cat. 162 📖 p. 153
Suit
Autumn–Winter 1960–61
White wool by Burg, navy wool braid, silk pongee, gilded metal
Paris, Patrimoine de CHANEL, inv. HC.AH.1960.2

Cat. 163 📖 p. 153
Suit
Autumn–Winter 1963–64
Ivory wool tweed, ivory silk pongee, chiné braid in navy and ivory wool, gilded metal
Paris, Patrimoine de CHANEL, inv. HC.AH.1963.1

Cat. 164
Suit
Between 1960 and 1965
Ivory tweed, navy and ivory wool braid, gilded metal
Paris, Patrimoine de CHANEL, inv. HC.INC.1960-1965.2

Cat. 165
Suit worn by Princess Grace of Monaco
c. 1960
Off-white embossed wool, navy braid
Monaco, Prince's Palace, inv. 13405

Cat. 166 📖 p. 285
Dress and coat ensemble
Spring–Summer 1962
Ivory tweed bouclette and silk crêpe, gilded metal
Paris, Patrimoine de CHANEL, inv. HC.PE.1962.3

Cat. 167 📖 p. 233
Coat
Spring–Summer 1954
Ivory wool and silk crêpe, mother of pearl
Paris, Patrimoine de CHANEL, inv. HC.PE.1954.2

Cat. 168
Suit with jacket, skirt and belt, worn by Marlene Dietrich
1970
Black fancy wool jersey by Marescot
Berlin, Deutsche Kinemathek, inv. 4.12-93/16-10006

Cat. 169
Suit with jacket, skirt and belt
1970
Ivory fancy wool jersey by Marescot
Paris, Musée des Arts Décoratifs, gift of Fried, inv. UF78-6-5ABC

Cat. 170
Suit
Spring–Summer 1966
Navy tweed bouclette, white gabardine, navy grosgrain, gilded metal and navy Galalith
Paris, Patrimoine de CHANEL, inv. HC.PE.1966.8

Cat. 171
Suit
c. 1965
Navy tweed, white cotton poplin, navy grosgrain, gilded metal
Paris, Patrimoine de CHANEL, inv. HC.INC.1965–71.2

Cat. 172 📖 p. 161
Suit
Spring–Summer 1962
Ivory tweed, navy shantung, gilded metal
Paris, Patrimoine de CHANEL, inv. HC.PE.1962.4

Cat. 173 📖 p. 160
Dress and coat ensemble
Spring–Summer 1962
Navy wool, ivory shantung
Paris, Patrimoine de CHANEL, inv. HC.PE.1962.5

Cat. 174 📖 p. 164
Dress and coat ensemble
Autumn–Winter 1965–66
Navy tweed, red wool, gilded metal
Paris, Patrimoine de CHANEL, inv. HC.AH.1965.13

Cat. 175 📖 p. 165
Suit
Autumn–Winter 1965–66
Navy tweed, red silk cloqué, navy Galalith, gilded metal
Paris, Patrimoine de CHANEL, inv. HC.AH.1965.3

Cat. 176
Coat
Autumn–Winter 1957–58
Red wool, navy silk velvet and crêpe, navy Galalith
Paris, Patrimoine de CHANEL, inv. HC.AH.1957.2

Cat. 177
Suit worn by Marlene Dietrich
1968
Navy and pink striped silk serge
Berlin, Deutsche Kinemathek, inv. 10012

Cat. 178 📖 p. 181
Suit
Autumn–Winter 1965–66
Silver lamé, white mink, gold metallic braid, ivory silk satin
Paris, Patrimoine de CHANEL, HC.AH.1965.10

Cat. 179 📖 p. 183
Dress and jacket ensemble
Autumn–Winter 1963–64
Gold lamé cloqué by Bucol, sable, pink silk pongee
Paris, Patrimoine de CHANEL, HC.AH.1963.9

Cat. 180
Suit
Autumn–Winter 1962–63
Gold lamé, absinthe ottoman silk
Paris, Patrimoine de CHANEL, inv. HC.AH.1962.9

Cat. 181
Suit
Autumn–Winter 1963–64
Ivory figured silk with gold lamé, yellow silk braid and cord, gold braid and sequins, ivory silk gauze, gilded metal
Paris, Palais Galliera, acquired by the Ville de Paris, inv. 1990.12.1

Cat. 182
'Golden Hind' ensemble
1960
Gold lamé Lurex and figured silk
Paris, Musée des Arts Décoratifs, gift of Chanel, inv. UF71-30-36ABC

Cat. 183
Coat
c. 1927
Kimono fabric in black and white ombré silk, gold lamé
New York, Metropolitan Museum of Art, gift of the Irene Lewisohn Bequest and Catharine Breyer Van Bomel Foundation, inv. 1984.30

Cat. 184
Dress
Autumn–Winter 1964
Gold and silver lamé cloqué
Paris, Palais Galliera, gift of Chanel, inv. 1977.20.3

Cat. 185 📖 pp. 278, 279

Dress
Spring–Summer 1960
Ivory cotton tulle embroidered
with cotton and gold thread,
gold lamé, white organdy,
ivory silk crêpe
Paris, Palais Galliera,
gift of Chanel, inv. 1977.20.4

Cat. 186

Evening dress and cape ensemble
Autumn–Winter 1967–68
Gold lamé cloqué, gold silk
organza, gilded metal,
mother of pearl
Paris, Palais Galliera,
gift of Chanel, inv. 1972.75.4

Cat. 187 📖 p. 281

Dress and coat ensemble
Autumn–Winter 1967–68
Gold lamé cloqué, gold cord,
gilded metal
Paris, Palais Galliera,
gift of Chanel, inv 1977.20.12AB

Cat. 188

Evening trousers and jacket
ensemble
1970
Black figured silk, gold lamé,
black velvet
Paris, Musée des Arts Décoratifs,
gift of Chanel, inv. UF76-29-40AB

Cat. 189

Sweater and skirt ensemble
Autumn–Winter 1970–71
Gold lamé and linen knit, gilded
metal, beige silk pongee
Paris, Musée des Arts Décoratifs,
gift of Chanel, inv. UF76-29-42AB

Cat. 190

Suit
Autumn–Winter 1961–62
Gold metallic thread and wool
tweed, raspberry silk pongee,
gilded metal
Paris, Patrimoine de CHANEL,
inv. HC.AH.1961.4

Cat. 191

Suit
Autumn–Winter 1957–58
Pink wool jersey, Lurex lamé
and 'Bal blanc' nylon by Bucol
Paris, Patrimoine de CHANEL,
inv. HC.AH.1957.1

Cat. 192

Bib necklace
c. 1925
Silver-plated metal, polychrome
rhinestones
Paris, Patrimoine de CHANEL,
inv. ACC.HC.INC.1924-1926.1

Cat. 193

Pair of cuff bracelets
c. 1925
Silver-plated metal, polychrome
rhinestones
Paris, Patrimoine de CHANEL,
inv. ACC.HC.INC.1924-1926.2

Cat. 194 📖 p. 201

Necklace and earrings
Spring–Summer 1928
Silver, rock crystal
Paris, Patrimoine de CHANEL,
inv. ACC.HC.INC.1928.1

Cat. 195

Bracelet
1934
18K yellow gold, tourmaline,
peridot, aquamarine,
citrine, beryl, amethyst
Paris, Patrimoine de CHANEL,
inv. JOA.3.1930-1934.1

Cat. 196

Necklace
Between 1935 and 1940
Gold, topaz
Paris, Patrimoine de CHANEL,
inv. JOA.8.1935-1940.1

Cat. 197 📖 p. 199

Cross-shaped brooch, formerly
belonging to Diana Vreeland
Between 1930 and 1939
Yellow gold, sapphire, ruby,
emerald, citrine, tourmaline,
peridot, aquamarine,
moonstone, beryl
Paris, Patrimoine de CHANEL,
inv. JOA.4.1929-1934.2

Cat. 198 📖 p. 199

'Maltese Cross' brooch, formerly
belonging to Diana Vreeland
Between 1930 and 1939
Yellow gold, sapphire, ruby,
emerald, citrine, tourmaline,
peridot, aquamarine,
moonstone, beryl
Paris, Patrimoine de CHANEL,
inv. JOA.4.1929-1934.1

Cat. 199

Ring
Between 1930 and 1939
Yellow gold, emerald, ruby
Paris, Patrimoine de CHANEL,
inv. JOA.1.1930-1939.2

Cat. 200

Bracelet
1934
18K yellow gold, emerald,
tourmaline, pink sapphire
Paris, Patrimoine de CHANEL,
inv. JOA.3.1934.1

Cat. 201

Square brooch
Between 1930 and 1939
Yellow gold, amethyst,
green tourmaline, topaz,
citrine, aquamarine
Paris, Patrimoine de CHANEL,
inv. JOA.4.1930-1939.1

Cat. 202

Ring
1934
Yellow gold, emerald,
ruby, sapphire
Paris, Patrimoine de CHANEL,
inv. JOA.1.1934.1

Cat. 203

Brooch
c. 1933–34
Yellow gold, silver, sapphire,
pink sapphire, white sapphire
Paris, Patrimoine de CHANEL,
inv. JOA.4.1933-1934.1

Cat. 204

Ring
c. 1933–34
Yellow gold, silver, sapphire,
pink sapphire, white sapphire
Paris, Patrimoine de CHANEL,
inv. JOA.3.1933-1934.1

Cat. 205

Cigarette case
c. 1933–34
18K gold, sapphire, pink sapphire
Paris, Patrimoine de CHANEL,
inv. JOA.15.1933-1934.1

Cat. 206 📖 p. 213

Bracelet
CHANEL design made
by François Hugo
Spring–Summer 1938
Gilded metal, cut glass
Paris, Patrimoine de CHANEL,
inv. ACC.HC.PE.1938.1

Cat. 207 📖 p. 215

Necklace
Autumn–Winter 1938–39
Gilded metal, polychrome
glass, pearls
Paris, Patrimoine de CHANEL,
inv. ACC.HC.AH.1930-1940.5

Cat. 208

Necklace
Autumn–Winter 1938–39
Gilded metal, polychrome glass
Paris, Patrimoine de CHANEL,
inv. ACC.HC.AH.1938.1

Cat. 209

Brooch
CHANEL design made by Gripoix
Between 1930 and 1939
Gilded metal, polychrome
glass, rhinestones
Paris, Patrimoine de CHANEL,
inv. ACC.HC.INC.1930-1940.11

Cat. 210

Necklace
CHANEL design made by Gripoix
c. 1930
Silver-plated metal, green
glass, rhinestones
New York, Mark Walsh Leslie Chin
collection, Vintage Luxury

Cat. 211

Necklace
1930
Gilded metal, red glass
New York, Mark Walsh Leslie Chin
collection, Vintage Luxury

Cat. 212

Necklace
CHANEL design made by Gripoix
c. 1938–39
Gilded metal, polychrome
glass, pearls
Paris, Patrimoine de CHANEL,
inv. ACC.HC.INC.1938-1939.1

Cat. 213

Necklace
CHANEL design made by Gripoix
1939
Gilded metal (probably brass),
polychrome glass
New York, Mark Walsh Leslie Chin
collection, Vintage Luxury

Cat. 214

Necklace
CHANEL design made by Gripoix
1939
Gilded metal, translucent
and opaque polychrome glass
New York, Mark Walsh Leslie Chin
collection, Vintage Luxury

Cat. 215 📖 p. 195

Brooch
CHANEL design made by Gripoix
1937
Gilded metal, translucent
and opaque polychrome glass
Paris, Patrimoine de CHANEL,
inv. ACC.HC.INC.1937.2

Cat. 216 📖 p. 193

Necklace
CHANEL design made by Gripoix
Spring–Summer 1938
Gilded metal, translucent
polychrome glass
Paris, Patrimoine de CHANEL,
inv. ACC.HC.PE.1938.2

Cat. 217

Earrings and brooch set
CHANEL design made by Gripoix
c. 1938
Metal, translucent polychrome
glass, rhinestones
New York, Mark Walsh Leslie Chin
collection, Vintage Luxury

Cat. 218

Necklace
CHANEL design made by Gripoix
Spring–Summer 1938
Gilded metal, polychrome glass
Paris, Patrimoine de CHANEL,
inv. ACC.HC.INC.1938.1

Cat. 219

Necklace
CHANEL design made by Gripoix
c. 1937
Gilded metal, pink glass
New York, Mark Walsh Leslie Chin
collection, Vintage Luxury

Cat. 220

Necklace
c. 1937
Gilded metal, polychrome glass
New York, Mark Walsh Leslie Chin
collection, Vintage Luxury

Cat. 221

Necklace
c. 1937
Gilded metal, red glass
New York, Mark Walsh Leslie Chin
collection, Vintage Luxury

Cat. 222

Pair of bracelets
Between 1930 and 1939
Gilded metal, polychrome
glass, pearls
Paris, Patrimoine de CHANEL,
inv. ACC.HC.INC.1930-1939.5

Cat. 223

Brooch
Between 1930 and 1939
Gilded metal, black and
red glass, pearls
Paris, Patrimoine de CHANEL,
inv. ACC.HC.INC.1930-1939.16

Cat. 224

Pair of brooches
Between 1930 and 1939
Gilded metal, red, green
and blue glass beads
Paris, Patrimoine de CHANEL,
inv. ACC.HC.INC.1930-1939.8(1)

Cat. 225

Bracelet
Between 1930 and 1939
Gilded metal, polychrome
glass, rhinestones
Paris, Patrimoine de CHANEL,
inv. ACC.HC.INC.1930-1939.8(2)

Cat. 226

Brooch
CHANEL design made by Gripoix
Between 1930 and 1939
Gilded metal, green, red and
purple glass, pearls, rhinestones
Paris, Patrimoine de CHANEL,
inv. ACC.HC.INC.1930-1939.18

Cat. 227

Belt buckle
Between 1930 and 1939
Gilded metal
Paris, Patrimoine de CHANEL,
inv. ACC.INC.1930-1939.10

Cat. 228

Necklace
Autumn–Winter 1937–38
Gilded metal
Paris, Patrimoine de CHANEL,
inv. ACC.HC.INC.1937.1

Cat. 229

Belt
CHANEL design made
by Robert Goossens
Autumn–Winter 1967–68
Gilded metal, red glass, elastic
Paris, Patrimoine de CHANEL,
inv. ACC.HC.INC.1967.3

Cat. 230

Belt
CHANEL design made
by Robert Goossens
Spring–Summer 1970
Gilded metal
Paris, Patrimoine de CHANEL,
inv. ACC.HC.PE.1970.4

Cat. 231 📖 p. 269

Belt
CHANEL design made
by Robert Goossens
Spring–Summer 1971
Gilded metal, red and green glass,
imitation pearls
Paris, Patrimoine de CHANEL,
inv. ACC.HC.PE.1971.2

Cat. 232

Belt
CHANEL design made
by Robert Goossens
1960s
Gilded metal, elastic
Paris, Patrimoine de CHANEL,
inv. ACC.HC.INC.1960-1974.4

Cat. 233 📖 p. 197

Crucifix pendant
CHANEL design made
by Robert Goossens
Between 1954 and 1974
Gilded bronze
Paris, Patrimoine de CHANEL,
inv. ACC.HC.INC.1954-1974.8

Cat. 234

Reliquary cross
9th–11th century
Bronze
Paris, Patrimoine de CHANEL,
inv. ACC.INC.INC.800-1200.1

Cat. 235 📖 p. 200

Brooch
CHANEL design made
by Robert Goossens
1960s
Vermeil, tourmaline
Paris, Patrimoine de CHANEL,
inv. JOA.5.1972.2

Cat. 236

Pair of fibula brooches
Late 6th century
Bronze, garnet
Paris, Musée de Cluny,
Musée National du Moyen Âge,
inv. Cl.3479 & Cl.3480

Cat. 237

Pendant
CHANEL design made
by Robert Goossens
1960s
Silver, red and green glass
Paris, Patrimoine de CHANEL,
inv. ACC.HC.INC.1954-1974.65

Cat. 238

Crucifix pendant
CHANEL design made
by Robert Goossens
Autumn–Winter 1969–70
Gilded metal, red and green glass
Paris, Patrimoine de CHANEL,
inv. ACC.HC.AH.1969.4

Cat. 239 📖 p. 207

Crucifix pendant
CHANEL design made
by Robert Goossens
Autumn–Winter 1965–66
Gilded metal, red and green glass
Paris, Patrimoine de CHANEL,
inv. ACC.HC.AH.1965.1

Cat. 240

Necklace with crucifix pendant
CHANEL design made
by Robert Goossens
1960s
Vermeil, polychrome glass
Paris, Patrimoine de CHANEL,
inv. ACC.HC.INC.1954-1974.7

Cat. 241

Necklace with pendant
CHANEL design made
by Robert Goossens
Spring–Summer 1971
Gilded bronze, red and green glass
Paris, Patrimoine de CHANEL,
inv. ACC.HC.PE.1971.1

Cat. 242

Necklace with crucifix pendant
CHANEL design made
by Robert Goossens
Spring–Summer 1971
Gilded metal, imitation pearls,
red and green glass
Paris, Patrimoine de CHANEL,
inv. ACC.HC.PE.1971.4

Cat. 243

Necklace with crucifix pendant
Between 1930 and 1939
Gilded metal, red and green glass,
imitation pearls
New York, Mark Walsh Leslie Chin
collection, Vintage Luxury

Cat. 244

Pendant
Between 1954 and 1964
Gilded metal, polychrome glass,
imitation pearls
New York, Mark Walsh Leslie Chin
collection, Vintage Luxury

Cat. 245

Bracelet
CHANEL design made
by Robert Goossens
1960s
White resin, gilded metal,
green glass
Paris, Patrimoine de CHANEL,
inv. ACC.HC.INC.1954-1974.88

Cat. 246

Bracelet
CHANEL design made
by Robert Goossens
1960s
Black resin, gilded metal,
translucent white and green glass
Paris, Patrimoine de CHANEL,
inv. ACC.HC.INC.1954-1974.89

Cat. 247

Pendant
CHANEL design made
by Robert Goossens
1960s
Vermeil, quartz, tourmaline
Paris, Patrimoine de CHANEL,
inv. JOA.5.1972.3

Cat. 248 📖 p. 209

Pendant
CHANEL design made
by Robert Goossens
1960s
Yellow gold, turquoise,
tourmaline, pearls
Paris, Patrimoine de CHANEL,
inv. JOA.5.1972.1

Cat. 249 📖 p. 196

Pendant
CHANEL design made
by Robert Goossens
1960s
Yellow gold, rock crystal,
smoky quartz
Paris, Patrimoine de CHANEL,
inv. JOA.5.1954-1974.4

Cat. 250 📖 p. 203

Pendant
CHANEL design made
by Robert Goossens
1960s
Vermeil, rock crystal, tourmaline
Paris, Patrimoine de CHANEL,
inv. JOA.4.1954-1974.1

Cat. 251 📖 p. 202

Crucifix pendant
CHANEL design made
by Robert Goossens
1960s
Yellow gold, rock crystal
Paris, Patrimoine de CHANEL,
inv. JOA.5.1954-1974.5

Cat. 252

Crucifix pendant
CHANEL design made
by Robert Goossens
1960s
Yellow gold, rock crystal
Paris, Patrimoine de CHANEL,
inv. JOA.5.1954-1974.6

Cat. 253

Crucifix pendant
CHANEL design made
by Robert Goossens
1960s
Yellow gold, rock crystal,
rose quartz, tourmaline
Paris, Patrimoine de CHANEL,
inv. JOA.5.1954-1974.2

Cat. 254 📖 p. 204

Brooch
CHANEL design made
by Robert Goossens
1960s
Gilded bronze, tourmaline
Paris, Patrimoine de CHANEL,
inv. JOA.5.1954-1974.3

Cat. 255 📖 p. 205

Brooch
CHANEL design made
by Robert Goossens
1960s
Gilded bronze, tourmaline
Paris, Patrimoine de CHANEL,
inv. JOA.5.1954-1974.1

Cat. 256 📖 p. 214

Necklace
CHANEL design made
by Robert Goossens
Autumn–Winter 1969–70
Gilded metal, red and green
glass, imitation pearl
Paris, Patrimoine de CHANEL,
inv. ACC.HC.INC.1969.1

Cat. 257

Necklace
CHANEL design made
by Robert Goossens
Spring–Summer 1970
Gilded bronze, imitation pearl
Paris, Patrimoine de CHANEL,
inv. ACC.HC.PE.1970.1

Cat. 258

Brooch
CHANEL design made
by Robert Goossens
1960s
Gilded metal, imitation
pearls, rhinestones
Paris, Patrimoine de CHANEL,
inv. ACC.HC.INC.1954-1971.10

Cat. 259

Necklace
CHANEL design made
by Robert Goossens
Autumn–Winter 1965–66
Gilded metal, baroque
pearls, rhinestones
Paris, Patrimoine de CHANEL,
inv. ACC.HC.AH.1965.4

Cat. 260

Bracelet
CHANEL design made
by Robert Goossens
1960s
Gilded metal, red and turquoise
glass, imitation pearls
Paris, Patrimoine de CHANEL,
inv. ACC.HC.INC.1960-1973.1

Cat. 261

Bracelet
CHANEL design made
by Robert Goossens
1960s
Gilded metal, red and white glass
Paris, Patrimoine de CHANEL,
inv. ACC.HC.INC.1954-1970.1

Cat. 262

Necklace
CHANEL design made
by Robert Goossens
Autumn–Winter 1967–68
Gilded metal, imitation pearls
Paris, Patrimoine de CHANEL,
inv. ACC.HC.INC.1967.6

Cat. 263

Necklace
CHANEL design made
by Robert Goossens
Spring–Summer 1971
Gilded metal, imitation pearls
Paris, Patrimoine de CHANEL,
inv. ACC.HC.PE.1971.3

Cat. 264

Necklace
CHANEL design made
by Robert Goossens
Autumn–Winter 1964–65
Metal, green glass, imitation
pearls, rhinestones
Paris, Patrimoine de CHANEL,
inv. ACC.HC.AH.1964.1

Cat. 265 📖 pp. 216, 217

Brooch
CHANEL design made
by Robert Goossens
Autumn–Winter 1961–62
Gilded metal, crystal,
translucent glass
Paris, Patrimoine de CHANEL,
inv. ACC.HC.AH.1961.1

Cat. 266

Bracelet
CHANEL design made
by Robert Goossens
Autumn–Winter 1961–62
Gilded metal, deep red glass
Paris, Patrimoine de CHANEL,
inv. ACC.HC.AH.1961.2

Cat. 267

Belt
CHANEL design made
by Robert Goossens
1960s
Gilded metal, green glass
Paris, Patrimoine de CHANEL,
inv. ACC.HC.INC.1954-1974.92

Cat. 268 📖 p. 217

Brooch
CHANEL design made
by Robert Goossens
Spring–Summer 1959
Gilded metal, turquoise glass,
rhinestones
Paris, Patrimoine de CHANEL,
inv. HC.PE.1959.2a

Cat. 269

Brooch
CHANEL design made
by Robert Goossens
1965
Gilded metal, turquoise glass,
imitation pearls, rhinestones
Paris, Patrimoine de CHANEL,
inv. ACC.HC.INC.1965.2

Cat. 270

Brooch
CHANEL design made
by Robert Goossens
Spring–Summer 1959
Gilded metal, turquoise
glass, rhinestones
Paris, Patrimoine de CHANEL,
inv. ACC.HC.INC.1959.6

Cat. 271

Brooch
CHANEL design made
by Robert Goossens
Autumn–Winter 1959–60
Gilded metal, rhinestones,
imitation pearls
Paris, Patrimoine de CHANEL,
inv. ACC.HC.INC.1959.5

Cat. 272

Pendant
CHANEL design made
by Robert Goossens
1960s
Gilded metal, white glass
Paris, Patrimoine de CHANEL,
inv. ACC.HC.INC.1954-1974.10

Cat. 273

Pendant
CHANEL design made
by Robert Goossens
1960s
Gilded metal, red glass
Paris, Patrimoine de CHANEL,
inv. ACC.HC.INC.1954-1974.11

Cat. 274

Necklace
CHANEL design made
by Robert Goossens
1960s
Gilded bronze
Paris, Patrimoine de CHANEL,
inv. ACC.HC.INC.1954-1974.12

Cat. 275
Necklace
CHANEL design made
by Robert Goossens
1960s
Gilded bronze, red glass
Paris, Patrimoine de CHANEL,
inv. ACC.HC.INC.1954-1974.13

Cat. 276
Necklace
CHANEL design made
by Robert Goossens
1960s
Gilded bronze, vermeil
Paris, Patrimoine de CHANEL,
inv. ACC.HC.INC.1954-1974.14

Cat. 277
Bracelet
CHANEL design made
by Robert Goossens
1960s
Gilded bronze
Paris, Patrimoine de CHANEL,
inv. ACC.HC.INC.1954-1974.15

Cat. 278
Belt
CHANEL design made
by Robert Goossens
1960s
Gilded metal
Paris, Patrimoine de CHANEL,
inv. ACC.HC.INC.1957-1974.6

Cat. 279
Necklace
CHANEL design made
by Robert Goossens
Autumn–Winter 1965–66
Gilded bronze
Paris, Patrimoine de CHANEL,
inv. ACC.HC.AH.1965.3

Cat. 280 📖 p. 210
Necklace
CHANEL design made
by Robert Goossens
Autumn–Winter 1965–66
Gilded bronze
Paris, Patrimoine de CHANEL,
inv. ACC.HC.AH.1965.2

Cat. 281 📖 pp. 282–283
Necklace
CHANEL design made
by Robert Goossens
1970s
Vermeil, rock crystal
Paris, Patrimoine de CHANEL,
inv. ACC.HC.INC.1965-1975.1

Cat. 282 📖 p. 206
Bracelet
CHANEL design made
by Robert Goossens
1960s
Vermeil, polychrome glass
Paris, Patrimoine de CHANEL,
inv. ACC.HC.INC.1954-1974.56

Cat. 283
Bracelet
CHANEL design made
by Robert Goossens
1960s
Vermeil, polychrome glass,
imitation pearls
Paris, Patrimoine de CHANEL,
inv. ACC.HC.INC.1954-1974.54

Cat. 284
Bracelet
CHANEL design made
by Robert Goossens
Autumn–Winter 1960–61
Gilded metal, polychrome glass,
iridescent glass beads
Paris, Patrimoine de CHANEL,
inv. HC.INC.1954-1971.19

Cat. 285
Bracelet
CHANEL design made
by Robert Goossens
1960s
Vermeil, gilded metal,
polychrome glass
Paris, Patrimoine de CHANEL,
inv. ACC.HC.INC.1954-1974.91

Cat. 286
Necklace
CHANEL design made
by Robert Goossens
Autumn–Winter 1967–68
Gilded metal, polychrome glass,
imitation pearls, rhinestones
Paris, Patrimoine de CHANEL,
inv. ACC.HC.AH.1967.1

Cat. 287
Earrings
CHANEL design made
by Robert Goossens
1969
Gilded metal, red and green glass
Paris, Patrimoine de CHANEL,
inv. ACC.HC.INC.1969.4

Cat. 288
Bracelet
Between 1930 and 1936
Yellow gold, silver, emerald,
diamond, ruby, sapphire
Paris, Patrimoine de CHANEL,
inv. JOA.3.1930-1936.1

Cat. 289
Oval brooch
Between 1950 and 1960
Gold, silver, red and green
synthetic stones,
diamond, emerald
Paris, Patrimoine de CHANEL,
inv. JOA.4.1950-60

Cat. 290
Bracelet
Between 1930 and 1939
Gold, sapphire, ruby
Paris, Patrimoine de CHANEL,
inv. JOA.3.1930-1939.1

Cat. 291
Necklace
CHANEL design made by Gripoix
1939
Gilded metal, polychrome glass
New York, Mark Walsh Leslie Chin
collection, Vintage Luxury

Cat. 292
Earrings
CHANEL design made
by Robert Goossens
1950s
Silver, Mabé pearl, diamond
Paris, Patrimoine de CHANEL,
inv. JOA.2.1955-1965.1

Cat. 293
Earrings
CHANEL design made
by Robert Goossens
c. 1955
Platinum, white gold,
Mabé pearl, diamond
Paris, Patrimoine de CHANEL,
inv. JOA.2.1954-1955.1

Cat. 294
Earrings
CHANEL design made
by Robert Goossens
Spring–Summer 1964
Gilded metal, glass
Paris, Patrimoine de CHANEL,
inv. ACC.HC.INC.1964.1B

Cat. 295
Brooch
CHANEL design made
by Robert Goossens
Spring–Summer 1964
Gilded metal, imitation
pearl, rhinestones
Paris, Patrimoine de CHANEL,
inv. ACC.HC.INC.1964.1Abis

Cat. 296
Brooch
CHANEL design made
by Robert Goossens
Autumn–Winter 1956–57
Silver, silver-plated metal,
glass, rhinestones
Paris, Patrimoine de CHANEL,
inv. ACC.HC.INC.1954-1974.62

Cat. 297
Necklace and two brooches
CHANEL designs made
by Robert Goossens
Between 1954 and 1974
Gilded metal, rhinestones
Paris, Patrimoine de CHANEL,
inv. ACC.HC.INC.1957-1974.7/8

Cat. 298
Clip brooch
CHANEL design made
by Robert Goossens
1961
Gilded metal, imitation pearls
Paris, Patrimoine de CHANEL,
inv. ACC.HC.INC.1961.2

Cat. 299
Clip brooch
CHANEL design made
by Robert Goossens
1961
Gilded metal, imitation pearls
Paris, Patrimoine de CHANEL,
inv. ACC.HC.INC.1961.3

Cat. 300
Clip brooch
CHANEL design made
by Robert Goossens
1961
Gilded metal, green glass
Paris, Patrimoine de CHANEL,
inv. ACC.HC.INC.1961.4

Cat. 301
Pendant
CHANEL design made
by Robert Goossens
1970
Brushed yellow gold, pearl,
baroque pear-shaped pearl,
old-cut diamond
Paris, Patrimoine de CHANEL,
inv. JOA.5.1970.2

Cat. 302
Earrings
CHANEL design made
by Robert Goossens
1960s
Gilded metal, imitation
pearls, rhinestones
Paris, Patrimoine de CHANEL,
inv. ACC.HC.INC.1954-1974.45

Cat. 303
Earrings
CHANEL design made
by Robert Goossens
1960s
Gilded metal, imitation pearls
Paris, Patrimoine de CHANEL,
inv. ACC.HC.INC.1954-1974.84

Cat. 304
Brooch and earrings
CHANEL designs made
by Robert Goossens
c. 1960
Gilded metal, imitation
pearl, rhinestones
Paris, Patrimoine de CHANEL,
inv. ACC.HC.INC.1959-1961.1

Cat. 305
Earrings
CHANEL design made
by Robert Goossens
1960s
Gilded metal, copper, imitation
pearl, rhinestones
Paris, Patrimoine de CHANEL,
inv. ACC.HC.INC.1960-1974.2

Cat. 306
Watch
CHANEL design made
by Robert Goossens
1960s
Yellow gold
Paris, Patrimoine de CHANEL,
inv. HOR.1.1954-1974.1

Cat. 307
Necklace
CHANEL design made
by Robert Goossens
1960s
Gilded metal, green and red glass
Paris, Patrimoine de CHANEL,
inv. ACC.HC.INC.1960-1971.3

Cat. 308
Necklace
Between 1954 and 1974
Gilded metal, amethyst, purple
glass beads, imitation pearls
Paris, Patrimoine de CHANEL,
inv. ACC.HC.INC.1954-1971.7

Cat. 309
Necklace
CHANEL design made
by Robert Goossens
1960s
Gilded metal
Paris, Patrimoine de CHANEL,
inv. ACC.HC.INC.1954-1973.3

Cat. 310
Necklace
CHANEL design made
by Robert Goossens
1960s
Gilded metal, red glass beads,
imitation pearls
Paris, Patrimoine de CHANEL,
inv. ACC.HC.INC.1957-1974.5

Cat. 311
Necklace
CHANEL design made
by Robert Goossens
1971
Gilded metal, green and red glass,
imitation pearls
Paris, Patrimoine de CHANEL,
inv. ACC.HC.INC.1971.1

Cat. 312
Necklace
CHANEL design made
by Robert Goossens
1960s
Gilded metal, green and red glass,
imitation pearl
Paris, Patrimoine de CHANEL,
inv. ACC.HC.PE.1974.1

Cat. 313
Necklace
CHANEL design made
by Robert Goossens
Autumn–Winter 1969–70
Gilded metal, red glass
Paris, Patrimoine de CHANEL,
inv. ACC.HC.AH.1969.2

Cat. 314
Necklace
CHANEL design made
by Robert Goossens
1960s
Gilded metal, red glass,
imitation pearls
Paris, Patrimoine de CHANEL,
inv. ACC.HC.INC.1954-1965.3

Cat. 315
Necklace
CHANEL design made
by Robert Goossens
1960s
Gilded metal, green glass,
imitation pearls
Paris, Patrimoine de CHANEL,
inv. ACC.HC.INC.1954-1965.4

Cat. 316
Necklace
CHANEL design made
by Robert Goossens
1960s
Gilded metal, blue and green
glass, rhinestones
Paris, Patrimoine de CHANEL,
inv. ACC.HC.INC.1954-1960.2

Cat. 317
Necklace
CHANEL design made
by Robert Goossens
1960s
Silver-plated metal,
polychrome rhinestones
Paris, Patrimoine de CHANEL,
inv. ACC.HC.INC.1954-1971.16

Cat. 318 📖 p. 262
Formal dress
Spring–Summer 1960
Black silk chiffon and satin
Paris, Patrimoine de CHANEL,
inv. HC.PE.1960.5

Cat. 319 📖 p. 247
Cocktail dress
Spring–Summer 1959
Black lace by Dognin
Paris, Patrimoine de CHANEL,
inv. HC.PE.1959.5

Cat. 320 📖 p. 219
Formal dress
Spring–Summer 1959
Black silk chiffon,
black silk satin ribbon
Paris, Patrimoine de CHANEL,
inv. HC.PE.1959.2

Cat. 321 📖 p. 263
Cocktail dress
Spring–Summer 1965
Black silk chiffon, black
silk satin ribbon
Paris, Patrimoine de CHANEL,
inv. HC.PE.1965.2

Cat. 322 📖 p. 261
Dress
Autumn–Winter 1966–67
Black silk chiffon, black
lace appliqué
Paris, Palais Galliera,
gift of Chanel, inv. 1972.75.2

Cat. 323 📖 p. 265
Dress
Autumn–Winter 1969
Black silk chiffon and fringing,
gilded metal
Paris, Palais Galliera,
gift of Mme Mantou, inv. 1996.174.1

Cat. 324 📖 pp. 216, 217
Dress
Spring–Summer 1964
Black organza and cotton cloqué
Paris, Palais Galliera, gift
of the Comité de Développement
et de Promotion de l'Habillement,
inv. 1989.86.2

Cat. 325
Dress
c. 1930
Silk tulle, embroidered all over
with white sequins
New York, Metropolitan Museum
of Art, gift of Gabrielle Chanel,
inv. C.I.55.61.1A-C

Cat. 326 📖 p. 171
Tunic and skirt ensemble
Spring–Summer 1960
Black silk crêpe with Lurex lamé,
black silk cord
Paris, Palais Galliera, gift
of the heirs of Henry Viguier,
inv. 1968.55.40AB

Cat. 327
Dress worn by Romy Schneider
Autumn–Winter 1963–64
Silk tulle, embroidered all over
with black sequins
Paris, Patrimoine de CHANEL,
inv. HC.AH.1963.8

Cat. 328
Cocktail dress
Autumn–Winter 1961–62
Black nylon and cellophane
'Flochebrille' tulle by Bucol,
black lacquered satin ribbon
Paris, Patrimoine de CHANEL,
inv. HC.AH.1961.1

Cat. 329
Formal dress
Spring–Summer 1954
Embroidered ivory cotton tulle,
gold netting, gold lamé,
white organdy
Paris, Patrimoine de CHANEL,
inv. HC.PE.1954.4

Cat. 330
Dress
1962
Ivory broderie anglaise
and cotton organdy
Paris, Palais Galliera,
gift of Chanel, inv. 1972.75.1

Cat. 331
Dress and stole
Autumn–Winter 1960–61
Leavers lace in beige silk
Paris, Patrimoine de CHANEL,
inv. HC.AH.1960.5

Cat. 332
Suit with jacket, skirt and blouse
Autumn–Winter 1961–62
Black cellophane velvet, ivory
duchess satin, black Galalith
Paris, Palais Galliera, gift of Nicole
Alphand, inv. 1987.1.199ABC

Cat. 333
Formal dress
Autumn–Winter 1929–30
Ivory silk lace embroidered with
iridescent sequins, ivory silk serge
Paris, Patrimoine de CHANEL,
inv. HC.AH.1926.3

Cat. 334 📖 p. 255
Dress worn by Delphine Seyrig
in *Last Year in Marienbad*
Autumn–Winter 1960–61
Gold lamé, gilded metal
Paris, Cinémathèque Française,
inv. C 0062

Cat. 335 📖 p. 257
Dress worn by Delphine Seyrig
in *Last Year in Marienbad*
Autumn–Winter 1960–61
Black silk chiffon
Paris, Cinémathèque Française,
inv. C 0061

Cat. 336 📖 p. 269
Dress
Spring–Summer 1971
Ivory figured organza, gold lamé
Paris, Palais Galliera,
gift of Chanel, inv. 1972.75.6-1

Cat. 337
Evening dress
Autumn–Winter 1970–71
Ivory figured silk chiffon, gold lamé
Paris, Patrimoine de CHANEL,
inv. HC.AH.1970.7

Cat. 338 📖 p. 271
Evening dress
Autumn–Winter 1967–68
Nylon netting, white silk chenille,
iridescent Lurex, ivory silk
crêpe, chiffon and charmeuse,
gilded metal, rhinestones
and mother of pearl
Paris, Palais Galliera,
gift of Chanel, inv. 1977.20.9

Cat. 339 📖 p. 267
Evening dress
Autumn–Winter 1965–66
Silk embroidered all over
with pearlized white sequins
Paris, Patrimoine de CHANEL,
inv. HC.AH.1965.11

Cat. 340 📖 p. 267
Bolero and skirt ensemble
Autumn–Winter 1963–64
Silk embroidered all over
with pearlized white sequins
Paris, Palais Galliera, gift
of Mme Leonelli, inv. 1994.92.4AB

Cat. 341
Evening dress
1954
Black silk tulle, applied embroidery
with black cord piping
Paris, Patrimoine de CHANEL,
inv. HC.PE.1954.3

Cat. 342
Evening dress and bolero
c. 1937–38
Black silk crêpe and lace
New York, Metropolitan Museum
of Art, gift of Yann Weymouth,
inv. 1981.348.2AB

Cat. 343
Evening dress
1930
Black silk lace
Paris, Patrimoine de CHANEL,
inv. HC.AH.1932.2

Cat. 344
Evening dress
Spring–Summer 1933
Black silk tulle, ivory silk pongee
Paris, Patrimoine de CHANEL,
inv. HC.PE.1933.4

Cat. 345 📖 pp. 258, 259
Evening dress
Autumn–Winter 1970–71
Red silk chiffon
Paris, Palais Galliera,
gift of Chanel, inv. 1977.20.18

Cat. 346 📖 pp. 258, 259
Evening dress
Spring–Summer 1955
Red silk chiffon
Paris, Patrimoine de CHANEL,
inv. HC.PE.1955.1

Cat. 347
Evening dress
c. 1950
Black silk gauze and velvet
Paris, François Hurteau-Flamand
collection

Cat. 348
Evening dress
Autumn–Winter 1967–68
Figured black chenille, black Lurex
Paris, Patrimoine de CHANEL,
inv. HC AH.1967.1

Cat. 349
Evening dress
Autumn–Winter 1957–58
Red silk velvet, black crêpe
silk chiffon
Paris, Patrimoine de CHANEL,
inv. HC.AH.1957.5

Cat. 350
Evening dress
Autumn–Winter 1967–68
Navy silk crêpe, pale blue silk
taffeta and chiffon
Paris, Patrimoine de CHANEL,
inv. HC.AH.1967.2

Cat. 351
Evening dress
Autumn–Winter 1929–30
Black silk tulle, silk crêpe
and mechanical lace
Paris, Patrimoine de CHANEL,
inv. HC.AH.1929.1

This book was published on the occasion
of the exhibition 'Gabrielle Chanel:
Manifeste de mode' at the Palais Galliera, Paris.

With the support of CHANEL

PARIS MUSÉES

Curators

Miren Arzalluz
and Véronique Belloir,
assisted by Nadia Albertini

Art Direction

Olivier Saillard

Exhibition design
Dominique Brard
Sandra Courtine

Graphic design
Loran Stosskopf (Mucho)
assisted by Seikyung Louise Son

Lighting
Alexis Coussement

Exhibition management
Aurore Pierre

Christophe Girard,
president of Paris Musées

Afaf Gabelotaud,
vice-president of Paris Musées

Delphine Lévy,
Executive director

Céline Marchand,
Head of International Relations

Anaïs Quinsat,
International Project Manager

Palais Galliera,
Musée de la Mode
de la Ville de Paris

Director
Miren Arzalluz

Board
Bénédicte Breton
Julien Lessecq
Monique Bouard
Alice Danger

Press and Marketing
Anne de Nesle
Caroline Chenu

Curators
Véronique Belloir
Laurent Cotta
Pascale Gorguet-Ballesteros
Christian Gros
Sophie Grossiord
Marie-Laure Gutton
Sylvie Lécallier
Alexandre Samson
Jacqueline Dumaine
Marie-Ange Bernieri

**Digitization of Collections
department**
Patricia Khayati
Emmanuelle Audooren-Lecointre

Library and central archives
Sylvie Roy
Nathalie Gourseau

Collection Care department
Corinne Dom
Joëlle Duhoo
Thierry Fripier
Catherine Gervais
Angélique Illiet
Rebecca Léger
Christine Mebtoul
Dominique Merliot
Évelyne Poulot
Angeline Théatin
Delphine de Trégomain

Restoration workshop
Sylvie Brun
Camille Lallemand
Anastasia Ozoline

Technical assistants
Prosper Thomas
Jacques Belleau

Cultural department
Evren Adanir-Rispal
Doris Arlot
Laure Bernard
Catherine Chapiseau
Janick Deshoulliers
Myriam Loussaief

and all the hospitality and security
teams at the Palais Galliera

Exhibitions
and Publications
Management

Olivier Donat,
director

Julie Bertrand,
**deputy director, head
of exhibitions department**
Fanny Hollman,
project leader
Laura Farge,
head of production

Éric Landauer
and the workshop team
at the Musées
de la Ville de Paris

Isabelle Jendron,
head of publishing
Hélène Studievic,
lead editor
Laurence Goupille,
head of picture research
Amélie Segonds,
Victoire Varenne,
picture researchers
Saint-Véron Pompée,
head of production
Marion Assémat,
business manager
Claude Ribeiro,
sales administrator

Visitor Development,
Partnerships
and Press

Josy Carrel-Torlet,
director

Philippe Rivière,
**deputy director and head of
marketing and digital departments**
Nina Garnier,
**deputy director
and head of marketing**
Blandine Cottet,
**marketing, partnerships
and publicity manager**
Andréa Longrais,
head of press and public relations
Hélène Boubée,
head of online content

Nathalie Coulon,
**head of patrons and business
department**
Laura Mingam
and Ariane Schweitzer,
patrons coordinators

Frédérique Leseur,
head of visitor development
Anne Stephan,
project mediation manager

Administration
and Finance

Solveig Mondy,
director

Jérôme Berrier,
head of purchasing and logistics
Clémence Raunet-Breger,
deputy head and public buyer

and all those who collaborate
with Paris Musées

Gabrielle Chanel on the staircase
of the Haute Couture salons,
31, rue Cambon, Paris, 1953.
Photograph by Robert Doisneau.

ACKNOWLEDGMENTS

The Palais Galliera would like to thank all of those whose generous support and cooperation made this exhibition possible.

Our very special thanks are owed to the **Maison CHANEL**
Bruno Pavlovsky, president of Chanel's fashion and of Chanel S.A.S.
Laurence Delamare, international director, fashion press and public relations department
Marie-Louise de Clermont-Tonnerre
Hélène Fulgence, head of the Patrimoine
Odile Prémel, collections coordinator
Rosa Ampudia, Anne-Charlotte Beaussant, Julie Deydier, Marika Genty, Cécile Goddet-Dirles, Marie Hamelin Dufief, Sarah Piettre

The museum would also like to express its thanks to the following people and institutions for their generous loans.

Archives Balenciaga Paris
Gaspard de Massé

Bibliothèque Historique de la Ville de Paris
Emmanuelle Toulet, director
Alain Durel,
Marie-Françoise Garion,
Pauline Girard, Juliette Jestaz

Château Borély – Musée des Arts Décoratifs (Marseille)
Marie-Josée Linou, director

Collection of the Prince's Palace (Monaco)
Hervé Irien, general secretary of the private collections of H.S.H. the Prince of Monaco

Deutsche Kinemathek – Museum für Film und Fernsehen (Berlin)
Florian Bolenius, executive director
Barbara Schröter,
Andrea Ziegenbruch

Fine Arts Museums of San Francisco
Thomas P. Campbell, director and CEO
Laura Camerlengo,
Jill D'Alessandro

Cinémathèque Française
Frédéric Bonnaud, director
Charlyne Carrère,
Marion Langlois, Régis Robert

Max Mara Archives (Reggio Emilia)
Laura Lusuardi

MINT Museum (Charlotte, North Carolina)
Annie Carlano, senior curator of craft, design and fashion

Modemuseum Hasselt
Karolien de Clippel, director

MoMu (Antwerp)
Kaat Debo, director
Frédéric Boutié

Musée des Arts Décoratifs (Paris)
Olivier Gabet, director
Florence Bertin,
Emmanuelle Blandinières Beuvin,
Marie-Sophie Carron de la Carrière, Évelyne Possémé,
Éric Pujalet-Plaà,
Marie-Pierre Ribère,
Myriam Teissier

Musée de la Mode et de la Dentelle (Brussels)
Caroline Esgain, chief curator

Musée National d'Art Moderne – Centre Pompidou
Bernard Blistène, director
Kim Dang

Musée de Cluny – Musée National du Moyen Âge
Élisabeth Taburet-Delahaye, director
Isabelle Bardiès-Fronty

The Costume Institute, Metropolitan Museum of Art (New York)
Andrew Bolton, head curator
Wendy Yu, Sarah Scaturro,
Elizabeth Shaeffer, Julie T. Le,
Karen Van Godtsenhoven,
Anna Yanofsky

The Museum at the Fashion Institute of Technology (New York)
Valerie Steele, director
Sonia Dingilian

Museo de la Moda de Chile
Jorge Yarur Bascuñán, director
Acacia Echazarreta

Museum of Applied Arts and Sciences (Sydney)
Lisa Havilah, executive director
Jessica McLean

Victoria & Albert Museum (London)
Tristram Hunt, director
Sonnet Stanfill

Private collectors
Hamish Bowles
Leslie Chin
Nadine Milhaud
Mark Walsh

Our special thanks are also due to all those who provided help and advice during the preparation of the exhibition and its catalogue.

Archives de Paris
Jean-Charles Virmaux, head of the department of private archives and special collections
Dominique Juigné
Marie-Pierre Lambelin

Archives Départementales des Pyrénées-Atlantiques
Jacques Pons, director
Nadine Rouayroux, director of the Bayonne and Pays Basque archive centre
Véronique Hayet

Archives Départementales du Tarn
Jean Le Pottier, director
Françoise Hubault

Archives Pathé Gaumont
Manuela Padoan, director

Association Sem
Xavier Chiron, honorary president
Élisabeth Bonnelle-Rombach,
Dominique Gouyou-Beauchamps

Bibliothèque Forney
Lucile Trunel, director
Martine Boussoussou

Grosvenor Estate (UK)
Louise Benson

Institut National de l'Audiovisuel
Laurent Vallet, president/director general
Christine Braemer,
Dominique Thiercelin

Médiathèque de Saint-Quentin
François Calame,
Nathalie Niay

Finally, our thanks to everyone else who contributed to this project in various ways:

Jérôme Aubé,
Michel Baldocchi,
Catherine Blanc,
Élisabeth Boucheron,
Francine Carpon,
Rosine Delaplace Moser,
François Hurteau-Flamand,
Theron Kabrich,
Guillaume Villemot,
Madgalena Vukovic

and our heartfelt thoughts to Julien Lessecq.